REDESIGNING
TEACHING

SUNY Series, Teacher Preparation and Development
Alan R. Tom, Editor

Sponsored by
the Consortium for Policy Research in Education,
a consortium of
the Eagleton Institute of Politics at Rutgers University,
Harvard University,
the University of Wisconsin, Madison,
Michigan State University,
the University of Southern California,
and Stanford University;
funded by
the Office of Educational Research and Improvement,
U.S. Department of Education,
under grant number
OERI G008690011

REDESIGNING TEACHING

Professionalism or Bureaucracy?

WILLIAM A. FIRESTONE
BETH D. BADER

STATE UNIVERSITY OF NEW YORK PRESS

Published by
State University of New York Press, Albany

Printed in the United States of America

For information, address State University of New York
Press, State University Plaza, Albany, N.Y., 12246

Production by E. Moore
Marketing by Fran Keneston

Library of Congress Cataloging-in-Publication Data

Firestone, William A.
    Redesigning teaching : professionalism or bureaucracy? / William
A. Firestone, Beth D. Bader.
        p.   cm. — (SUNY series,teacher preparation and development)
    Includes bibliographical references and index.
    ISBN 0–7914–1123–0 (alk. paper) . — ISBN 0–7914–1124–9 (pbk. :
alk. paper)
    1. Teachers—United States—Case studies. 2. Education and state-
-United States—Case studies. 3. Educational change,United States-
-Case studies.   I. Bader, Beth D. II. Title. III. Series: SUNY
series in teacher preparation and development.
LB1775.2.F57   1993
371.1'00973—dc20
                                                              91–30791
                                                                  CIP

CONTENTS

Acknowledgments   vii

Introduction   1

1. The Design of Teacher Reforms   11

2. Mossville: Bureaucratic Redesign   36

3. Hill City: A Mixed-Mode Reform   75

4. Academy: Professional Redesign   111

5. The Dynamics of Bureaucracy and Professionalism   154

6. The Politics of Redesign   182

7. Conclusion   203

Appendix A: Research Methods   219

Appendix B: Site Visit Guide   229

Appendix C: Academy Survey   249

Notes   257

References   259

Subject Index   269

Author Index   273

ACKNOWLEDGMENTS

The writing of any book entails tremendous amounts of work on the part of many people, not just those whose names appear on the cover. This book has been no exception. It is with great appreciation that we acknowledge the many contributions that have made this book possible.

First mention goes to Susan Fuhrman, the Director of the Center (now Consortium) for Policy Research in Education, who afforded us essential institutional support for our research, patiently critiqued earlier reports and conceptions, and generously provided us with the time away from CPRE's primary project to develop and write this text.

Ann Weaver Hart and Susan Moore Johnson read the draft manuscript and provided invaluable insights and critiques for rewriting. Richard Elmore offered assistance with an earlier conceptualization, and Rein van der Vegt helped us refine our field protocols and data collection approaches. At Rutgers University, Mary Orr helped with some of the field work, and Tom McMahon did some of the coding.

Linda Van Vlack, with amazing patience, made countless revisions and reprints as the manuscript went back and forth between us. She also input survey data, and managed the Ethnograph coding and searching for the interview data base. Her work is greatly appreciated.

It is difficult not to identify people in the district for special thanks. We promised them anonymity, but many were so generous in their helpfulness, openness, and patience that we regret not being able publicly to acknowledge their contribution. All three superintendents, many other district officials, the principals of the schools we visited, board members, teachers, and parents were extremely helpful. All interviewees were open and forthright. Some endured several hours of our questioning with cheerfulness. One board member in Hill City spoke with one of us for five hours.

Special mention of the "Mossville" district administrative assistant and the "Hill City" and "Academy" executive secretaries must be made. They went out of their way to be helpful, arranged endless schedules and endless schedule changes, facilitated our document collection, and endured endless interruptions without making us feel that we were interrupting. The districts are fortunate to have their services.

The three districts, each very fine, work very diligently to do the best possible job for their students. Although some of our analysis may be viewed as negative, it in no way lessens our respect and admiration for the energy and dedication of everyone in all three. We hope that some of our observations, at least, might be helpful to them.

We also want to thank the state officials and university faculty who helped us to identify three appropriate districts. Their perceptions greatly assisted us in narrowing our search. Although others have contributed to the development of this book, we alone are responsible for any errors that we may have made.

WILLIAM A. FIRESTONE
BETH D. BADER

INTRODUCTION

Less than a decade ago the National Commission on Educational Excellence (1983, 5) asserted that "if an unfriendly foreign power had attempted to impose on America the mediocre educational performance that exists today, we might well have viewed it as an act of war." In the wake of that report, there has been a major effort to reform teaching. Most of the rhetoric focuses on the concept of professionalism. The Carnegie Forum on Education and the Economy (1986, 2) asserts that "without a profession possessed of high skills, capabilities, and aspirations, any reforms will be short lived." Other organizations, including the Holmes Group and the American Federation of Teachers, among others, offer advice to their members on how to professionalize. Districts like Cincinnati, Ohio; Miami-Dade County, Florida; and Rochester, New York; are pointed to as constructive examples of workplace reform.

But what does professionalizing teaching mean? Consider two recent conversations we had with educators. In one district, the superintendent told us:

> Our organization is flexible but we have a central theme. All we do focuses on improving teaching and learning. We'll do all we need to do, but the decisions should be made as close to the action as possible. Everyone is a professional. Everyone wants to be the best they can be.... We have an environment with a great deal of internal support, but also a fair amount of questioning.

In another district, a principal attributed teacher morale problems to accountability. Teachers can't close their doors and do what they want. They're being looked at and inspected, and teachers have not had the kind of supervision and accountability we have now.... We're asking them to be treated as professionals and looked at as professionals. The newness of it is what's making these things seem a problem.

In the first district, professionalism involved making decisions close to the action, intrinsic motivation, and external support. In the second, it involved external supervision and accountability.

This confusion about the real meaning of professionalism often appears when people consider how to reform teaching. Underlying the confusion are real disagreements about the direction such reforms should take. Though many seem to agree that teaching should be professionalized, it turns out that they have very different ideas in mind. Some people's ideas refer to the classical professional occupations: medicine, law, engineering, and others. In this view a professional has a special body of knowledge, a sense of self-directedness and a commitment to important values. However, application of that knowledge and those values is a complex judgmental task; problem solving is the order of the day. To perform adequately, professional teachers must be highly trained. They also require considerable discretion to apply their knowledge. But discretion does not mean isolation. The application of informed judgment benefits from sharing and interaction among professionals. Professional organizations use network structures more than hierarchical controls for sharing information and advice. Decisions must be made closer to where teaching happens and must include teachers. Teachers must be motivated intrinsically rather than controlled externally. Second-wave reforms such as school restructuring, site-based management, teacher empowerment, and some career ladders reflect these principles (Passow 1989).

Other people who use the term "profession" to refer to teaching, actually adopt a bureaucratic perspective on management of the occupation. In this view, there is a scientific body of research that prescribes the most effective teaching strategies; this research is often known better by administrators, staff, and researchers than teachers themselves. Moreover, this view requires simplified, clarified educational goals that can be clearly measured. The technology of teaching becomes routinized to the point where the complex judgment of professionals is less important. Education can be centrally managed by standardizing inputs through textbooks, outputs through mandated testing programs, and work processes through standardized teacher-evaluation systems. In the first wave of educational reforms in the 1980s, which embraced this approach (Passow 1989), frequently adopted policies included increased high school graduation requirements, increased teacher testing for certification, merit pay, and in a few states certification based on standardized in-class assessments (Firestone, Fuhrman, and Kirst 1989).

In some ways the debate over whether to professionalize or bureaucratize teaching is new, but the underlying issue reflects a recurring dialectic in educational reform. Indeed, Dewey (1938) said over five decades ago that the history of educational theory is

> marked by opposition between the idea that education is development from within and that it is formation from without; that it is based upon natural endowments [versus] that [it] is a process of overcoming natural inclination and substituting in its place habits acquired under external pressure. (17)

What complicates matters is that the language used in the debate often obfuscates important differences. When one digs beneath the rhetoric, however, each side has different images of what teaching reforms should accomplish and how teachers should operate. Both sides have some research on their side, but that research is mixed with a good deal of ideology. As a result those policy makers, administrators, and teachers and their associations interested in reforming teaching are as likely to work out their approach through conflict and negotiation as through reasoned judgment. Moreover, reforms touted as ways to empower teachers may actually reduce their discretion because teachers and administrators do not understand the implicit assumptions built into the changes they make.

QUESTIONS AND ANSWERS

This book is an effort to clarify the current efforts to reform teaching by addressing the following questions:

1) What are the underlying assumptions behind the professional and bureaucratic approaches to reforming teaching?
2) How do specific schools and districts decide to adopt particular reforms, and what role do state policy and local politics play in that process?
3) What do these reforms look like in practice?
4) How do these reforms change teachers' behavior and motivation?

To answer these questions we conducted case studies of school districts implementing two kinds of reform in teaching: job differentiation and changes in internal governance. Job differentiation creates sets of ranks or special positions to which teachers can aspire according to two principles. With merit, the bureaucratic principle, teachers are paid more for doing the same work better—that is, for exceeding some absolute standard or comparison point with other teachers. With job enlargement, the professional principle, teachers' income increases when they do more work, usually involving training or curriculum development. For example, increasing teacher participation in internal decision making is a professional reform; reducing teacher discretion in the classroom is a bureaucratic one.

The case-study strategy affords the advantage of a depth of understanding of how particular reforms work; its limitation is the difficulty of generalizing from the settings studied to other situations. Nevertheless, our cases strongly suggest what we believe are useful answers to the questions posed. In particular, we conclude that professional reforms for improving teaching are more effective than bureaucratic ones. When teachers have opportunities to help their colleagues and to have input into decisions, they take steps to improve their own effectiveness. Because teachers' satisfaction comes from intrinsic rewards, changes that make them more effective on their own terms have the further advantage of increasing their motivation, thereby enhancing the potential for improving their teaching. Because professional reforms increase collegial interaction and encourage teachers to be more active in the improvement process, they also have the potential to increase teacher reflectiveness about their own practice.

Bureaucratic reforms do have some value. They establish external criteria of good teaching and reward teachers who comply with them. The results are quicker and neater, but bureaucratic reforms undermine teacher motivation and do not provide a basis to move to more complex modes of teaching. From an investment point of view, bureaucratic reforms promote accountability but buy only one benefit: compliance. Professional reforms are more complex—they look messier but accrue multiple benefits.

We also conclude that the process of redesigning teaching is quite political. The plan adopted by any given district may be shaped by state policy, but it will also reflect a complex interaction among teachers, administrators, and the school board. The superintendent is often the catalyst for change but can rarely control the final outcomes. Administrators tend to propose or support changes that are more bureaucratic than professional. Professional reforms are more likely when teachers exert influence to modify programs in that direction. How the contest between teachers and the administration is resolved will depend on both administrator openness to teacher influence and board effectiveness in encouraging acceptance of teacher proposals.

STUDY METHODOLOGY

To address these questions, we conducted case studies of three school districts. The districts were in different states and were selected for their reputations as trend setters in teacher reform. Two (Academy and Mossville to use their pseudonyms) were leaders in implementing state policies that featured some element of differential pay for teachers. Hill City (also a pseudonym) also implemented a state teacher policy, but its response to the state was part of its comprehensive local program, Mutual Governance, developed to promote closer working relationships between teachers and administrators. (Table 1 provides demographic information on these three districts.)

TABLE 1
Description of Districts

	Mossville	Hill City	Academy
Pupil Population	19,041	6,800	13,100
State per Pupil Expenditure as Percent of National Average[1]	87	118	57
District per Pupil Expenditure	$3,043	$4,265	$2,634
Percent Minority Enrollment	31	10	5
Percent Below Poverty Level[1]	28.6	15.2	25.2

[1] Taken from National Education Association (1989).

We spent approximately twenty days in each district talking to teachers, principals, district administrators, board members, parents, and media representatives as well as collecting program descriptions, demographic and student data, program evaluations, newspaper articles, and school board minutes. In two districts we also had access to surveys of teacher opinion. In Mossville, the state surveyed all teachers in districts participating in the pilot program we studied; we were able to get item means for Mossville from the state report. Academy's superintendent asked us to conduct a survey while we were there to help both district planning and our study. (More details on our research methods are provided in Appendix A.) We brought from each district a good sense of its history and culture, reasons for reforming teaching, the design of the change, and how teachers' sentiments and behaviors were modified.

One other observation on our methodology is important because it addresses the problem of the biases that may have been brought to the study: this is not the book we set out to write. In qualitative research, important themes and issues often emerge in the course of the study. This was especially true here. Our original goal was to understand why some school districts were especially effective in implementing state policies. Our interest was strictly in issues of implementation rather than of policy content. Midway through our second case study, when we realized we had an opportunity to explore important questions related to the design of teaching, we chose our third case to make sure that it implemented an important policy affecting teachers.

We mention this because it was not our intention to write a book extolling the virtues of professional designs and criticizing bureaucratic ones. We began all our case studies with the assumption that we were studying districts where results were extremely positive. Only as we began to interview teachers did we begin to see any problems, and only as we conducted the analysis did we understand how changes in teaching and teacher motivation were related to the new job designs that were being implemented. The emergent quality of our conclusions, we believe, lends them credibility.

PLAN FOR THE BOOK

Before describing the districts, Chapter 1 expands on the issues that were addressed. Its primary purpose is to describe the two approaches to reform by examining their conceptions of what students should learn and how teachers should teach before exploring organizational designs that are theoretically expected to promote such teaching. It also examines how the current condition of teaching fits with each approach and what is known about how school district politics may affect the local design of reform.

The next three chapters present the stories of three districts' efforts to redesign teaching. Each story begins with a historical background that presents the district's environment and events leading up to the adoption of the restructuring program. The teacher program is then described in its district context, and issues of implementation are analyzed. Finally, we examine the consequences of the program for both teacher motivation and instructional practice.

If each case covers the same issues, the details as presented in Chapters 2, 3, and 4 vary greatly. Mossville's is a tale of increased bureaucracy. After over a decade of economic change and community unrest, a new superintendent initiated a number of changes, including new policies to test students more often and to use the data to evaluate principals. When his state initiated the teacher development program that would give teachers who received strong evaluations salary increases, he encouraged his director of personnel to apply to pilot the program. The new system assessed teachers on their use of direct instruction, and a special cadre of observers was hired from the teaching ranks to help principals evaluate teachers. The district provided extensive training to teachers on both the principles of instruction involved and the new evaluation system. Teachers were leery of the new system, and the failure to give some well-respected instructors top salary increases led to lawsuits in the program's early days. After four years, teachers and administrators agreed that staff applied the principles built into the evaluation system much more frequently in the classroom. However, teachers complained about the heavy-handed implementation of the program, and were less enthusiastic about their work than they had been before.

Hill City provides a mixed case. After over a decade of labor unrest and budget battles, a new superintendent brought a management style that entailed much more consultation with teachers. After extended conversations with the local union leadership, he unveiled the plan for Mutual Governance that called for more cooperation among himself and the central office, the school board, teachers, and principals. Teachers were given regular positions at school board and administrative cabinet meetings, and a series of new consultative bodies were instituted at the district and school level. These bodies were formally charged with developing new positions for teachers and a new evaluation system wanted by the school board. Teachers hoped they would provide a way to address a series of long-standing complaints, and the superintendent wanted to make specific curricular changes. At the end of three years, the board's agenda and part of the superintendent's had been achieved, but the teachers complained that their real influence in the district had not increased.

Academy's is a story of professional reform that increased teacher influence in district governance, curriculum development, and teacher training. A new superintendent arrived from out of state to energize a sluggish instructional program by way of a combination of clinical supervision and curriculum revision. After staff strongly expressed their displeasure with his directive approach, he began a more collaborative approach to planning. Meanwhile he was instrumental in designing his state's career ladder program. Using state funds, Academy then designed a program that gave teachers 1) extra days for collective in-service and individual preparation before classes began, 2) a series of special jobs for two-fifths of the teachers, which paid them to redesign existing curricula and train their colleagues, and 3) a small merit-pay element required by the state. This program was used in different ways in each building, but teachers appreciated the opportunity to influence program design and the chance to develop their skills and enrich the districts' offerings. They saw the program as contributing directly to their effectiveness as teachers.

Chapter 5 examines how the three districts implemented divergent conceptions of teacher reform. After comparing the educational outcomes from the three districts, it examines how each dealt with changes that differentiated jobs among teachers and changed their role in governance. It examines the extent to which these changes reflected bureaucratic or professional approaches to reform. It then explores how each approach creates incentives that motivate teachers differently. It shows how professional reforms motivate teachers by facilitating their efforts to teach children, and how bureaucratic reforms demotivate by stressing compliance.

Chapter 6 analyzes the politics of redesign by examining the roles of different groups in shaping district policies. It examines each group's interests and sources of influence, and suggests reasons for differences among districts. We conclude that two groups play crucial roles in the design of those policies: superintendents and teachers. When the state chooses to play a role, the funds and regulations it provides will have major impacts on local efforts, but it is not necessary for major restructuring efforts.

Chapter 7 synthesizes the arguments of the book. It first summarizes the evidence presented for the two approaches to redesign teaching. It emphasizes that the short-run benefits of the bureaucratic approach cannot lead to long-term improvement but that the professional approach can in fact lead to greater improvements in the quality of teaching. It then identifies a series of challenges that must be addressed to professionalize teaching. First, public pressure for accountability, an important impetus to bureaucratic reforms, must be met in more comprehensive ways. Second, teachers must become active in lobbying for professionalization, but in the process they will have to modify some of what have been their key beliefs. Third, government entities will have to provide additional financial support and a stable policy environment. Finally, administrators will need to incorporate teachers into decision making while maintaining the focus on truly improving practice.

1. THE DESIGN OF
   TEACHER REFORMS

THE LAST DECADE witnessed a great deal of education reform, but also much confusion and ambiguity. Impatient with the incremental growth of standards in the early 1980s, some reformers called for a substantial restructuring of American education, but it was never clear what restructuring meant. As Kirst notes, "restructuring is a word that means everything and nothing simultaneously" (Olson 1988, 1). It includes, but is not limited to, the reform of teaching. Even in that area, the array of recommendations is bewildering and sometimes contradictory. Some want to micromanage teachers and enhance administrative control whereas others want to strengthen teachers' expert judgment and give them more autonomy. What confuses things is that people use similar language to describe very different reforms (Popkewitz and Lind 1989).

Underlying the florid rhetoric is a poorly formulated debate about whether to make teaching more bureaucratic or more professional. This book attempts to clarify the debate, to illustrate some advantages of professionalization, and to describe some organizational changes that can help bring it about. At the same time it explores why some districts choose professional reforms and other select bureaucratic ones. The next section of this chapter describes the assumptions underlying both approaches. It is followed by an introduction to the concrete reforms attempting to implement those approaches, and a brief discussion of teachers' sentiments that helps to anticipate how reforms are likely to change their behavior and motivation. Finally, we turn to local decision making to provide a framework for examining the local politics of teacher reform.

BUREAUCRATIC AND PROFESSIONAL DESIGNS

In the designing of organizations, there is a technical component that fits organizational structures to the work that must be done. There is also a normative part, however, because organizations systematically embody socially sanctioned purposes (Meyer and Rowan 1977). Organizational charts and regulations reflect values, expectations, and definitions of satisfactory performance; they make it easier to achieve some purposes and prohibit others (Ranson, Hining, and Hughes 1980). The normative element is especially strong in schools where task definition is more a social than an engineering problem. Hence, redesigning teaching is partly a technical problem but it also has a political side.

Consensus is growing that schools are "loosely coupled" (Bidwell 1965; Weick 1976). Loose coupling implies that educational goals are numerous, ambiguous, and difficult to prioritize and that knowledge as to what instructional approaches facilitate student learning is weak. In such circumstances schools are organized to look rational from the outside but avoid inspection of what happens inside: close inspection and strong lines of authority would show that people disagree about how to proceed, and cannot improve substantially on teachers' own performance.

Loose coupling papers over disagreements about what schools and teaching should entail. There are better ways to achieve educational goals. Two strategies have been suggested to help schools become more effective at achieving educational ends (Rowan 1990): schools can be organized as self-governing professions, or as centrally directed bureaucracies (Bacharach and Conley 1989; Weick and McDaniel 1989). The first relies on the commitments of professionals and the second on external control to assure coordination and effectiveness.

There is a substantial normative component to the decision between the bureaucratic and the professional option, and each has generated its own rhetoric. The dominant discourse of the last decade emphasizes professionalism. The Carnegie Forum (1986, 56) lists four characteristics of a "professional environment for teaching":

1. Teachers should be provided with the discretion and autonomy that are the hallmarks of professional work.

2. Districts should foster collegial styles of decision making and teaching in schools in which "Lead Teachers" play a central role.
3. Teachers should be provided the support staff they need to be more effective and productive.
4. School districts should consider a variety of approaches to school district leadership.

The bureaucratic view is less well articulated but has been pervasive. Around 1984 districts and states began tightening up school standards and practice. Monitoring and close inspection became a regular practice. Districts and state departments of education began emphasizing accountability. One manifestation of this concern was an interest in merit pay, an innovation popularized by the National Commission on Educational Excellence. The Southern Regional Education Board (1990) declared:

> Results...performance...outcomes—call it what you will but for education it is now a more highly visible priority for the public, governors, legislators, and many educators.... Rewards for schools, teachers, and principals are being linked to performance.

It described the spread of merit-based programs to over twenty states. Because differences between these two theories are not well understood, attempts to professionalize can lead to unintended bureaucratization. Table 1–1 and the discussion following clarify some of the important differences between these theories.

Strictly speaking, professions—connoting the organization of an occupation—and bureaucracies—connoting structure—are not comparable. However, certain organizations—universities, law firms, research laboratories, and in some ways hospitals—are designed to house professionals and facilitate their work. What differentiates these organizations from bureaucracies most fundamentally is the technology they use (Perrow 1970). Some technologies entail a great deal of certainty. People can solve problems through established analysis strategies rather than inspired intuition. Moreover, the number of problems that need to be solved is relatively low. Most situations are familiar and the course of action is clear. Bureaucracies are well designed to handle such work. On the other hand, the work conducted by professional organizations entails great uncertainty. Each case has its own special problems and the strategies for solving those problems are not entirely clear. These technological differences lead to others in the kind of workers preferred by each type of organization, and the way the organization should be structured. The professional needs to be an expert, so more is expected and the organization is designed to facilitate that person's work. In the bureaucracy, expertise rests in upper levels of the hierarchy, which is designed more to control than facilitate the worker. In these circumstances less is expected of the worker. The big question, then, is, How certain is the technology of teaching? Separate research traditions can be used to argue for both high and low certainty. The next step is to look at those research traditions. Then we can look at the implications for what teaching and schools should entail.

TABLE 1–1
Differences between Bureaucratic and Professional Designs for Teaching

	Bureaucracy	*Professional Organization*
Task Certainty	High—there are few problems; and means have been established to solve them	Low—situations have more unique elements and analysis strategies are not well codified
Research Justification	Process-product research supporting direct instruction	Research on teacher thinking as reflective practice
Expectations for Teachers		
Knowledge of teaching	Basic levels only are required	More complex knowledge is necessary
Importance of high commitment	Useful but not crucial	Crucial, as are specific values
Organizational Arrangements		
Strategic decisions	Made by managers alone	Made by managers and workers together
Operational decisions	Controlled through direct supervision (teacher evaluation), standardization of work process (curriculum and texts) and outputs (tests)	Managed through mutual adjustment (collegial interaction) and standardization of inputs (preparation and certification)
Incentives	Financial	Financial and intrinsic

Conceptions of Teaching

Two paradigms for studying teaching make different assumptions about the underlying technology. Process-product research, which leads to direct instruction, provides the intellectual underpinning for bureaucratic designs; research on teacher thinking, which highlights the need for reflective practice, supports professionalism.

The process-product paradigm (Gage 1978) uses correlational and experimental studies to link teaching behaviors (and attitudes) to student achievement. A substantial body of research links three classroom factors to the learning of basic skills: 1) Time. Students spend more time on some curricular areas than others, and more time is linked to increased achievement, especially when it is devoted to the skills tested (Brophy and Good 1986). 2) Teacher expectations. Teachers call on high-achieving students more often, praise them more, criticize them less, and give them more time to recover from failures. These differences in teacher responses exacerbate poor students' poor performance (Good 1983). 3) Teacher management. Teachers who manage instructional functions appropriately increase achievement (Rosenshine 1983). Appropriate management includes frequent review and checking of past work so errors will not go undetected; presentation of material in small steps with considerable modeling; frequent, guided practice to the point of "overteaching"; extensive monitoring; and designing problems or exercises so that students get most answers right. Reducing teaching to a small number of principles would go a long way toward adding confidence on how to proceed.

Although process-product research has been very powerful, it has recently come in for substantial criticism. According to Carter and Doyle (1989), this research showed only that experienced volunteers could use some of the principles involved to modify their classroom practices. It told teachers little about how to create the conditions for time-on-task and frequent questions. It provided minimal information on how the subject matter determined what teaching tasks were important, and did not suggest what knowledge teachers needed to interpret classroom events or to establish and maintain a positive learning environment.

Whereas process-product research viewed teaching from the outside, the reflective practice paradigm focused explicitly on the effective teacher, and embodied explicit theories about learners, curriculum, subject matter. The effective teacher has an approach to planning that is both subtle and spontaneous but also understands how to read cues in the situation and when to deviate from the plan.

He or she can analyze events and take corrective action (Clark and Peterson 1986). This new paradigm does not view teaching as a stable problem situation to which a small set of principles can be regularly applied. Instead, it assumes considerable uncertainty and attends to the internal process by which teachers solve problems created by that uncertainty. Researchers examine how teachers use a rich, specific understanding of their work settings to facilitate the efficient interpretation and disposition of new problems (Carter and Doyle 1989).

These two paradigms are linked to different educational outcomes. Direct instruction clearly promotes achievement of basic skills (Brophy and Good 1986), but may work against higher-order thinking. Its emphasis on fast pacing, student success, and modeling solutions can redefine the skills taught, from synthesis and creativity to mimicry. The tendency to break teaching into small steps reflects the emphasis on discrete basic skills. By contrast, the reflective practice of the professional teacher exemplifies higher-order thinking and draws on some of the same research on expert cognition. Thus, reflective teachers would probably model higher-order thinking.

Images of the Teacher

In sum, direct instruction and the process-product research provide an underpinning for the bureaucratic design of schools, whereas research on teachers' reflective practice supports the professional design. These two designs require employees that differ in the depth of both their knowledge and commitment. In education, much attention has been given to teacher knowledge. Typically, the most talented undergraduates do not major in education, and the best of those who do either never become teachers or leave the field early (Lanier and Little 1986). This talent gap is much less critical to the bureaucratic than the professional design. Bureaucratic organizations are based on the premise that they require less teacher knowledge because teachers' work will be guided more extensively by central administrators and staff experts. This is apparent in state teacher-certification policies. While forty-four states require teacher candidates to take some kind of test to become certified, these are typically paper-and-pencil tests of basic skills in communications, mathematics, and other areas (McCarthy 1990).

Professionalism requires a higher standard because it is based on the premise that teachers must be capable of exercising more discretion. Lanier and Sedlak (1989) argue that "teacher knowledge is at the core of teacher efficacy. It is central to teachers' ability to bring about sustained student learning of the sort judged critical to quality schooling" (135). In their view, teachers must have a deep knowledge of their subject area, expertise in pedagogy, and the understanding to deal with the endemic uncertainties of classroom life. Shulman (1987) lists seven domains of professional knowledge for teachers, among them understanding of subject matter, knowledge of the principles of classroom management, knowledge of learners and their characteristics, and knowledge of educational purposes and values. Much more complex certification examinations are required to test such knowledge (Peterson and Commeaux 1989).

Whatever conception one has of an occupation, commitment is a useful quality. Committed workers give more effort to their employers and clients, are more inclined to follow directives, are absent less frequently, stay with their jobs longer, and generally reduce costs of training new workers and overseeing existing ones (Mowday, Porter, and Steers 1982). Nevertheless, commitment is not as crucial for bureaucratic as professional organizations. With routine technologies, bureaucratic schools can use supervisors to ensure that teachers are performing properly.

In the professional setting, however, workers not only carry out pre-programmed work routines but also decide what must be done and how. Outside experts cannot easily predict what teachers will have to do because they inevitably fail to understand the nuances of specific situations. While they may have more generalized scientific knowledge, that knowledge is hard to apply without a concrete understanding of the setting.

This is more than a technical problem; it also implies choices about the ends to be achieved. Professionals not only have a special field of knowledge, they are also elites responsible for the protection of social values (Selznick 1957). Moreover, the uncertain situations in which they work often make it difficult to understand what values are appropriate at a given time. Without general rules, professionals must decide what ends to meet as well as how to meet them. Therefore, it is especially important that a person be deeply committed to the organization and its purposes (Weick and McDaniel 1989).

Organizational Arrangements

The bureaucratic design uses a mechanistic strategy to control workers by monopolizing decision making and standardizing work activities. The professional design employs an organic strategy that develops networks among workers at different levels, incorporates more people in decision making, and coordinates work through frequent interaction (Rowan 1990). These differences are apparent when one examines strategic and operational decisions separately. Strategic decisions affect the organization's overall work. They include questions of policy, work allocation, discipline, and staff development and evaluation. Operational decisions are directly related to the work at hand; they include what to teach and how to teach it (Bacharach and Conley 1989). The differences between bureaucracy and professionalism are also apparent in the use of incentives.

Strategic Decisions. In the bureaucratic organization, strategic decisions are centralized. The highest-level policy decisions may be made by an elected board or other entity, but top managers translate those broad policy directives into specific operational and allocation directives (Weber 1947). Workers' concerns are not solicited because managers are assumed to know them best. In the professional organization, strategic decisions are shared because managers and workers have different kinds of knowledge (Bacharach and Conley 1989). The workers better understand work processes, challenges, and complexities whereas the managers know more about the outside environment and have a broader overview of the organization. Moreover, as carriers of special values, professionals will advocate critical concerns that might otherwise be ignored (Weick and McDaniel 1989). Worker participation in decision making is said to build commitment to the decisions that result, making compliance easier to accomplish (Berman and McLaughlin 1975). Worker participation also promotes commitment to the organization more generally (Bacharach and Conley 1989; Newman, Rutter, and Smith 1988).

Operational Decisions. The same distinction between centralization in the bureaucracy and shared decision making in the professional organization applies to operational decisions, but with different means. Mintzberg (1983) lists five ways to coordinate operational activity. Two involve face-to-face interaction. Mutual adjustment is informal, direct discussion, often among equals. Two people can communicate a great deal of information; both contribute their judgment. Mutual adjustment can also build skills by providing situations where individuals are forced to examine what they are doing and to consider alternatives (Shulman 1987). It also facilitates building, the implementation of new practices and a greater sense of certainty in teachers' work (Little 1982; Rosenholtz 1989). However, the process is time-consuming and expensive. As information does not travel well, mutual adjustment can only coordinate the work of a few people. With direct supervision one person oversees the work of others, issues orders to them, and monitors their progress. This process is faster, less expensive, and ensures greater comparability of practice. It can include a few more people, though that limits somewhat the information exchanged and the judgments contributed.

The other three mechanisms standardize or prespecify some aspect of the work. When one standardizes work processes, one specifies how tasks are done. Curriculum guides and textbooks standardize educational work processes. Standardizing outputs specifies what the results should be instead of how the work gets done. District and state testing programs, a form of output standardization, are even faster and cheaper than direct supervision and can be applied on a very broad scale. However, they further constrain the amount of information that is exchanged, and judgment is exercised primarily at the point of setting standards.

Finally, one can standardize skills and values by detailing the training workers should receive. Such training can include scientific knowledge and book learning, but it also features long hours of apprenticeship or supervised practice of the sort doctors receive in their internships and residencies. In addition to developing technical skills, standardization through extensive training effectively socializes trainees to significant values of the group. This approach can be time-consuming and expensive. In fact, skills and values are often standardized where they are especially complex. However, with standardized skills, a great deal of discretion is left to the worker.

Bureaucratic and professional organizations use different means to coordinate operational decisions. Bureaucratic organizations use direct supervision and standardization of work processes and outputs to control operational decisions. These techniques shift judgment from the worker to the supervisor or standard-setter. One indication that process-product research supports the bureaucratic perspective is that it has been used to justify narrow, behaviorist procedures for teacher evaluation (Peterson and Commeaux 1989). By contrast, professional organizations emphasize mutual adjustment and standardization of skills and values. These mechanisms channel the professional's discretion without removing it. They also require more complex certification tests that make explicit the mental process teachers use to make instructional decisions.

Incentives. Bureaucratic and professional organizations use different incentives and distribute them differently. The bureaucratic organization relies on extrinsic incentives—that is, those distributed by others that do not come directly from the work itself (Staw 1980). Money is the ultimate extrinsic reward in work settings, but externally conferred honors and prestige are also incentives. Bureaucracies often use extrinsic incentives to reinforce standardization (Weber 1947); then rewards are conditional upon compliance with external standards. A complete system for distributing incentives will specify a standard, provide a means of observation, and link rewards to observed performance (Dornbusch and Scott 1975). Extrinsic reward systems can be very effective motivators; but if improperly designed, they can actually reduce motivation and also lead to unanticipated consequences—like concentrating on measured performance at the expense of other valued activities (Lawler 1973).

Professional organizations emphasize intrinsic incentives that take their value either from doing the task—the activity itself—or from what is accomplished (Staw 1980). Moreover, the incentives are not geared for shaping behavior to administrative ends so much as for building worker commitment (Porter, Lawler, and Hackman 1975). Intrinsic incentives include skill variety, or engagement in many different activities using a variety of talents; task identity, or the completion of an identifiable piece of work from start to finish; task significance, or importance to the overall work or to others; autonomy, or freedom in scheduling work and determining the procedures to use; opportunity to interact with peers or colleagues; and feedback, or clear information on the effectiveness of one's work (Oldham and Hackman 1980). Moreover, one can increase intrinsic incentives by removing barriers to task accomplishment (Staw 1980).

Since intrinsic incentives come from the work itself, administrators cannot link them to performance. However, opportunities for job enlargement or enrichment that increase intrinsic incentives may be distributed as rewards. In the professional organization, these should be distributed by peers because they have the contextual knowledge to make the most informed decisions and because, as champions of key values, they are best placed to determine who should be rewarded. Moreover, professionally oriented organizations are designed so that all professionals are adequately reimbursed.

REFORM OPTIONS

Job differentiation and modified governance were among the most often discussed reforms of teaching in the 1980s. The first varies the remuneration teachers receive to reflect either the amount or quality of their work. Rank distinctions may also be introduced. The second brings teachers to the decision-making process. Both changes can professionalize teaching, but job differentiation can also make it more bureaucratic.

Job Differentiation

States and districts have implemented many programs to differentiate teachers' jobs (SREB 1990). Two issues separate the various plans: whether the changes are based on merit or job enlargement and whether they are permanent or temporary (Darling-Hammond and Berry 1988; Malen, Murphy, and Hart 1988). The first issue is the most fundamental. The merit principle assumes that all teachers do the same work, but pay varies depending upon the quality of the work. Success using this strategy depends on finding means to measure teacher quality that are acceptable to teachers. Merit is a bureaucratic reform because it ties financial rewards to direct supervision. Its popularity stems from its link to efforts to increase external accountability and discipline of teachers. Moreover, it assumes that teachers can be effectively motivated by extrinsic incentives (Rosenholtz 1989); its primary effect is to increase such rewards. When they are in place, teachers who conform to externally defined standards of excellence[1] will benefit.

Job enlargement creates situations for some teachers to do more or different work from others. This work may include mentoring for beginning teachers, providing training to all teachers, or developing new curricula. Sorting good teachers from bad is secondary, although the question of which teachers should get enlarged positions still arises. The principle requires identifying tasks teachers can do, achieving agreement that such tasks are worth additional reimbursement, and clarifying the relationship between the added work and regular teaching responsibility.

Job enlargement has two professionalizing features. First, it expands intrinsic benefits as well as extrinsic ones. Those who perform special tasks get paid more for more varied work and opportunities to develop new skills. In addition, the results of their work should be available to others, who then benefit from enhanced training opportunities and enriched curricula. Second, teachers selected for enlarged positions have augmented opportunities for influence, which should increase the motivation of those involved and ensure that a teacher perspective is better reflected in instructional decisions.

The permanency issue pits the conceptions of reformers against current norms of teacher equity. The hierarchy of teaching is nearly flat, with teachers receiving their maximum salary increase within fifteen or twenty years of entry and with the top salaries not a great deal above those of beginners' when compared to other occupations. With salaries typically allocated on the basis of seniority and level of education, there is little incentive to maintain one's productivity. Many teachers reach their peak within five years of entering the field (Rosenholtz 1985). Reformers have argued that teachers would be more motivated to continue improving if they had a series of career milestones that involve some mix of increased remuneration and greater responsibilities to work toward (Carnegie Forum 1986). This strategy assumes that generally acceptable ways can be found to identify improved performance so that teachers can move to the next level when their work has progressed to a measurable extent. Considering that teachers' concerns about equity and vulnerability make judgments about progress difficult, rotating positions is preferable (Malen and Hart 1987). Although the concept of progressive increases in money, status, and responsibility is thereby lost, abuses can be avoided.

Taken together, these dimensions suggest four alternatives for job redesign (Table 1–2). Merit-pay plans give teachers temporary bonuses for good performance. Before the recent interest in redesigning teachers' work, they were tried in the 1920s and 1950s and then faded from view (Johnson 1984). In the 1980s they were much criticized by teachers. Florida initiated and later discontinued such a program. The only difference between merit-pay and master-teacher programs is that the latter reward good teachers with permanent salary increases. Tennessee modified its initial merit-pay program into one that emphasized master teachers. Generally, merit-based programs have been most popular with state legislatures (Malen et al. 1988).

Job enlargement programs are more rare, although informal project add-ons have been part of teaching for many years. Any time a teacher receives summer work to develop new curricula or teach summer school, it is a project add-on. State programs in Tennessee and South Carolina included this element (Malen et al. 1988). Professionally oriented reformers like the Carnegie Forum (1986) have been the biggest advocates of career ladders. The Holmes Group (1986) model includes three career steps:

1) *Instructors* are first and second year teachers who have not yet made a career commitment to teaching and who lack practical experience. They are not given full responsibility for a classroom on their own as are beginning teachers now, but are overseen by colleagues.
2) *Professional teachers* are in many ways like teachers found in most

schools today. They have demonstrated a commitment to teaching and knowledge of subject matter. Their responsibilities would not necessarily extend beyond the classroom, although their input would be solicited.

3) *Lead teachers* continue to teach but are interested in broader educational policy issues and want to work formally with other adults. They take on such instructional leadership responsibilities as supervising instructors, curriculum development, training and coaching all staff, developing testing and measurement systems, helping professional teachers who want it, or action research. They also supervise and evaluate instructors and professional teachers and collegially manage school buildings.

Whether a career ladder is a pure case of job enlargement or a mixed one with a strong merit component depends on how teachers are selected. Where there is a heavy emphasis on administrative selection using fixed performance criteria, the merit element is reintroduced.

While the term "career ladder" is very popular and was adopted by twelve states (Southern Regional Education Board 1989), few use this approach in its pure form. Utah's and Tennessee's programs are among those that include provision for it.

TABLE 1–2
Job Redesign Alternatives

| Stability | Differentiation Principle | |
	Merit	Job Enlargement
Temporary	Merit Pay	Project Add-Ons
Permanent	Master Teacher	Career Ladder

Governance

The most often discussed changes in governance professionalize schools by including teachers when making strategic decisions. The Carnegie Forum (1986), for instance, advocates "a profession of well-educated teachers prepared to assume new powers and responsibilities to redesign schools for the future" (2). How much power teachers should have over these decisions is not entirely clear. Some of the language of the Carnegie Forum suggests that schools should be totally run by lead teachers. Bacharach and Conley (1989) suggest that the critical question is how to increase teacher participation without sacrificing the ability of management to coordinate. Even though some decisions are clearly in the realm of administrative authority, they argue, teachers should have formalized opportunities to influence them.

One popular means to engage teachers in strategic decisions is site-based management, which authorizes schools to make decisions previously controlled at the district level and to involve teachers in the process. In these programs, schools can make decisions about curriculum, personnel—especially hiring—and budgets (Clune and White 1989). Site-based management need not empower teachers; all these decisions could be made strictly by the principal. However, such changes usually include a school council or steering committee. Teachers typically dominate such committees, but parents and high school students can also be included. Teacher influence typically depends on the authority vested in the council and the proportion of teachers on it. In Santa Fe, New Mexico, teachers are authorized to select their own principals. In one case, when a principal left council members chose not to replace that person but to run the school themselves. Because of state laws, opportunities to change reading and mathematics curricula at the elementary level are limited, but in other areas councils have substantially modified the typical classroom format to use nongraded groups of various ages and team teaching. They have also added curricular goals like teaching all children to speak Spanish (Carnoy and McDonnell 1989).

Teacher influence need not be limited to the school level; it can also include district decisions. In the ABC District in Cerritos, California, the Curriculum Master Plan Council designs the curriculum. With a representative teacher from each school and overseen by the teachers' union, it is supported by a district-level "management facilitator," and detail work is done by ten district-wide subject-area committees also made up of teachers. The council has an annual budget of approximately $170,000 for a variety of purposes including paying teachers for summer development work. Its curriculum guides are reviewed by all teachers in the district, and final decisions are subject to the approval only of the school board (Sickler 1988).

TEACHERS' SENTIMENTS ABOUT REFORM

While teachers' associations have participated in the debate about how to reform teaching (e.g., Shanker 1990), teachers' preferences and perceptions have not been consistently incorporated. Those preferences should be considered for two reasons. First, they illustrate that neither the bureaucratic nor the professional design really fit today's schools, and point to some of the changes that need to be made to implement either one. Second, both redesign strategies require some teacher cooperation. Teacher support is essential for the professional redesign. Active opposition can end bureaucratic programs, as happened with Florida's merit-pay program (Firestone et al. 1989). For these reasons, we review what is known about teachers' beliefs as to the uncertainty surrounding their work, their commitment to teaching, control and coordination, incentives, and their views about popular reforms.

Uncertainty

Teachers, whose work is rife with uncertainty, have great difficulty assessing their work for three reasons. First, there is ambiguity about what their work should achieve. In addition to cognitive goals, teachers have moral ones like promoting good citizenship and developing an interest in learning for its own sake. Moreover, while they must maintain their own authority, they still want to be liked (Lortie 1975). Second, teachers have trouble assessing student progress (Kottkamp, Provenzo, and Cohn 1986). They are much less sanguine about the value of tests than are psychometricians, policy-makers, and the public. Since credible feedback from adults is relatively rare, teachers rely extensively on their own observations (Kasten 1984). Finally, it is difficult to know if success reflects one's own efforts, the child's, the parents', the work of other teachers, or even the materials provided. Efforts to reduce the uncertainties of teaching are erratic; over a fifth of teachers say that the staff development available to them is inadequate (Bacharach, Bauer, and Shedd,1986).

While uncertainty is much more pervasive than fits the bureaucratic design, the kind of reflective practice that should be associated with professionalism is also atypical. The dominant mode of teacher presentation is a highly nonreflective use of teacher lecturing, passive students, and testing for basic skills with very little variation in instructional strategy to reflect contingencies created by students or material (Cuban 1990; McNeil 1986). Moreover, when cultural norms encourage teachers to exclude formal theory and outside experience from their thinking about the classroom, they discourage more reflective approaches (Hargreaves 1984). When considering innovations, teachers often accept the underlying principles of innovations uncritically and focus on the implications for day-to-day work (Berman and McLaughlin 1975). They sometimes acquiesce to curricula designed around behavioral objectives (Bullough, Gitlin, and Goldstein 1984) or teacher-evaluation systems geared to specific behaviors (Popkewitz and Lind 1988) without questioning how those systems constrain what will be taught or how. They will also adopt the procedures that should lead to more reflective teaching without understanding or properly applying the underlying principles (Cohen 1990).

Commitment

Teaching rarely generates the commitment predicted by theories of professionalism. Historically, teaching was something men did for a while and women did because it fit with their family responsibilities. While it is becoming a more permanent occupational choice, part of its appeal is an annual schedule that permits travel, family activities, and other pursuits not related to work. (Kottkamp et al. 1986). This is not necessarily a sign of strong commitment to one's work.

Actual emotional commitment to teaching has declined in recent decades, but the great variation suggests that changes in working conditions could build stronger ties to the occupation in the future. The proportion of teachers who reported that they certainly or probably would become a teacher again peaked in 1966 at 78 percent, dropped to a low of 47 percent in 1981, then rose slightly over the decade (NEA 1987). Things may continue to improve. In 1984, 45 percent of teachers said they would advise a young person to pursue a career in teaching, but in 1989 67 percent said they would do so (Taylor et al. 1989). These data suggest a modest renewal of enthusiasm for teaching but also point to its frailty.

Control and Coordination

The pattern of coordination and control in schools is mixed. Mutual adjustment is atypical. Teaching is a lonely occupation where teachers may have only limited social contact with each other; interaction around educational issues is even more limited (Johnson 1990). However, supervision is equally rare. Teachers' interactions with principals rarely deal with instructional problems, course content, school goals, or general educational concepts (Bacharach et al. 1986). If anything, the pattern here is more one of loose coupling than either the bureaucratic or professional design.

The distribution of decision making varies with the issue, giving teachers substantially more influence over operational than strategic issues (Bacharach et al. 1986). The portion of teachers who occasionally, seldom, or never participate in decisions ranges from 25 percent for decisions about how to teach, to 44 percent for decisions about grade- or subject-level assignments, to 94 percent for staff hiring decisions.

The absence of control over strategic decisions reflects the bureaucratic model, but it is not clear how much influence teachers want. Lack of influence is experienced as a deprivation. When asked how opportunity to participate should change, more than half the teachers in one survey wanted more input in fifteen out of sixteen areas. Yet in the same survey, 82 percent were very or somewhat satisfied with their current authority (Bacharach et al. 1986). Interviews suggest that teachers do not want active involvement in making strategic decisions, but they do want to protect their instructional autonomy and to get more of available resources (Firestone and Rosenblum 1988; Johnson 1990). They particularly resent the artificial participation that occurs when committees of teachers are formed and asked to make recommendations that are subsequently ignored, as sometimes happens with site-based management (Sirotnik and Clark 1988).

A major constraint on greater influence is time. Many teachers already have trouble finding time to counsel students (59 percent), grade papers (55 percent), and plan for future lessons (48 percent) (Bacharach et al. 1986). They would rather take care of these routine, but difficult-to-schedule, tasks than meet on strategic issues—unless they believe decisions on those issues will be badly made otherwise. In sum, teachers will resent bureaucratic changes that limit their present influence. How enthusiastic they will be about programs to empower them will depend on the practical implications of those programs.

Incentives

Teachers are very sensitive to intrinsic rewards. Large majorities report that their biggest reward comes when their students learn more effectively (Kottkamp et al. 1986; Lortie 1975). Other studies by Bredeson and colleagues (1983), Johnson (1990), and Kasten (1984) confirm the importance of work-based rewards. At the same time, salary makes a difference. Teachers say it is a major reason for leaving teaching (Harris and Associates 1985; Kasten 1984), and those who are paid more actually stay in teaching longer (Murnane, Singer, and Willett 1989). In fact, some combination of salary and intrinsic incentives seems to be necessary to keep people from leaving teaching (Chapman and Hutcheson 1982), but *how* they combine to motivate teachers remains an unanswered question.

Views of Reforms

When asked about job differentiation reforms, teachers preferred those that stressed job enlargement. Merit pay does not appeal to them (Kasten 1984). Given a choice they prefer career ladders. They fear that all forms of job differentiation will create "artificial and unfortunate distinctions among teachers" (Taylor et al. 1989, p. 49) and question the fairness of selection processes. Given the problems teachers have assessing their own performance, it is not surprising that these concerns were associated mostly with merit pay. Moreover, when they evaluate reforms, extrinsic rewards (income) are important but less significant than intrinsic ones related to peer interaction and task variety or opportunities to learn new things (Smylie and Smart 1990; Taylor et al. 1989).

Teachers also prefer governance changes to merit pay. In one study, two-thirds thought every school should establish a leadership committee with principals, teachers, and students to set and enforce rules, and four-fifths thought teachers and principals should share time after school to formally plan staff development, curriculum, and management (Taylor et al. 1989).

Teachers' sentiments fit neither the bureaucratic nor the professional design. Their opposition to decision deprivation and merit pay suggest that efforts to increase bureaucracy will not be well received. They prefer professionalizing reforms, but there are few signs even in that direction that they are truly enthusiastic about major changes.

THE POLITICS OF REFORM

While our primary objective is to clarify the differences between bureaucratic and professional designs and understand their implications for teaching, we are also interested in understanding why districts choose the reforms they do. The ambiguity and controversy surrounding the reform of teaching is similar to what is found in many other settings. Beliefs about how to design jobs and organizations are often a source of conflict (Ranson et al. 1980). This conflict may result from ideological differences, like those between advocates of professionalism and bureaucracy in teaching; divergent training, which leads groups to see the same problem in different ways; or varying perceptions of personal advantage (Pfeffer 1978).

For any new design to be implemented, these disagreements must be resolved. Recent experiments with restructuring, including the redesign of teaching, have created new alliances—sometimes between historical adversaries, and often with groups outside the district (David 1989). Political theories help one understand how this alliance-building process works and where it breaks down. A well-developed research tradition treats the organization and its environment as a set of conflicting groups with divergent values, interests, and sources of power (Morgan 1986). It suggests that some groups have more access than others to decisions about organizational design. Yet it is rare that anyone can make such decisions alone. Instead, decisions result from periodic bargaining. Such bargaining will lead to coalitions of groups that determine the organization's structure for varying periods of time (Bacharach and Mitchell 1987). The resulting decisions will reflect the interests of some groups more than others. To understand this decision-making process, we first examine its dynamics and then the groups that participate.

The Dynamics of Organizational Politics

The politics of organizational reform are determined by the preexisting formal structure. School districts are sets of interacting parts, each a system in its own right. These primary systems include the state, the community, the school board, the administration, and teachers (Bacharach and Mitchell 1987). Each system has its own functions: the school board represents community interests, the administration turns statements of interest into action plans and resource allocations, and teachers convert plans and resources into actual teaching. These functions help specify each system's rights, responsibilities, and interests.

The formal organization also specifies the decision-making authority of each system. Authority is different from influence (Gamson 1968). The first refers to the formal right to make binding decisions over a range of issues. The second refers to the capacity to get others to respond to one's will. Those with authority may conspicuously lack influence as often happens with constitutional monarchs. Yet authority is a source of influence. American presidents cannot pass legislation, but they can set the agenda and use the veto to shape the bills that come before them.

Of the many sources of influence that have been identified in addition to authority, five are especially important. The first is *control over resources*, like money and labor (Pfeffer 1978). The federal government gives small special-purpose grants to gain considerable influence over local districts. Interest in this money allowed the government to attach special conditions to its use through the regulations guiding programs for poor and minority children in the Chapter 1 program, and the handicapped in Public Law 94–142. The labor of individuals is rarely in short supply, but that of groups can be. Unions gain influence by controlling access to whole categories of people, including teachers, bus drivers, and so forth.

A second source of influence is *knowledge and information* (Pfeffer 1978). To make decisions, people need to know what is happening and what alternatives are available. Superintendents gain considerable influence over board members by both flooding them with information and withholding it (Kerr 1964). Staff specialists derive influence from their expertise, which helps them suggest solutions and marshall evidence for their effectiveness.

Time is a third source (Cohen, March, and Olsen 1972). People who have time to participate in the whole process have more opportunities to ensure that decisions meet their interests than those who do not. Some individuals have more discretion in how to use that time than others. Most teachers spend too much time in classrooms to participate extensively in schoolwide decision making. Release time can increase their opportunity to participate. Principals have much more time to make decisions for their schools, but their time in the district office is limited.

A fourth source of influence is the *ability to apply decision criteria* (Pfeffer 1978). In spite of ongoing politics, organizational decisions are normally justified in terms of how they contribute to the greater good. However, because criteria are in conflict, that greater good is often difficult to define. Sometimes what is cheapest makes sense; sometimes what helps students does. One might rely on a combination of other sources of influence, not to gain votes directly for one's position, but to convince others of the importance of rulings that indirectly favor that position. Argument and persuasion can sometimes achieve the same effect.

A final source is the existence of a *coalition of like-minded individuals* (Bacharach and Mitchell 1987). As organizations grow larger, opportunities for individual influence grow smaller. Then individuals may band together in groups to have a greater voice. Though this is especially likely to affect electoral decisions where numbers count, the strategy works in other areas as well. Thus, a superintendent is less likely to adjust bus schedules for one family than for a school's Parent Teacher Organization. Coalitions take place at two levels. Members of the same subsystem—such as teachers or community members—may band together. Diverse subsystems may also come together to influence others, as when teachers ally with the school board to influence the superintendent.

The influence of various groups operates differently at various stages of the decision cycle. Two crucial stages are adoption, when the formal decision is made, and implementation, when it is put into practice (Fullan 1982). The adoption of a decision is usually made by a relatively small number of people. Formal authority is crucial at this stage, but the exercise of that authority can be shaped by individuals with the time and knowledge to explore options and present evidence for their usefulness, by persuasive people who can make arguments for particular decision criteria, and by coalition leaders.

Implementation is more inclusive, so the cooperation of those not involved in making the decision is necessary. While a formal decision can rarely be directly vetoed at this stage, it can be interpreted in ways that shape its impact or carried out selectively so that its intent is not fully realized. Resources, time, and knowledge facilitate the actions needed to enact the decision. Decision criteria are applied to obtain the cooperation of those who do the work rather than "decision makers." Finally, coalitions become important for their ability selectively to withdraw their energies from the effort to make the decision work. As a result, teachers have more influence at this stage, and persuasive efforts are usually directed at them rather than at formal authorities.

The Participants in Reform

While one can identify general patterns in organizational politics, the array of groups, interests, and sources of influence will be historically determined for each district and decision (Bacharach and Mitchell 1987). The school board, top district administrators, principals, teachers, and the state all play key roles in redesigning teaching (David 1989). What those roles will be and how much influence each group will have is not always clear.

The Superintendent and Board. Where design decisions are not constrained by custom or legislation (Meyer and Rowan 1977), they should be the province of the superintendent and the school board. As the elected representatives of the district, the board is the policy-making body responsible for such fundamental decisions. Its key source of influence is its authority, as well as its right to hire and fire superintendents. However, the superintendent has two other sources of influence—greater time to pursue these issues and the knowledge and information to develop and evaluate proposals. How will these different sources of influence play out in practice?

In the short term, superintendents can dominate their boards (Burlingame 1988). In addition to the sources already mentioned, the superintendent can take advantage of the ideology of expertise, which reinforces formal authority, the variety of ways to socialize board members to agree with a chief executive, and the difficulty a group has in building agreement on how to oppose an individual (Tucker and Zeigler 1980; Zeigler, Jennings, and Peak 1974).

Over the long haul, however, boards have more influence (Burlingame 1988; Cuban 1976; Iannaccone and Lutz 1970). Major social changes, such as battles over integration or the immigration of new client groups (e.g., executives to new suburbs), can activate the board to oppose the superintendent. Rarely during these periods can the board overcome the superintendent's policy preferences. Over time, however, continued board-superintendent conflict leads to the replacement of the incumbent with someone who more often will agree with the board.

When the district's identity is in place and normal politics prevail, the superintendent will seem to dominate board activity, but with the acquiescence of the board. During critical periods when the district's identity is in question, the board will be more active (Zald 1969). These are also the times when major reform is most likely. Top administrators are most open to reform during crises—that is, at exactly the times when the board is most active in policy decisions. In the few cases where districts voluntarily reform, the relative influence of the superintendent and the board are difficult to assess. Where change is successful, the board and superintendent share a vision of how the district should proceed. Where they do not, presumably there is too much factionalism for substantial change. However, it is not clear whether the vision necessary for success is initiated by the board or the superintendent (Cuban 1989).

District Administrators.   The role of the district administration is more difficult to assess because of the paucity of research in this area (Fullan 1982; Fullan et al. 1986). Some interesting clues can be gleaned from the research on school-level implementation. Hall (1987a, b; Hord, Hall, and Stiegelbauer 1983), for instance, has identified and elaborated on the "consigliere" role. This person is a second change leader, someone who helps the principal implement change. This is not a formal role. It can be played by a regular classroom teacher or someone in a position that can be redefined for a special purpose, such as a resource teacher. Typically, the consigliere complements the principal—for instance, by providing the concrete assistance the principal lacks the time to offer. With weak principals, the district office may try to work around the person in formal authority. However, circumventing the formal authority is less effective for implementation than having a strong leader in the formal position assisted by a second in command. Carlson (1972) identifies variants on this role at the district level.

One would expect to find a subgroup of district administrators acting as consiglieres for the design and implementation of reforms. This subgroup should fall within the formal structure of the district office, but not entirely. In a typical pattern, the subgroup should support the superintendent in his decisions—either by providing staff assistance in formulating options (increasing the superintendent's time and expertise) or by carrying them out during implementation. However, the possibility exists, at least theoretically, for district administrators working around a weak superintendent to keep the district operating, sometimes in direct contact with influentials on the school board.

Teachers. Traditionally, teachers have not participated in the adoption of major reforms because of their limited access to strategic decision making. Teachers' associations working in an industrial labor relations model limited their bargaining to narrowly conceived questions of salary and working conditions, sometimes because of their own conceptions of their self-interest and sometimes because of restrictive collective-bargaining legislation (Mitchell 1989). One of the most pathbreaking developments of the 1980s was the inclusion of teachers' associations in decisions about reform (David 1989). In several instances, the formal mechanism has been either the labor-management contract or some other agreement between the district and the union (Casner-Lotto 1988; Johnson 1989; Sickler 1988). In several instances, even where teachers did not initiate change, the magnitude of what was accomplished and the amount of conflict depended on the relations between the district and the union (Johnson and Nelson 1987). Sources of teacher influence are not clear, but they appear to include formal access to district decision making that is based on, but separate from, the collective-bargaining process; the time, knowledge, and persuasive abilities of association leaders; and the capacity of members to withdraw cooperation from policies they opposed during implementation. Finally, as in the case of the superintendent-board relationship, extensive change seems to result more from an equitable, cooperative working relationship rather than domination by either side.

Principals. Historically, principals' influence has come during implementation. According to Arends (1982) principals are crucial to successful change. In a more fine-grained analysis, Firestone and Corbett (1988) suggest that the principal's contribution is to provide resources, protect a change program from disruptive influences, and encourage staff to participate. Principals have not historically participated in major district decisions (Tucker and Zeigler 1980). Especially in larger districts, they may have no more authority to participate than teachers. The accounts of current reform efforts often give them little attention. In fact, there is some indication of active principal opposition to such efforts, most notably in a lawsuit filed by principals in Rochester, New York.

The State. The state is rarely an active participant in local decisions on whether or how to reform teaching. Instead, it provides the legal framework and sometimes resources within which reform takes place. This can be done directly through special programs. For instance, during the 1980s Missouri, Tennessee, Texas, and Utah initiated statewide career-ladder programs that provided money for differential pay for teachers and specified how to evaluate staff to award salary increments. Other states—including Arizona, Georgia, and North Carolina—piloted such programs in a limited number of districts (Southern Regional Education Board 1990).

State regulation can also affect organizational designs indirectly. For instance, teacher certification requirements contribute to high schools' departmental structure by creating separate specialties in various subject areas. Laws specifying the responsibilities of school boards determine the extent to which teachers can legally participate in decision making. Collective-bargaining regulations determine how much teachers' associations can use formal negotiation channels to work out new organizational arrangements with a school board. States that are willing to grant selective waivers of any of these laws or regulations can facilitate local reforms.

State regulation also contributes to the influence of district administrators. Changes in regulation often result from the persuasive efforts of school people, and those most likely to represent a district to the legislature (and to interpret regulations to the district) are the superintendent and top district administrators. On occasion, these people can have substantial input into state regulations (Fuhrman, Clune, and Elmore 1988). Administrators' interaction with the state can be a crucial source of information and resources that can be used to shape the adoption of reform proposals.

CONCLUSION

The bureaucratic and professional views of teaching derive from different conceptions of how teachers should teach and imply different designs for schools and districts. The bureaucratic view assumes that teaching is relatively certain and codifiable. As a result, decision making should be centralized and teaching should be controlled through direct supervision and the standardization of work processes (curriculum and texts) and outcomes (tests). This view provides a justification for reforms like merit pay. The professional view emphasizes the uncertainty of teaching and the need for informed judgment. For that reason, it requires better-trained and more committed teachers. It also supports greater decentralization to include teachers in decision making and more mutual adjustment, or collegial interaction. The professional view offers a rationale for proposals to empower teachers and adopt job enlargement plans.

Differences between these viewpoints are often blurred by ambiguous language, confusion about how the elements of each viewpoint fit together, and misunderstandings of the fundamental conflicts between them. Such conflicts become apparent, however, when districts seek to adopt reforms. Therefore, we can expect that district efforts at teacher reform will become highly political with the board, the central administration, teachers, and others playing a role. To understand how these differences are worked out, what the resulting programs look like, and how they affect teaching, we turn now to the three case studies.

2. MOSSVILLE:
BUREAUCRATIC REDESIGN

MOSSVILLE SHOWS THE strengths and weaknesses of bureaucracy. The district was one of a small number piloting its state's Teacher Development Program (TDP). This program provided teachers with incentives in the form of permanent salary increases if they were evaluated as successfully using the form of direct instruction built into the state's Teacher Evaluation System (TES). The state's specifications gave the district very little leeway in designing its program, but the state philosophy was compatible with that of district leaders who played a major role in designing it. The program was initiated by the district's superintendent and assistant superintendent for personnel who responded to a state pilot program. Because of both state policy and administrative predilections, teachers were given little voice in program design. When they opposed the program and appealed to the board, the administration held firmly to its initial position. This firmness maintained the original design although it probably contributed to the superintendent's departure from the district. As implemented, the program standardized instruction and reduced teacher motivation. Classroom instruction was substantially influenced by the evaluation system and became more rigorous, but teachers became frustrated and anxious as a result of the program and the bureaucratic implementation.

To explain why the program had the effects it did, this chapter will describe the district context that created interest in the TDP, summarize the relevant state policies, examine the operation of the program in Mossville, and then present information on its effects as perceived by teachers and administrators.

MOSSVILLE'S HISTORY

Mossville's interest in piloting the state's Teacher Development Program and the particular approach the district took reflected the tempestuous history that preceded implementation and continued after the effort was underway. Mossville began a more innovative chapter of its history when Jack O'Brien became superintendent in 1981. During 1988–89—the year of field observations and the last year the TDP was authorized—his contract was not renewed. In 1989–90 a new superintendent presided over the process of folding the TDP into the state's new improvement program. Before turning to the district's history, a demographic description is presented.

Background

Mossville was a regional trading and industrial hub. Most people in the county lived in Mossville itself, but the city was dying and most growth took place in the smaller surrounding towns. The student enrollment of just under 20,000 had been shrinking over the last few years. The proportion of black students, 30 percent, was consistent with the rest of the state. Slightly more than a quarter of the students received free or reduced lunches while a tenth were enrolled in the Chapter 1 program. These students were housed in three high schools and twenty-seven other buildings. About a fifth of the staff of just under 1,300 was black. About two-thirds of the district's income came from the state and a quarter was generated locally. The balance was federal funding. These figures approximated the state averages. Still, the local contribution was in the top quintile in the state.

The Old Regime

Jack O'Brien was hired to respond to the problems of the two previous decades. Until the 1960s Mossville, like other districts in the state, was segregated. Serious desegregation efforts began with a lawsuit filed in 1964. The resulting court order required students to be assigned to schools so that each building reflected the racial makeup of the whole district. Staff were also shifted; each junior high or high school had one black administrator.

The court case was accompanied by extensive riots. Desegregation academies opened and flourished as—according to one long-time administrator—"the fundamentalists and the affluent left the system." As many as 20 percent of the school-aged population may have been in the academies. By the middle 1970s the worst civic unrest was past, but the system still lacked a compromise that would please both the courts and the community. The less public adjustment was to loosen the curriculum. The more public change was a frequent modification in age-group configurations and school boundaries to achieve desegregation. These were changed so regularly that one board member remembered having a child attend five different schools in seven years.

At the same time, Moss County experienced a major economic readjustment. Mossville was essentially a company town in the 1950s. When that company moved out, unemployment moved into the 14–20 percent range, and Mossville lost much of its civic elite. Efforts were begun to bring in new businesses. New development began in earnest in the early 1970s, when three Fortune 500 companies built plants in the region. Later, smaller companies began relocating from the north. Managers of these businesses found the schools wanting, so the Chamber of Commerce became more active in education. Ernest Faulkner, the superintendent who took the Moss County Schools through desegregation, had worked his way up within the system. His supporters said, "Ernest was home-centered. We never went anywhere. We didn't participate in state activities." Some board members were critical of his insularity, saying, "Faulkner was homegrown. With his leadership, the Moss County Schools had become inbred."

Two new issues arose late in the Faulkner administration. First, when many outdated buildings had to be replaced, Faulkner could not develop a building plan. Second, the board believed the district was hiring underqualified people. Earlier, people had been hired as much because of kinship ties as academic qualifications. Faulkner usually paid more attention to academic qualifications, and "word got out that you couldn't get hired if you had a D on your transcript." In fact, he may have generated school-board opposition because members' relatives were not hired. Still, one person with a weak academic background but kinship ties to a district administrator was hired as a teacher, and at least one teacher was promoted to principal with insufficient formal qualifications. The board was convinced there was a serious problem.

Meanwhile, community support for the schools remained weak. For example, turnover in school-board seats is usually voluntary.

Even a few cases of incumbents losing elections suggest substantial discontent (Iannaccone and Lutz 1970). Yet, between 1975 and 1980, five of the nine cases of board succession resulted from election losses.

In 1981, four of the county's seven board members were new. Four were from outside the county. Three were professionals, one was the wife of an engineer in a new business that had come into town, one was a secretary and the wife of a small businessman, and two were retired teachers. The husband of one of these ran a funeral home. Three were extremely discontented with the status quo; and one, according to a district administrator, "was a stated enemy of Faulkner."

The board chose not to renew Faulkner's contract and began a search for a new superintendent. High on the priority list was someone who would be what the board called more "PR oriented." According to one member,

> The board said the first thing was community support. We needed someone who could get business and parent support. Also someone who understood instruction. That was third on my list. Buildings were also crucial.

In this context a national search was held and culminated in the selection of Jack O'Brien.

The New Superintendent

O'Brien's administration provided the context for Mossville's Teacher Development Program, but he also had to deal with other issues. He began his tenure with strong board support and quickly pushed through a number of tough improvement measures. Over time, however, his support eroded in the community, among staff, and with the board. His contract was renewed in 1985—the year TDP began—but not in January 1989. The issues that arose during O'Brien's eight-year tenure fall into two clusters: 1) desegregation, buildings, and community and 2) evaluation and accountability, including TDP.

Buildings and Desegregation. Early on O'Brien concluded that the district's K–4, 5–6, 7–9, 10–12 system "was part of the integration effort, but it didn't deliver instruction." He wanted to move to a middle school system. For that, he said,

> we had to have a $24 million construction program to get rid of obsolete construction. There was a lot of changing schools as a

result. We closed seven buildings, built four new ones, and added wings to others that were the equivalent of two new buildings.

To do that, he passed a bond issue. That success may have been the highlight of his public relations orientation.

Along with the building program, periodic readjustment to school boundaries was needed to comply with the desegregation court order. Although the boundaries were drawn with great sensitivity to neighborhood interests, O'Brien said he was "blistered" by the public for those changes. He says he resigned from two clubs because of the constant pressures opposing desegregation. Still, the issue remained. When the board had to redistrict late in his tenure, board meetings were jammed by 120–150 people. According to newspaper articles,

> [two board members] complained that the new plans do not address the longstanding problem of some elementary school pupils having to ride buses past nearby schools to ones far away.... "When I see a five-year-old child sitting by the side of the road waiting for a school bus, I don't like it," said Ron Gormley, who later acknowledged that he thinks safety concerns should override racial concerns at least at the elementary school level.

In January 1988 a new redistricting plan that achieved racial balance passed on a 4–3 vote.

Evaluation and Accountability. According to O'Brien, the context for accountability policies was set by the 1981 board's perception of the district's internal disarray:

> When I was interviewed in February 1981...the board had changed significantly.... What they wanted as a change was accountability. Thirty schools were doing what they wanted.... Some [administrators] were not certified. The board wanted more central control. The district had eliminated all testing but what the state required. They wanted someone with knowledge of curriculum, testing, and evaluation.

Moreover, the problem was not just a lack of control systems. According to O'Brien, the board criticized several individual administrators: "The board wanted a lot of personnel changes. I said I couldn't guarantee anything until I'd been here a year. Some were bad; some were good. I didn't want to be a hatchet man." To O'Brien, accountability had two elements. The first was the use of formal, objective data for monitoring performance. "Hell yes," he said, "I look at data!" He was especially proud of introducing quick, basic-facts tests that elementary students took every year. Second, people had to measure up to expectations. Negative incentives or "pressure" were often used in the process. In his own words,

> I have meetings each year where I bring together the principals of the five schools that do the best on the tests with the principals of the five schools that do the worst. I ask the principals who did the best how they succeeded. Then I ask the other five, "why can't you do that?" That's pressure.

To strengthen accountability, O'Brien did not just develop the new basic-skills tests. He also began publicizing the results of district and state tests for the whole district and for individual schools in enough detail to allow a parent to assess how well his or her child's school was doing in comparison to other schools in the district, the whole district, the state, and itself over time. Just publishing the test scores had some effect, as O'Brien explains:

> I publish scores in the newspaper. Tom Mix is principal of Winnetka with its elitist, old-time Mossville money. Two years ago, his school was fourteenth in the district on the basic skills test. Parents came in and asked him why. Now his school is second.

O'Brien also developed an administrative evaluation system with written expectations for each administrator. These were supplemented by formal individual sessions with him and several kinds of group coaching sessions. Through the individual sessions he helped principals develop measurable or observable indicators for expectations, create strategies to meet those expectations, and learn to use the same approach to shape teacher behavior. Moreover, he modeled the process by working out expectations for his own performance with the board and having the board publicly discuss his own evaluation each year.

This system was not popular with administrators. According to O'Brien,

> At the first principal's meeting of the year...in front of all seventy-five administrators, [a principal] handed me a piece of paper.

It was a letter signed by the principals. It said, "we respectfully request that you eliminate written expectations. Our time is too scarce to work on those expectations with all the other things we are expected to do." I said, "I'll answer that right now. With all due respect, I refuse to grant your request. I have them here, and I'll pass them out."

Another response was to remove staff. In the past almost all nontenured teachers were given tenure at the appropriate time. O'Brien tried to tighten up, but the board's support for this change was not as solid as he expected, as one board member from that time explains:

[O'Brien's] desire was to improve accountability by evaluation at all levels. He asked us when he got here, "do you want average teachers or good teachers?" We said, "good teachers." He asked us, "do you know what you're biting off?" We swore we did, but when he brought us seven average teachers only three were terminated.

The board's difficulty in releasing nontenured teachers created a need to document teacher performance. Over time the district's documentation procedures became fuller, and the proportion of nontenured teachers retained declined. Still, such decisions continued to be difficult for the board.

Similar problems occurred with top administration. O'Brien replaced one person, and another resigned early in his tenure. However, his idea of what should be done with two people differed sharply from the board's. One was Joan Dark, the assistant superintendent for personnel, whom two board members criticized for "favoritism" in personnel practices. O'Brien found her to be his "best administrator." He attributed the history of favoritism to the previous superintendent rather than Dark, and he supported her with the board. On the other hand, O'Brien believed that his assistant superintendent for curriculum and instruction, John Metropolis, was inadequate; but Metropolis was a local. When the board would not remove him, O'Brien gave him "busy work" and took on much of the curriculum leadership himself. All told, efforts to remove staff generated considerable resistance by those involved and friction with the board but relatively little personnel change.

O'Brien also changed hiring practices. Faulkner had allowed principals to hire their own assistants and then had hired principals from among the district's assistant principals. This resulted in locally grown principals who contributed to the district's "inbred" nature. O'Brien wanted to hire technically competent administrators who shared his interest in evaluation and student achievement even if he had to look outside the system. Therefore, principal selection was centralized and formalized. He created teams to select candidates for all certified positions and usually joined administrator-selection teams. He saw this as strengthening the merit component of the selection process. Others saw it as ensuring that those selected fit his image of an effective principal.

One board member opposed O'Brien's efforts to bring in outside candidates for administrative positions. This issue was explicitly discussed with the board, and an agreement was reached that no more than half the principals selected would be from out of the district. In fact, of the nineteen principals hired during O'Brien's eight years, only two were truly brought in from the outside.

Another board member and the local NAACP complained that too few black administrators were hired. When the old black and white school systems were combined, the district had a number of black administrators. However, several of them were old, and at least two opposed O'Brien's program to increase student achievement through testing and evaluation. Several retired, in at least one case after encouragement from O'Brien. For the most part, they were replaced by white administrators. Only two out of nineteen principals O'Brien hired were black and one other was partly Native American.

The Superintendent, the Staff, and the Board

This overview of the issues during the O'Brien years indicates considerable tension between the superintendent and the board, much of it over personnel evaluation issues. This was only part of the story, as becomes clear from a more detailed examination of the orientations, actions, and influence of O'Brien, the teachers, and the board.

The Superintendent. Jack O'Brien was in his mid-forties when he came to Mossville. He had worked his way up from teacher to central administration in two midwestern states and received his doctorate from a large state university in one of them. His views on education emphasized accountability for instruction and desegregation. His approach to educational management emphasized strong ties to the outside world but centralized direction of the district.

O'Brien's stand on desegregation was quite clear. In his own words, "I don't hesitate to tell the community it's right for your kids to go to school with blacks." The limit to his dedication to equal opportunity for minorities came in his dealings with professionals. There he was fundamentally committed to making personnel decisions on the basis of performance, an attribute which he believed could be assessed through the use of test scores, in-class ratings, or other standardized procedures.

At the same time, he worked hard to build ties outside the system. To improve relationships with the county and increase financial support for education, he became the spokesperson for the schools that his predecessor had not been. He joined clubs, spoke frequently with the press, and was generally seen as "an excellent PR man. He appears well on the media." He also developed relationships with the closest branch of the state university to give his staff greater access to professional development opportunities, and raised the involvement of the board in the National School Boards' Association.

Within the state he was much more active than his predecessor in educational politics. Some of this he did himself. In some cases, he encouraged others to participate in state pilot programs. Joan Dark clearly saw the difference between O'Brien and Faulkner:

> Take our involvement in the pilot of the beginning teacher program. [The department] called and asked if we wanted to play. [Jack] jumped on it in a heartbeat. Ernest would have said no. I'd not have known about the phone call.

At the same time, O'Brien clearly believed in a strong central administration:

> My attitude is you hired me to run this railroad. I know how. If you don't like it, get rid of me.... There'll be no progress if seven people try to be superintendent. In an enterprise this size, you've got to have someone to run it.... I put people into two categories: strong and weak. The strong ones like me. The weak ones don't. I don't like to mess around too long with the weak ones.

This vision did not encourage building support among separate constituencies.

While he could delegate clearly, he maintained control over what he considered to be important decisions. Speaking of the plans for the schools built under his administration, he said:

> I don't have time to ask principals how to spend money. They did that for 30 years and the mouthiest, brightest principals had

the nicest buildings.... When I came, I had all the furniture ranked A, B, and C.... I didn't ask the principals. I looked at the data. If a building had 85 percent C furniture, no other building got the money.

He also insulated himself from the board according to both top administrators and board members:

One thing that contributed to [Jack's] downfall was his reluctance to have special board meetings.... Jack didn't want to meet with the board more than he had to.

The things he didn't give me were the information I thought I needed on day-to-day operations of the schools. I wasn't involved in curriculum unless I talked to others. We found out about unfortunate things in the newspapers.

Teachers.   Teachers were among the least influential participants in district policy making. A major contributing factor was the state context. By law, Mosstate specified features at the state level that were often locally determined elsewhere. Most important, there was a statewide professional salary scale. Since salaries were determined by the legislature, local professional associations were relatively weak; and collective bargaining was unknown. By contrast, the state teachers' association was very active. While the research was underway it mounted an extremely aggressive effort, complete with demonstrations at the state capitol, to raise the salary scale for the first time in several years.

It did not help that teachers were split into two factions with separate organizations. The president of the more militant American Federation of Teachers local spoke on some issue at each board meeting. The AFT formally screened candidates for the 1988 school board election and endorsed three of them, but only one won. The National Education Association affiliate was much larger than its AFT counterpart but also much less active. This group did not have a regular presence at board meetings and played no active role in board elections.

The Board.   The rapid electoral turnover in the years before O'Brien was hired continued for another year. Two board members lost elections in the fall of 1982. Then followed a period of relative stability until 1988. Four of the members who elected O'Brien were still in office in January 1988.

During this period, board leadership came from two midwesterners who generally supported O'Brien. Early in his administration, the frequency of meetings declined compared to the last years of the Faulkner administration, although the number of meetings increased over time. His support from the board was quite strong. His December 1984 public evaluation was positive with two exceptions: keeping the board informed and his relations with teachers.

Things began to change rapidly in 1988. In January one board leader moved out of town. A newspaper account describes his successor as follows:

> Last August, Melody Jackson picked up a placard and joined 40 other angry parents outside the Moss County Schools office to protest a ban on hardship transfers. In September, she helped write a memo to school board members, accusing them of making children "pawns" in a game of racial quotas.... Last week she was picked to replace [the outgoing board member] by the county GOP.

The 1988 board election for three positions involved seats held by two board members who had hired O'Brien. One was defeated in the primary. Newspaper accounts of interviews with candidates indicate two major issues. One was the recent redistricting plan and other desegregation-related issues. The other was Jack O'Brien himself.

> I don't think it's any secret what I think about Dr. O'Brien.... He is deceptive and manipulates everyone that has to make a decision to his way of thinking. I have not met a teacher yet, or a student, or a parent who feels that he is doing even an adequate job.

A third incumbent who had not supported O'Brien was reelected. The most extreme critics of O'Brien and the redistricting effort lost, but the two winners had been critical of district operations. Moreover, the board now consisted of three former Mossville teachers, including two who had made public statements about "teacher morale." Demographically, it had not changed much. Four of the candidates had been raised outside the district. There was the same number of women (four) and a comparable mix of professionals, small-business people, retirees, and wives of those employed by larger businesses.

When O'Brien's contract was reviewed a month after the new board was sworn in, the vote was 6–1 not to renew. Nadine Kurtz, the sole member remaining from the board that had hired him, gave the only positive vote.

In fact, indicators of a gap between O'Brien and the board had occurred earlier. According to a principal, "The handwriting was on the wall one and a half years ago. Suddenly, he wasn't winning any more. He was doing too much too fast." In the previous year two of his recommendations for hiring principals had been overruled. Moreover, when the associate superintendent retired in the summer of 1988, the position was not filled so a new superintendent could choose his own deputy.

THE STATE TEACHER DEVELOPMENT PROGRAM

Although Mosstate's per pupil expenditures on education placed it in the bottom fifth for the nation, it was one of several southern states that initiated significant educational reforms in the late 1970s and early 1980s. Between 1985–86 and 1988–89, it piloted the Teacher Development Program in fifteen districts. In 1989, when a new policy was initiated, the TDPs in the pilot districts were folded into the new effort.

The legislation establishing the TDP listed as its purposes "to improve the quality of classroom instruction, to increase the attractiveness of teaching, and to encourage the recognition and retention of high quality teachers." The mechanism was an incentive system for teachers, but it built on the previously developed Initial Certification Project to support and evaluate more effectively beginning teachers. It also employed the state-developed Teacher Evaluation System that was introduced at the same time as the TDP and mandated for use in teacher evaluation throughout the state. Thus, the TDP in practice combined three pieces of legislation: for beginning teachers, for evaluating teachers, and for rewarding high performers financially.[1]

Differentiated Ranks

The TDP expanded on the use of the new evaluation system by paying higher salaries to teachers who demonstrated superior skills on the teaching behaviors that it assessed. The salary increases were reflected in the introduction of career ranks. These were as follows:

1) *Initial status* for teachers in their first two years of service and not yet fully certified.
2) *Provisional status* for teachers in their third year and fully certified.
3) *Career Status I* (CS I) for teachers who had completed three years of service and thirty hours of a state-designed effective teacher train-

ing program and who had been evaluated as at least "at standard" in all functions assessed through the Teacher Evaluation System.

4) *Career Status II* (CS II) for Career Status I teachers who had completed a total of four years of service, were judged "above standard or higher" on the TES, and had compiled a portfolio showing years of service, valid state certification, attendance records, indicators of professional growth, unique assignments or leadership roles, and additional duties and responsibilities.

The CS I and CS II ranks were the results of the TDP. Teachers were rewarded for reaching their ranks in two ways. First, they received pay increases. The steps in Mosstate's statewide salary schedule were based primarily on years of experience. Teachers who received CS I were moved up one extra step on the scale. Those who received CS II were moved up another step. Each step increase amounted to about five percent of the teacher's salary. CS II teachers were also eligible for extra work assignments that would receive extra pay. Jobs available to CS II teachers included mentoring initial status teachers, chairing departments and other groups that met regularly, and making staff-development presentations. Mentoring a beginning teacher or chairing a large department could increase a teacher's salary by $100 per month.

Selection

Promotions were based on teacher quality as defined by the Teacher Evaluation System. Through it, teachers were to be evaluated on eight criteria. Five referred to the teacher's classroom work: management of instructional time (intended to utilize time more effectively), management of student behavior (to ensure an orderly environment governed by clearly specified rules), instructional presentation (which assessed the effectiveness of lessons), instructional monitoring (the teacher's ability to collect information on student learning and the pace of instruction), and instructional feedback (or the accuracy, timeliness, and quality of information the teacher gave students on their own progress). These areas were content-free and reflect recent research on direct instruction (Brophy and Good 1986). In theory they were aspects of classroom management that could be assessed without knowledge of the content of the lessons observed.

The other three assessment areas referred to out-of-class work. Facilitating instruction examined the quality of lessons and their fit with district goals and curriculum. Communication in the educational environment had to do with teachers' interactions with colleagues and the community, and students in classroom and nonclassroom settings. Noninstructional duties covered adherence to state laws and other orders.

Two other features of the program were the professional development plans and the appeals procedure. The professional development plans were designed to encourage growth in teachers' performance and to guide individual efforts to gain or refine skills. Thus, there was a training component to accompany the incentive system built into the program. The appeals procedure came into play when there were disagreements over what a teacher's career status should be. In the case of a disagreement a two-step process was followed. The first review was by a special panel of three chosen jointly by the teacher and the principal in question. The second step was a review by the board.

Observer-Evaluators

To operate the program in the pilot districts, the legislation created two new positions to be supported by the state. One was a TDP coordinator. The other was the observer-evaluator (OE). The OE was a teacher on assignment for two to four years at supervisor's pay with two responsibilities. First, the OE observed other teachers. When teachers were assessed four times, two assessments were by the OE and two by the principal. The OE's role in the end-of-year assessment changed over time. Initially, the task was strictly the principal's since that individual was legally responsible for evaluation. By 1988–89 the OE was required to "sign off" on the final evaluation to ensure a higher level of objectivity. Second, OEs delivered most teacher training in the district. At first they were to deliver a state-mandated effective teacher training program to all educators. Later, they became the vehicle through which Mossville developed its own teacher-training program. The state supported one OE for every 96 teachers in the district.

Teacher Development Program Governance

The state made two provisions for governance of the TDP. At the state level there was a steering committee with one teacher, one principal, and the superintendent or designate from each district. Locally, each district was to have its own steering committee with representatives from various groups of certified staff. This local committee was to make recommendations for changes and improvement in the program and to keep personnel at each school informed about program progress.

MOSSVILLE'S TEACHER DEVELOPMENT PROGRAM IN ACTION

The TDP addressed several of Jack O'Brien's interests: in tightening accountability, in the necessity to strengthen the district's personnel system, and more specifically, in the need for a better system to document teacher quality so poor teachers could be dismissed. Because of his external orientation, he helped design the TDP legislation. Later, he encouraged Joan Dark to apply for a grant (which the district won) to pilot the program.

In practice, the TDP had four key elements: 1) a system for evaluating teachers for promotion, 2) training to facilitate high evaluations, 3) new staff, and 4) a system of governance. In describing these elements we rely not only on documents and our own interviews but also a survey conducted as part of an evaluation of the statewide TDP pilot. Usable returns were received from 84 percent of the teachers and 97 percent of the principals in the district. The survey items asked respondents to report how much they agreed with statements about the program using a 5-point scale where 1 equaled "strongly disagree," 3 was "neutral," and 5 was "strongly agree."

The Evaluation System

For district administrators, the new evaluation system was a mechanism to control teachers. It offered a means to find out more about what happened inside the classroom. According to Joan Dark, "The key issue is the evaluation system. It's like teachers are working in a doll house. Now they can't go in and close the door. People can take the top off the doll house and look in." Many principals agreed with this view. One explained that "teachers can't close their doors and do what they want. They're being looked at and inspected, and teachers have not had the kind of supervision and accountability we have now." This emphasis on control fit with O'Brien's press for accountability, but there was also an implication that teachers had been irresponsible in the past. When reviewing this section of an earlier draft, Joan Dark agreed with that implication, saying, "I've seen teachers go to the lounge as soon as the principal left the building." Isolated comments of teachers suggested that at least pockets of such irresponsibility had existed: "Before [TDP] some of us took the freedom. People were out of class. I'd come to the office and see some of the same persons. I wondered how they got their jobs done."

There was also an interest in using the evaluation system for "growth," as one principal put it. Another one said:

I use the observations to help teachers remediate their practices.... I point out their strengths. During the course of the evaluations, I may pick up something. I'll talk about it at the post-conference. I check with the other observations to see if it's a trend.... [What do you do to remediate?] It might be a course, giving them some literature, visiting another teacher, participating in a different cluster.

In other words, the evaluation system was used for skills development as well as distributing rewards.

The actual instrumentation had been developed for statewide use by a state university. Two standardized forms were used. The data instrument provided a list of thirty-eight behaviors organized under the eight functions to be evaluated. These are listed in Table 2–1. The observer had a space to code each behavior as strong, appropriate, or weak, and to make comments. Over time, observers were trained to supplement the data instrument with a running written observation of classroom events. This additional documentation ranged from nine pages of notes on one session that were so "exact" that "it was like reliving the lesson," said one teacher, to nothing. The data instrument provided the basis for filling out the data analysis: a form where the observer could summarize observations by both function and strengths and weaknesses.

At the beginning of each year, the principal and OE for the building would divide the observations so each person would do some for each teacher. For each announced observation, the observer would meet with the teacher in advance to learn about the lesson and the teacher's plans and then sit in on the lesson while filling out the data instrument. After completing the data analysis, the observer and teacher would meet. Follow-up conferences were to verify that observations were accurate, provide positive feedback on strengths, and offer suggestions for dealing with weaknesses. As one OE explained,

I talk about what I saw. I ask them, "is it accurate? Am I interpreting this correctly?" We go through the raw data so they can follow the sequence of events. Just because I list "needs improvement" doesn't necessarily mean it's bad, but I know ways to do it better.

At the end of the year, the OE and principal met to rate each teacher on each function using a 6-point scale where 3 meant "at standard" and 6 meant "superior." These were discussed with the teacher

TABLE 2-1
Functions and Behaviors in the Data Instrument

1 *Instructional Time*

   1 Materials ready
   2 Class started quickly
   3 Gets students on task
   4 Maintains high time on task

2 *Student Behavior*

   1 Rules—Administrative Matters
   2 Rules—Verbal Participation/ Talk
   3 Rules—Movement
   4 Frequently monitors behavior
   5 Stops inappropriate behavior

3 *Instructional Presentation*

   1 Begins with review
   2 Introduces lesson
   3 Speaks fluently
   4 Lesson understandable
   5 Provides relevant examples
   6 High rate of success on tasks
   7 Appropriate level of questions
   8 Brisk pace
   9 Efficient, smooth transitions
  10 Assignment clear
  11 Summarizes main points

4 *Instructional Monitoring*

   1 Maintains deadlines, standards
   2 Circulates to check student performance
   3 Uses oral, written work products to check progress
   4 Questions clearly and one at a time

5 *Instructional Feedback*

   1 Feedback on in-class work
   2 Prompt feedback on out-of-class work
   3 Affirms correct answer quickly
   4 Sustaining feedback on incorrect answers

6 *Facilitating Instruction*

   1 Instructional plan compatible with goals
   2 Diagnostic information to develop tasks
   3 Maintains accurate records
   4 Instructional plan for curriculum alignment
   5 Available resources support program

7 *Communicating with the Educational Environment*

   1 Treats all students fairly
   2 Interacts effectively within school and community

8 *Noninstructional Duties*

   1 Carries out non-instructional duties
   2 Adheres to laws, policies
   3 Plan for professional development

in an end-of-year summative evaluation. The numerical ratings were what determined if a teacher would move from one step to the next.

The process was extremely time-consuming for administrators. One assistant principal described the load as follows:

We do the formal evaluation on the first five functions. You have to be in the classroom a whole period. You can't just come in for fifteen minutes.... There is tremendous paperwork. The actual formative is 55 minutes of constant writing. Then you write a summary on another page. You fill out the categories. It takes two hours per observation times 80 observations per year.

Without the OEs, that principals' time would have been consumed by observations.

The fact that individual observers might evaluate differently created a need to standardize the use of evaluation categories. Using two people to observe each teacher provided a check on individual variation, but the district still had to maximize commonality. The district developed a training program that familiarized observers with the strategies and practices suggested by the instrument and provided opportunities to practice script taping (writing verbatim notes) and evaluating videotaped lessons. By comparing one's own evaluations with those conducted by experts, an individual could come to approximate a districtwide standard. Moreover, a senior OE was assigned to building "interrater reliability" or agreement. She became someone to call when a principal and OE had problems and offered spot-training and calibration as needed.

One recurring issue for teachers was the fairness of the evaluation system. The state survey lists several items related to evaluation fairness (see Table 2–2). These suggest that principals believed in the fairness of the evaluation process whereas teachers were ambivalent. Most teachers did not object to their own evaluations. They generally agreed with the results. Strangely enough, they agreed that the TDP's overall procedures were fair, but disagreed that the evaluation process was fair and objective. They neither agreed nor disagreed with assertions about the accuracy of the data instrument and data analysis. They had modest questions about the fairness of the appeals process.

Data on appeals of promotion decisions suggests a somewhat different pattern. The state evaluation shows that 135 appeals were filed in all fifteen pilot districts between 1985–86 and 1987–88. Forty-one of these, or 30 percent, were from Mossville. The other 70 percent were spread over fifteen districts. The district with the closest number, a larger district, had twenty-six appeals. The state evaluation finds a strong rank-order correlation between district size and number of appeals. Mossville was the second-largest district in the program, approximately two-thirds the size of the largest one. Yet it had more than half again as many appeals suggesting that size was not the only factor involved.

TABLE 2-2
Views of the Fairness of the TDP Evaluation System

Item	Mean	
	Teacher	Principal
I agree with the results of my year-end evaluation	3.56	N/A
My system has fair and reasonable procedures for the TDP	3.24	4.27
Evaluation process is fair and objective	2.71	N/A
Data instrument provides accurate record of teaching performance	3.07	4.07
Data analysis provides accurate record of observation	2.92	4.13
Appeals process used by local panel is fair	2.89	4.36
Appeals process used by school board is fair	2.88	3.75

5 = strongly agree   3 = neither agree nor disagree   1 = strongly disagree

These statistics do not indicate the acrimony surrounding some of these appeals. Two involved presidents of the local NEA chapter who had recently been identified as teachers of the year, raising questions about bias in selection. While O'Brien denied any bias, these appeals led to two lawsuits that were still in court during the field research.

Another explanation for the high appeals rate in Mossville might be the difficulty of achieving promotions there. The state evaluation presents separate data for promotion to CS I and CS II. At the first level, Mossville did not stand out. Between 1985–86 and 1987–88, 96 percent of the teachers eligible for promotion were promoted throughout the state as compared to 93 percent in Mossville. The district's rankings for promotions among the fifteen districts in each of the three years were 7, 14, and 7. Thus, with the exception of one year, Mossville was very close to the state average. Achieving the CS II was more difficult. Data are available only for 1986–87 and 1987–88. Throughout the state 85 percent of the teachers who applied were promoted as opposed to 76 percent in Mossville. The district's rankings were 14 and 11.5 (the decimal reflecting a tie). Especially at the second level, Mossville maintained a tougher standard for promotion; but it was not radically out of line with the other pilot districts.

The interviews that probed more deeply into teachers' sentiments suggested more discontent with the evaluation process than does the survey. Sixteen out of eighteen teachers made thirty-four different comments on the unfairness of some aspect of the system. In contrast, only three saw the program as fair in some sense, including two who also identified unfair elements.

"Unfairness" was not a blanket condemnation. Instead, teachers mentioned four specific problems. One general concern was "interrater reliability," or variation among observers. As one teacher put it, "there's a lot of personal judgment involved. We're humans. The system is weak because it uses judgment." This general concern had three different parts. At the simplest level, eight teachers noted the inconsistencies between individuals:

> [The current principal] is the same as an evaluator. She knows instruction forward and backward. She's more thorough than the evaluator we've had for two years.... [This principal] reads back verbatim what you said!.... [The previous principal] didn't handle it like it's being handled now. There was no announced observation. She called you in and presented a sheet. She had you read it and sign it. She didn't have anything constructive to offer. It was not nearly as professional as now.

> Principals list more strengths than OEs cause you have a relationship so you're seen as a person. The person knows you more than 30 minutes twice a month.

> We have someone who understands. She got to be an OE simply because she's so good. The assistant principals are not as knowledgeable.

These inconsistencies point to differences in evaluation ratings between OEs and principals and among principals, although the direction of those differences is not clear.

While OEs and principals generally emphasized the similarities in their ratings, they were also aware of differences that they viewed as isolated events. According to one principal, a few of her older colleagues had little incentive to take the evaluation process seriously. Their evaluations tended to be uniformly high or low and disagreed with those of OEs committed to applying categories more uniformly. Two OEs describe extreme cases of this sort:

> [The principal] was very protective of the teachers. The principal would agree with what I saw but didn't want to tell them. Last year the principal had to tell them because they were going for CS II and they wouldn't make it. If I'd been a weaker OE, they would have made it.

These extreme cases were rare. However, they suggest that milder discrepancies also existed that were more upsetting to teachers than administrators.

Not only did individuals or roles vary, but also the expertise of observers varied depending on the past work. The TES was supposed to be content-free and applicable to any classroom. Yet teachers continued to believe that subject matter and student age made a difference. Four made comments to the effect that "an English teacher can't judge a trig class, because they don't know what to look for." Similarly, primary teachers complained that high school teachers did not apply appropriate standards of classroom management to kindergarten and first grade classes.

A variant on this problem was that the basic evaluation system did not apply to some fields. Teachers of severely handicapped children argued that it was not necessary to state their objectives, for instance, when working with eight-year-olds with IQs so low that they were still being toilet trained. In most cases, these wide discrepancies were dealt with either by developing modified procedures—as happened for special education teachers—or by recruiting specialists in the field to apply slightly modified standards, as happened with librarians.

A third problem, mentioned by seven people, related to individual discretion was the potential misuse of authority. Teachers continued to believe that

> What the principal decides goes. At the summation if the evaluator says 4 and the principal says 3, the person will get a 3...

> It has become an instrument to intimidate some teachers. The principals can disregard the observations.

Principals denied, as one put it, that they were "playing 'Gotcha'" and suggested that the evaluation system constrained their authority. The board was not likely to sustain an appealed decision on the basis of formal evidence from evaluations. Yet teachers continued to believe in this potential for abuse. Some of them were quite aware of the court cases about teachers who charged that they had been denied CS II status because of their activities in the teachers' association.

Not all fears raised concerned punitive use of the evaluation system. Teachers were also sensitive to favoritism. As one said, "I wonder about the situation where some teachers are CS II. Had I been principal, they wouldn't have gotten it."

A final concern, raised by four teachers and agreed with by two principals, had less to do with individual unreliability than with the sampling strategy; the teacher's evaluation for the whole year depended almost entirely on three or four hours of classroom work:

> Resentment comes because you're talking about having people come in for one hour. Is it fair to judge a year on an hour? What if you're off or the kids are awful? But how else can you do it?

> It's harsh to only have three lessons for evaluation out of the whole year. That might not be a true sampling. It is in my case. I don't *plan* for the evaluation. It might not be a true sample for people who plan for the evaluation.

These comments illustrate two problems with the small sample. On the one hand, something might go wrong during the sampled period that would lead to an undeservedly low evaluation. On the other, teachers and principals both suspected that some teachers "put on a show" for the short time the evaluator was present to achieve a high evaluation that did not reflect regular practice.

This sampling problem suggests that the issue of evaluator discretion was more complex than teachers made it out to be and that sometimes teachers benefited from that discretion. In fact, evaluations may have been more valid as a result. Consider the following instances described by one teacher:

> The evaluator here this year was wonderful. If you're sick when she comes in, she'll come back. That happened. I was going to let her observe me, but she said she'd come back.... Also she came in when we gave the California Achievement Test (CAT). She came in after the CAT test while the kids were on a break. The kids were climbing the walls, velcroed to the ceiling. She said, "I'm here to observe." She saw they were taking a break so she left the room for a few minutes. She came back and I had an excellent evaluation. I hoped she'd understand.

If nothing else the small sample of evaluations of each individual required discretion. A more formalized sampling plan would deny evaluators the opportunity to "get" teachers by observing when students were unusually unruly, but it would also force an evaluator to collect data during an atypically boisterous period. In effect, then, this classroom evaluation system required evaluator discretion.

Training

An observer who frequently dropped into the district office would gain the impression that a great deal of training was provided to staff. There always seemed to be a group meeting about something. Not all training was related to the TDP. For instance, O'Brien met regularly with groups of principals to discuss shared problems. His evaluation sessions with principals were often extensive periods of joint problem solving to bring up test scores.

Yet the TDP itself entailed a great deal of training, most of which was offered by the OEs. Some of this was mandated. The state required that every teacher who applied for promotions through the program take a thirty-hour course on Effective Teacher Training (ETT). In a two-month period in the summer of 1985, 70 specially prepared teachers trained another 941 of their colleagues. In subsequent years, ETT was offered to new teachers and by the spring of 1989 it was offered routinely.

The district offered four additional training programs for teachers beyond the mandated minimum training. Because experience with ETT indicated that some teachers needed specialized work in some areas to raise their evaluation scores, the OEs developed Strategies for Effective Teaching Sessions (SETS), a series of two-hour sessions developed to provide information, further clarification, and strategies for the five teaching functions identified on the data analysis form. These were intended to be reinforcement sessions. Often teachers would take one or two sessions on the recommendation of their principal, who identified specific functions with weaknesses.

Over time, teachers became concerned that the TES reinforced a limited approach to direct instruction that was not appropriate in all situations. As the OEs became more sophisticated in the application of that system, they concluded that the five teaching functions were compatible with a wide range of teaching strategies. To introduce teachers to such strategies and illustrate their compatibility with the evaluation system, a program entitled Beyond Effective Teaching Strategies (BETS) was offered in 1988–89. It introduced teachers to such approaches as cooperative learning and Socratic questioning as well as additional topics like writing lesson objectives and the importance of alternative learning styles.

In addition to these options, the performance assessment training (PAT) sequence that prepared future evaluators on how to conduct evaluations was made available to all teachers so they would better understand the system. The OEs, in conjunction with a professor from the local branch of the state university, also offered special training for experienced teachers who would be assigned to mentor beginners.

In addition to these five group-training opportunities, there was some customizing. For instance, principals were required to develop a professional development plan with each teacher. The complexity of the plan depended on teachers' specific needs and capacities. It might specify that a teacher should take a specific SETS workshop or attend BETS, but other curricular or instructional options were also available. The social studies department chair, for example, was given the opportunity to develop a state-level social studies curriculum.

There was even more individualized assistance for new teachers through the Initial Certification Project for new teachers. Each teacher was assigned an individual mentor—a teacher in one's own building who had successfully completed PAT and mentor training. These people were to meet regularly with new teachers. In 1988–89 the district also experimented with group mentoring because individual mentoring focused so much more on pedagogy than on content. Teachers would be grouped by subject area or grade level and meet periodically after school or on weekends to discuss common problems. Both the group and individual mentors were paid through the extra-pay-for-extra-work provisions of the TDP.

Some of these examples indicate the responsive nature of the district's training. As district staff learned more about the problems teachers faced, they adjusted their offerings accordingly.

While the training was flexible and reflected teacher concerns, it was all centrally offered. Beyond the formal mentor teaching situation, the TDP did not encourage teachers to share with teachers. In fact, competition for higher ratings appears to have inhibited sharing. Teachers disagreed mildly with an item in the state survey stating that "TDP encourages discussing instruction and sharing information" (2.85). (Principals did not share that view; they agreed with the item [3.33].) Eight of the interviewed teachers suggested that competition encouraged teachers to hoard ideas and not learn from each other, a view summarized by this comment:

> Teachers feel there is some competition. It used to be that everyone was on the same level, but when one makes Career Status II

and the other doesn't, it makes a problem between them. Some CS IIs used others to get where they are, so people keep ideas to themselves.

There appeared to be pockets of strong friendship ties that are especially immune to the problem of competition; where these pockets did not exist, competition among teachers was a real, but small, factor inhibiting sharing.

The survey data suggest that principals were enthusiastic about the training offered, but that enthusiasm was not shared to the same extent by teachers (see Table 2–3). To teachers, the benefits of training were that it helped them develop a common language to discuss instruction—although they were ambivalent about its actual impact on instruction—and that it helped beginners.

TABLE 2-3
Views on Training Offered

Item	Mean	
	Teacher	Principal
ETT has provided common language about instruction	3.59	4.40
ETT has helped improve my classroom instruction	3.09	4.31
TDP helped to make me a more effective teacher	2.87	3.76
Mentors and support teams have helped new teachers	3.40	4.18

These data may to some extent underestimate teacher enthusiasm for the training offered because they ask about the standard elements rather than the newer, more responsive ones like the teacher SETS and BETS. Still, the interviews reinforced this absence of a strong enthusiasm on the part of teachers. Only four teachers commented on the training at all although all observations were positive. One experienced teacher suggested that the biggest advantage of the TDP was that it brought "a structured program of help to new teachers." Given the sophistication and energy that went into the training, it was somewhat surprising that teachers were not more enthusiastic about it.

Staffing

The TDP involved three staffing changes: building up the district's personnel department, adding the OE role, and the extra-pay-for-extra-work option for the CS II teachers. Although Dr. Dark continued to direct the TDP, two positions were created to free up time to help her with her work. State money was used to hire a Teacher Development Coordinator who worked with the OEs on a day-to-day basis. The district also hired a benefits coordinator to oversee most of that work.

Observer-Evaluators. The biggest single change was the addition of the OEs, who helped the principals with evaluations and did most of the training associated with the TDP. In any given year, there were twelve to thirteen of these individuals. They had become sophisticated in the use of the Teacher Evaluation System. As one OE remarked:

> A teacher I worked with this year who came from another county said she'd never had an observation which told her what she was doing and how she did it effectively. I saw two of her data instruments [from the other county]. You couldn't tell what she was teaching or why ratings were given. There was only a one- or two-sentence write up.

OEs described how their own observing had become more sophisticated over the history of the program:

> Over the four years, the system has evolved.... We learned that variations are possible. There was no prescriptive writing at first. Evaluators recorded and rated. They weren't allowed to say, "you will improve if you do such-and-such."

The OEs felt well supported by the district:

> They allowed us to go to conferences.... We had mentors as OEs. We got a lot of in-service training. [The senior OE] does our in-service. If I have a question about a data analysis, I can go to [the senior OE], [the program coordinator], Dr. Dark. We exchange data analyses among ourselves. We're a good support team for each other, and we get support from the top.

Numerous OEs commented on their easy access to program administrators.

Being an OE was rewarding financially because individuals were paid at a supervisor's salary rather than a regular teachers'. In addition, OEs found the work intrinsically rewarding. Some enjoyed the challenge of observing:

> [The fun part of the work is] observing, going into classrooms. The challenge of script writing—that's a big challenge. Each class is different. I went into special education because I like to look at each child to analyze and prescribe. This is the same thing.

More typically, OEs found they learned a great deal about teaching by observing others. "When I go back to teaching, I'll be perfect. I've learned so much. What other job gives you a chance to see so many teachers? It's a growing, professional thing for me."

Another potential incentive was the opportunity for promotion. Several OEs suggested that they did not want to return to regular teaching jobs. They enjoyed working with adults and looked forward to positions as lead teachers working with teams of colleagues (a position that was not standardized in the district) or supervisors. In the past, several OEs had become assistant principals or principals in the district.

The OE position was marginal. Individuals were supposed to rotate into the role for two years and then return to the ranks of teaching. The idea was to create a situation where the individual teacher was evaluated by both an administrator and a "teacher," with the OE acting as a teacher. Some principals questioned whether this idea had worked as expected:

> Initially the OE was seen as a peer evaluator.... OEs are supposedly teachers, but they don't know the context. Their training is far too technical.... The principal is now preferred.... Things an observer might write down, I'd ignore because I know what's going on. Some things an observer might not appreciate, I understand. Teachers say as soon as OEs leave the classroom, they cease to be teachers.

This is not to say that relationships between OEs and teachers were difficult, but that OEs had to establish themselves with teachers and work with them:

> I'm pleasantly surprised. People don't have the negative attitude I expected. By being constructive and calling for a "needs improvement" only where I can make suggestions, I can be a positive resource. I like that.

I try to be accommodating to the teachers. I ask, "what class do you want me to see for the announced observation?" Also when I make my unannounced observation, I ask permission to enter because I want teachers to be able to refuse me if they have a legitimate reason.

For the most part OEs successfully developed working relationships with teachers. Mossville reactions to the state survey showed teachers to be generally positive about the OEs. Teachers agreed with statements like "my OEs have received sufficient training" (3.55), "my OEs have good interpersonal skills" (3.73), "my OEs try to understand my feelings about instruction" (3.65), and "my OEs' feedback improves my classroom performance" (3.41).

Difficulties did appear when the OE believed a teacher was performing inadequately:

> This year I had a problem where I went to see a CS II person who was said to be a good teacher and I saw lots of faults. That was hard. I might put the person on alert and take a rating away.

> The hardest part is prioritizing when you see a teacher with needs. Being succinct. What to work on first when there are a lot of needs. That's a big responsibility.

Extra Pay for Extra Work. The TDP also provided funds so CS II teachers could take on special assignments for additional pay. These assignments included mentoring beginning teachers, serving as a department chair, chairing school accreditation teams or teams that made special education placements, and doing staff development presentations. Teachers appreciated the opportunity to earn the extra income that these assignments afforded, but their enthusiasm for this work did not match that of the OEs about their jobs. In fact, there was some sense that though the funds available were one of the few ways to supplement teachers' income, they did not really cover the time required to do the work. As one teacher commented, "I get a $1,000 supplement for mentoring and five substitute paid days for observing and working with the mentee. I still have to prepare for the sub. There is not consideration given to one's own schedule and needs."

Governance

The major decisions affecting the TDP were made at the state and district level. Most of the procedures through which the program operated were developed by the state. The state staff worked closely with a mandated steering committee. Joan Dark was Jack O'Brien's representative on that committee, and she is described by the department's liaison person as

> very influential on a technical level. Very smart, hard working, articulate. Within the state career development organization, she was looked up to as a leader. She had prestige among the superintendents that no other assistant superintendent had because she was technically skilled, articulate, and willing to stand up and make her point.

In comparison, he says, O'Brien was never a major player in decisions about the TDP. Many state steering committee decisions appeared to reflect her (and the district's) concerns.

Locally, questions of influence began with the program design and seemed to change over time. Planning for the TDP began with an open meeting to which 200 teachers came. At that early stage, teacher input into planning appeared substantial. According to a union representative,

> We broke into subgroups and tried to define where we were going. We asked for information from the state. We developed criteria for the CS I. Then things changed so much that another group developed criteria for administrators.... Then we set the criteria for the CS II.

This person also saw a substantial change in teacher input after the program got under way:

> They are unwilling to change the instrument. It started from the ground up. Now it's coming from the state to us. We thought we developed the plan. When you buy into it, it's yours. But when people say you've got to do it this way, it's harder to sell.

Once TDP moved past the planning stage, two mechanisms were established to help guide it. The first, required by law, was the local steering committee. The twenty-six members included the superintendent, the assistant superintendent for personnel, the TDP coordinator, a parent, representatives of business and higher education, and about four teachers, but it had a substantial number of principals, assistant principals, and OEs. Dark described the local steering committee as

an advisory group.... The steering committee makes some decisions. I make some.... I got so broad a spectrum that the committee is unworkable. It's hard to get them together.... The steering committee designed the extra-pay-for-extra-work plan.

Because the local steering committee did not work well, the district
took the unusual step of forming a second body, a Teacher Development
Council, consisting entirely of teachers with one or two representatives
from each building. While the official purposes of this council included
"provid[ing] teachers and other educators with an avenue for direct
input into the Teacher Development Program" and "determin[ing] the
needs of particular schools as they relate to the Teacher Development
Program," its impact too was limited. Again according to Dark, "the first
year it was a bitch session. Now we funnel information to them." In
commenting on her role on the council, one member said, "I felt that a
lot is said there that assumes that I know a lot I don't. I don't ask questions where it looks like everyone knows but me."

While neither body provided an effective mechanism for teacher
input, two caveats are in order. First, local discretion in program
design was extremely limited. Most decisions were made at the state
level. Often these were quite detailed, dealing with matters like
changing the number of "5" or "well above standard" ratings
required to be promoted to CS II. As a result, Teacher Development
Council meetings were sometimes used to sound out teacher opinion
so Dark and other state steering committee members could more
accurately represent the district at meetings of that body.

Second, there were examples of changes that reflected teacher
interests. These included removal of objectionable elements from the
TES, such as the "six-point lesson plan" (described below) and the addition of training programs like BETS to respond to teachers' complaints.
Often, however, as in the case of BETS, such changes happened more
through unilateral administrative decisions that anticipated or reflected
teacher concerns than through negotiation or joint problem solving.
Consensus on the removal of the six-point lesson plan from the evaluation instrument was that this decision was made by Dark. She denied
doing so as a response to teacher pressure, saying instead she refused to
put it in because she knew teachers would not accept it. In fact, many
internal program decisions appear to have been made by Dark.

In the absence of effective internal representation, teachers took
two other routes, both involving the board. First, they made frequent
use of the mandated appeals procedure where the board of education
was the second level of redress. Second, they raised a whole host of

issues about program administration with the board. One board member said the TDP was "painful. There has been bloodletting and sweat." According to another, "We got phone calls at home. You talk to teachers. Some parents thought something was happening. Letters, but mostly phone calls." These led to a series of board meetings where teachers aired their complaints. The Teacher Development Coordinator said that in

> the first year, there were so many rumblings that the board invited teachers for a grievance session. I wasn't allowed to come. Neither were any of the district administrators or the OEs. Dr. O'Brien and Dr. Dark weren't there. The second year, I attended to answer questions.

These meetings led to newspaper coverage that publicized teachers' concerns more broadly. There was no clear-cut connection between them and changes in the operation of the TDP, but one board member suggested that just holding the hearings helped defuse teacher concerns.

In spite of past problems, teachers did not seek greater influence over the program or object to the input they had. According to the state survey, teachers leaned toward agreeing with the statement that the "local steering committee listens to my concerns" (3.31), with the principals' response only slightly more positive (3.79). On the other hand, no one pointed to any changes that had been made in the program as a result of teacher influence.

OUTCOMES OF THE TEACHER DEVELOPMENT PROGRAM

The TDP's first two objectives of "improv[ing] the quality of classroom instruction" and "increasing the attractiveness of teaching" are close to our own concerns with the effects of redesigning teaching on teacher motivation. It is clear that the first objective was met more successfully, at least in terms of what the district considered quality classroom instruction, than the second. Before addressing these concerns, however, we will examine student achievement in the district.

Student Achievement

The state educational agency conducted testing in the sixteen pilot districts and fifteen controls (matched on four dimensions: average daily membership, per pupil expenditure, percent of students planning to attend college, and geographical location). The students completed the California Achievement Test Total Battery. Achievement had increased in Mossville and across all pilots in comparison to the matched sample. At grades 3, 6, and 8, the number of TDP districts scoring above the national median increased, while in the match districts the number increased only in grade 3 and the number in grade 6 actually declined. Specifically in Mossville, scores in the third grade increased from the 61st to the 68th percentile from 1986 to 1988; sixth grade scores increased from the 58th to the 66th; and eighth grade scores increased from 51st to 57th.

In particular, Mossville's eighth grade rankings within the TDP units increased from 9th to 5th, and overall Mossville ranked 2nd for TDP pilots in average score increases across all three grades.

Teaching Practice

When we turn from student achievement to changes in teaching practice, we find a strong difference of opinion between teachers and administrators. The state survey data suggested that teachers doubted that the TDP helped students (see Table 2–4). To a lesser extent they questioned whether it improved teaching although they see it as encouraging improvement. Administrators were much more likely to agree with these statements about the benefits of TDP for teaching. The statement that teachers most agreed with—unlike administrators—is that TDP makes teaching "regimented."

TABLE 2–4
Assessments of the Effect of TDP on the Quality of Teaching

Item	Mean	
	Teacher	*Principal*
TDP has had a positive effect on students	2.58	3.88
TDP has increased effectiveness of teachers	2.90	4.17
TDP will improve the quality of teaching	2.81	4.08
TDP has encouraged teachers to improve teaching	3.12	4.23
TDP instructional process makes teaching regimented	3.62	2.02

The interview data are more positive than the survey. Of those who offered opinions about the overall effect of the program on teaching, four indicated in one way or another that "it made me a better teacher" or "it started out as a game I had to play. Now the game has become a habit, a good habit." Six suggested that the process did not make a great deal of difference, and one said "we're split. Half the building doesn't mind. The other half mind it or want changes."

These data also helped to explain why teachers were more ambivalent than principals. Teachers clearly modified their instructional strategies to fit with the new evaluation system. This was especially apparent to principals:

> It's made some teachers more organized in lesson delivery. Some practices are much more widespread now than they were. It's raised teachers' consciousness about those practices that we look for over and over again.

Teachers generally agreed with this assessment. The new evaluation system clearly gave them a language or set of categories for describing their pedagogical behavior that they did not have before:

> These processes have labels and you say, "Ooh! How can you do it all?" When they look at your work, they point out where you do it. You say, "Oh, did I do that?" I didn't need a lot of help. It made me more cognizant.

These cognitive changes were also reflected in behavior. Teachers particularly mentioned that they "are all in the classroom trying to keep time-on-task" or maximize the amount of time given to instruction as a result of the new system and related training. Other comments referred to general improvement in teachers' organization: "the strength is that teachers have been better prepared"; "the program made me better organized"; "there's a focus. It's not hit or miss. There's a plan." Some comments were more idiosyncratic, as by one teacher who reported, "I'm aware of how many times I say 'OK.' I now use all different positive statements. I don't just use 'OK.' I said 'OK' fourteen times in one hour."

What differentiates teachers and principals is not their conception of what changed so much as their evaluation of its importance. O'Brien stated the argument in favor of these changes in the introduction to the district document describing the TDP:

> Research in education has shown that specific teaching behaviors can positively influence student learning. We in Mossville

are demonstrating our commitment to the use of effective teaching practices with the research based Teacher Evaluation System. In so doing we are holding ourselves accountable to educational policy makers and the public.

While this paragraph argues that the new evaluation system increases accountability, it also specifies the link to achievement: the specific behaviors in the evaluation system have been shown to increase student learning.

Teachers made a different argument which revolved around what the state survey called rigidity. One complained:

> It's insidiously and gradually stifling individual style. Four times a year, teachers are too frightened to be innovative.... They learn how to play the game...the 6-point lesson plan has to be followed or you get minuses.

These comments suggest that in conforming to the criteria in the evaluation system, teachers' discretion was reduced. The effect was to stifle experimentation and learning on the part of teachers as well as their ability to adjust to differences among students.

Most objections were to the "6-point lesson plan," an aspect of the early evaluation plan that required each lesson to include a review of past material, a statement of the lesson objective, and feedback on student performance. While explicit use of the six-point lesson plan had been eliminated as a matter of policy, teachers believed it was still embedded in the evaluation system and that some principals continued to adhere to it inappropriately.

Moreover, teachers disagreed with administrators and OEs about the effects of the 6-point lesson plan on instruction. Most teachers saw it as rigid and stultifying, perhaps reflecting how it had been applied in the early days of the program. The OEs, more sophisticated principals, and a few teachers disagreed. One principal said:

> That makes me maddest of all. The 6-step lesson plan can be done two million different ways. You can do it with one child. If you leave something out, you leave out something important. You don't have to do the 6-step lesson plan with the whole class.

This view of the 6-point lesson as a set of general principles of good lesson design led to the development of the BETS training program. Achieving an understanding of the evaluation system that allowed for such flexible application required considerable sophistication and willingness to learn. These characteristics were found frequently among OEs but only among selected principals and teachers.

The concern about rigidity was more pervasive than a dislike of a particular policy. Some teachers saw the whole evaluation system as stressing minimums rather than effective teaching. One said, "It looks at minimal competencies. It tended to conform teachers to a boring pattern of teaching." Another pointed out that it reduced teacher discretion more broadly:

> If a kid walks in with some tadpoles, teachers feel if the OE comes in, she'll say you're not supposed to teach tadpoles. You're supposed to teach light. That's what's in the lesson plan. Lots of times, I teach tadpoles anyway, but people hold back because of the observations and stress and the 6-point lesson plan, and keeping records.

Joan Dark's response to such observations was that though teachers needed some room for spontaneity, too much "teaching tadpoles" led to "time-off-task."

A related concern among teachers not shared by administrators was that the evaluation system led to a form of goal displacement, where the criteria evaluated became more important than student learning: "When the evaluators are in there, you have to come up with ways to reach a student, but I think about what I'm showing them, not what will reach the student." This concern was not mentioned as often as the worry about rigidity.

In sum, the TDP increased the kinds of behaviors assessed and rewarded through the evaluation system. Administrators saw a direct link between those behaviors and student achievement and argued that such increases helped explain the rising achievement in the district. Teachers disagreed, arguing that the TDP rigidified teaching and displaced attention from helping students to carrying out specified behaviors as ends in themselves. These teachers appeared less impressed than the principals with the district's testing data but offered little data on their own about the effects of the program on students.

Teacher Motivation

When one turns to the attractiveness of teaching as a field, the same disagreement between teachers and principals about the effects of the TDP are evident (see Table 2–5). Teachers disagree about the incentive value of the TDP both in terms of its ability to attract new recruits to the field or to increase their own satisfaction. These data do not suggest why the TDP does so little to increase the attractiveness of teaching, but they do tend to rule out one explanation, that TDP creates excess demands on time. Once more, principals see much greater benefits to the program than do teachers.

TABLE 2–5
Effects of TDP on Teacher Motivation

Item	Mean	
	Teacher	Principal
TDP provides incentives for good teachers to remain	2.64	3.71
TDP will help attract more people into teaching	2.27	3.42
TDP has increased my satisfaction with my career	2.45	3.67
Amount of time required by TDP is reasonable	3.19	4.17

The TDP should have offered three benefits to teachers: increased capacity to teach, increased salary, and increased status. Insofar as the training provided by the TDP and the changed behavior resulting from the evaluation system increased teachers' professional skills, it should have helped them obtain the intrinsic benefits from working with students that teachers generally find so motivating. However, because these teachers saw the TDP as rigidifying their teaching and displacing concern from students to getting good evaluations, those intrinsic rewards were, if anything, reduced.

Administrators were generally impressed with the financial incentives the TDP offered. One of the superintendent's arguments for the program was that the state was going to insist on the new evaluation system, so "you might as well get paid for it." Six of the principals interviewed saw the added income as a plus, one saying that because of the program "teachers laugh all the way to the bank."

Teachers, too, appreciated the salary increase. There were seven positive comments to three negative ones. Yet the increased income did not change how teachers felt about their work. Sometimes its effects were limited because the income went to other people. Two teachers commented that "those who have got merit pay are happy about that." In fact, this number should have been relatively large, because about 80 percent of the teachers had reached CS I and 40 percent had reached CS II.

Sometimes teachers implied that they would take the salary increase whatever they thought of the program. When asked what the TDP meant to her, one teacher replied, "Honestly? It means a 20 percent raise in salary. I have learned from my training, but I did most of those things anyway." Yet for a few teachers the increased salary was not worth the effort required by the program:

> This isn't much of an incentive to make us feel appreciated. I don't know people who aren't working hard. They bust their butts. The little money you get for moving up the ladder isn't enough.... A lot of teachers say they would rather not bother with the money because of the stress factor.

In sum, teachers viewed the financial aspect of the program as part of an exchange of money for services. Where the exchange was profitable, they took it, but it did not change their thinking about their work. Where it was not profitable, they were not happy.

If the salary increase drew limited discussion, the status system and job differentiation drew hardly any. The only comment on the system of ranks was, "CS II won't earn them respect. If you were respected last year for your professional capacities, adding CS II won't make a difference."

In addition to these benefits, the TDP also created new costs. One already mentioned was competition among peers. A more pervasive concern was referred to as "stress" or "pressure," as indicated by the following statement: "We're frightened all the time. It has made good teachers neurotic. We are measurably more anxious than we used to be. It's our reality no matter how many times we are told not to be." Complaints about stress referred to two different problems. The first was an increase in the amount of work required of teachers. What discouraged teachers was not the quantity of work so much as the impression that it took away from their teaching. This concern was mentioned by eight people, but one said the program did not change the workload. The primary concern here was said to be an increase in paperwork:

> We're doing as much as we can in the classroom, but they're pulling us to do paper work and other things. We should teach

more and have less paperwork for accountability. When I'm happy and not stressed out, I do a better job of putting information to the kids.

The tension caused by being observed in class was an equally important concern mentioned by eight people. One said, "I'm being nice. Some people are very uncomfortable. They feel lots of pressure. When the OE comes in they get uptight. Some teachers get extremely uptight."

Observer Evaluators

While the TDP was designed to reward excellence and motivate teaching by creating a set of ranks that terminated with the CS II position, the people who truly found their work more attractive were the OEs. In fact, the OE position had more rewarding characteristics than did the CS II. The OE had more opportunity to develop new skills. In addition to learning all the new approaches to instruction made available to rank-and-file teachers, the OE had to learn how to conduct and carry out evaluations, how to negotiate with other adults in the sometimes tense situations involving teacher evaluations, and how to design and deliver training programs for adults. The OE had greater work variety, essentially a whole new job, while the only new elements for the CS II were the extra-pay-for-extra-work assignments. OEs had greater control over their work, negotiating schedules with principals, other teachers, and district office staff, while the new evaluation system actually reduced regular teachers' discretion in the classroom. OEs had more opportunities for collegial interchanges with teachers, principals, and their colleagues than the CS IIs who remained fixed in the classroom. Finally, the real differentiation in money and status was between the twelve to thirteen OEs and the 40 percent or more of the teachers who were CS IIs rather than between CS Is and CS IIs. Under these circumstances, it is not surprising that the OEs appeared much more enthusiastic about the TDP. Unfortunately, there was one other difference: For the length of their tenure as OEs, these individuals were totally out of the classroom as teachers, a situation that is contrary to the desire to keep the best teachers in the classroom.

SUMMARY

Mossville's board invited Jack O'Brien into Mossville's turbulent political situation to create an environment of educational excellence.

He did so by stressing the importance of educational improvement through accountability as well as centralized administration. Because Mosstate's TDP emphasized these same values, it fit well with local interests. His influence, the absence of effective teacher opposition, and the failure of the board to mediate between teachers and the administration when opposition arose allowed Joan Dark to implement this particular version of the Teacher Development Program.

As implemented in Mossville, the TDP stressed a promotion system that provided financial incentives for teachers who demonstrated carefully defined instructional management behaviors, the creation of a new role—the OE—to help with evaluation and provide training related to the instructional management model, and a system of governance that formally included teachers but left decision making largely in the hands of Joan Dark and the state. The evaluation process assumed that teaching fit the bureaucratic model outlined in the first chapter. The state legislation was heavily bureaucratic in its conception and in the way the program was presented to the district. Only limited local discretion was possible.

The board's vision at the time of implementation was of giving more pay for better teaching, a goal that seemed to be met by the TDP. However, the change from past practice in the district was a source of anxiety for teachers that, although diminishing, remained several years after the career ladder was initiated. This tension existed in spite of many teachers' impressions that their principals were sensitive, informed observers. What seemed to be at work was the newness of the phenomenon and teachers' doubts about the fundamental legitimacy of the evaluation system.

The TDP successfully promoted the approach to instructional management built into the new evaluation system. However, it failed to make teaching more attractive to teachers. The people who appear to have been most motivated by the program were the OEs, the group most professionalized by the process, but the Teacher Development Program did not realize its stated objective of raising teacher motivation for most classroom teachers.

3. HILL CITY:
A MIXED-MODE REFORM

HILL CITY PRESENTS an example of professional redesign but mixed professional and bureaucratic implementation, with the result that outcomes were also mixed. The district developed a new policy of inclusion, named Mutual Governance (MG), to bring teachers into the decision making process in the district. The program was developed by the superintendent in consultation with the regional NEA representative, and was expected further to develop good relationships and communication among the four principal sectors of the district—board, district office, principals, and teachers. Teachers were to be officially represented by elected teachers at their buildings and at district meetings. Differentiated staffing through the creation of master teachers and a peer assistance council was expected to strengthen instruction. However, inclusion proved to be partial and selective, resulting in increased teacher frustration and decreased motivation. As for differentiated staffing, there was no money for extra pay; it came to only partial fruition.

To explain why the program worked as it did, this chapter will describe the district context, discuss the design and implementation of Mutual Governance, explain what the outcomes were as described by district members, and show how the policy failed to deliver its promise as it was put into action.

HILL CITY'S HISTORY

Hill City was a small, industrial city built on seven hills in a northeastern industrial state. Robert Hardwick, the superintendent, told of a church on each hill representing one of the strong ethnic groups in the city. Many respondents at all levels in the district described the residents as having a strong work ethic and solid family values. One board member described the teachers as "an older faculty with a work ethic of 100 percent." According to Hardwick, the cultural revolution of the 1960s almost passed the city by. The pupil population at the time of the study was a little under 7,000. It had slowly declined for about ten years, until about 1986 when elementary enrollments began to climb. Over 70 percent of the graduating students attended a post-secondary institution, with 60 percent of those going to junior college or college.

The education orientation of the people was evident in the beautiful and well-kept buildings that housed the district schools, and in the fact that people from all occupations volunteered to serve on its board. No sector of the community was either over- or underrepresented on the board, as either regular members or leaders. Family support for students was generally high, and the drop-out rate was below 2 percent. The budget was over $30,000,000, high for the district's size and its relative economic position within the state.

The local economy had declined in the late 1970s and early 1980s as the industrial base dried up and was not replaced by service industry. On the main commercial street of the city were many boarded-up or marginal stores. Several board members and many other city people worked in the neighboring state because adequate employment was not available locally.

At the time of the study, a new interstate highway opened up transportation to a major metropolitan area, allowing people from its suburbs, which had very high property values, to sell their tract houses, buy more spacious homes in and around Hill City, and still be within reasonable commuting distance to the major city. A slow, steady influx of new people was helping the city rebuild its center. Considerable new housing and commercial construction was under way, held up only by environmental impact concerns.

The school district was an amalgam of five small entities that the state ordered consolidated in the late 1960s. The board took its current form, with nine members serving four-year terms, in the 1970s. Since then the board has been, on the whole, relatively stable. There had been times, especially during the considerable strife of the early

1980s, when board members rotated quickly, either resigning during their terms or not running for reelection. But two members who were serving at the time of the study had served for more than twenty years. Members had historically come from many walks of life, including the professions (including university professors, nurses, and teachers); high-technology jobs; industry, both management and labor; sales; banking; self-employment; and fast-food restaurant work. They represented many occupations and classes in the city. The district's 10 percent minority population was represented by an Afro-American member who later served as both president and vice-president. At the time of the research, the board consisted of a university professor, two communications professionals, two small-business owners, a labor relations manager, a banker, a homemaker, and a park maintenance officer.

Of the nine members who served when Robert Hardwick was appointed superintendent, five were still on the board. One of those who was not had died. In only one of the four seats that changed had more than one person succeeded a board member who voted on Hardwick's superintendency in 1984.[1] Only one member was defeated at the polls, and that person was widely thought to have been incompetent. In fact, since 1970 only three people had been defeated at the polls. The board lost more members to resignation or to other community organizations such as City Council, the School Authority, or the post-secondary boards that were managed and funded cooperatively with other districts in the regional service unit.

DISTRICT CONFLICT

The district had a history of sometimes violent conflict. In the late 1960s a race riot that began in the schools shook the town and the schools for several days. The memory and bad feelings lingered. Two teachers' strikes in 1976 and 1980 were long and bitter. The UniServ[2] representative, Bruno DiLisi, made an ingenious and rather Machiavellian move to force the board into a settlement of the second strike on the last day before the state would intervene. DiLisi had the membership preratify a contract. Copies were then delivered by hand to each board member and the board counselor, and DiLisi publicized the contract to ensure a large turnout at the board meeting. Several hundred people came and forced the board's collective hand. The ingeniousness and success of the strategy forced the then superintendent out of the district and fashioned the board's and the administration's behavior during the next round of negotiations. The administration made certain that it had plenty of money for salaries, and both the new superintendent and the personnel director went to the negotiating table.

The political infighting—bitter strikes, and long and sometimes violent board meetings—earned the district a reputation not only in the area but outside it as well. One new administrator was warned away by his colleagues when he was offered a position. A board member described the situation this way: "There was the local play, the movie theater, and the [Hill City] School board meeting. Some people would get what they wanted, some would not. It was so divisive it would take months to get over the process."

The succeeding superintendent, Rosa Miles, was the district's first woman in that position. A former nun, she was organized and detail oriented. "Dr. Miles was hands-on, paper trail. She knew all about everything at all times," said one district administrator. Miles had many problems during her tenure because of her personal style. She refused to interact personally and individually with any board members. Her insularity created bad feelings because disputes as well as board business then had to be worked out in public. One incident in particular rankled a number of members. The board president, Eunice Border, was dying of leukemia and requested that the board and superintendent meet at her home to set the agenda. When Miles refused to visit anyone's home, even under those circumstances, she incurred a lot of enmity.

Miles' interactions with teachers were also conflictual. Some teachers charged that she took a hard line. One reported that she said, "If you have a fire in your home, you must still call in to school, because if you don't you will not only not have a house you will not have a job." Her nickname, "Flying Nun," referred to both her former religious affiliation and her seeming ability to be everywhere at once.

One action taken by Miles was regarded highly even five years after she had left. She formulated a committee of community members and teachers to study the report of a consulting firm that had recommended closing an elementary school. One board member described the committee deliberations:

> Miles was very careful about planning.... She was very strict with the members. She told them, "If you miss the meeting you're off the committee. I'm not wasting the time to catch you up on what you missed." They put out a fine product. Very well organized and thought out. They told us to wait before closing a school, which was good advice because now we're growing

again. People remember the decision and the planning with great pleasure.

This was one of the few times the board listened to Miles. Her continuing isolationism allowed them frequently to ignore her. They began sniping at members of the administration. District personnel described the situation this way:

> Border would follow the carpenter around and say "Use nails instead of screws so it will go faster." No matter that it would also fall down faster. We didn't get respect for the administration team. We worked out of fear.

> Two to three administrators were talked into early retirement. They were almost forced out. It was not a happy time. Board members would pick out individuals. I was targeted because I had a history of getting teachers on strike. I didn't want to go to board meetings.

Border, the board president, was described as a very strong person, with a firm commitment to the district. She ran the board with determination and a strong ideology. Her powerful personality created a flashpoint among the board, the superintendent and administration, and the community. She did not approve of Miles and made her job very difficult. Border was joined in her confrontational style by another board member.

The final straw was the 1984 budget. Miles, whose financial acumen was discounted by some board members, was asked to bring in three budgets: an administrator wish list, a budget reflecting the continuation of present programs, and a budget with no increase in taxes. Miles constructed the budgets privately and presented them to the board during its public meeting at the beginning of May. The budget with the district's continuing needs would have required a $7.3 million increase with some capital loans, increases the board would be reluctant to ask for. By devising the budget without consulting the board, Miles forced them to respond in public with no time to formulate a position. Although she had complied with the board's specific request to submit several versions, the controversial nature of the resulting documents and their public debut created a whirlwind the board could not control.

These budgets highlighted a deficit that the district had carried for two or three years. The decision had been made previously not to raise property taxes, but not to cut the budget, either. The resulting deficit had reached $1 million, and was very troublesome to the board and the district. The need to be more conservative exacerbated the situation.

The no-increase budget—the "Shock List"—cut all interscholastic sports, driver education, many elementary programs, after-school activities, home economics, and industrial arts. By the end of May, the newspaper announced the superintendent's resignation. Board members reported that she was not asked to resign, but that she had experienced a good deal of pressure.

At the budget hearing 100 residents came to protest the cuts. In response, some programs were reinstated. By June 12, a tax increase of 6 mills was called for, and everything but driver education was reinstated. That one omission triggered the organization of a militant group of parents, provoked a long summer and fall of community unrest and bitter board meetings in an effort to continue that program.

None of the group's well-organized actions was successful. The board would not move. One member even read the newspaper during the testimony, and wrapped her gum in the group's literature, creating further hard feelings. The vote remained steadfastly 5–4.

During this time a superintendent search was also taking place. A subtle change in the attitude of one influential board member in particular may have been critical to the process within the community. Harold Zimmer, the president during the time of the study, was reported to have been antiteacher during the 1970s and early 1980s, and in fact had been in a fistfight at a board meeting with a member of the Hill City Education Association leadership. But two HCEA leaders reported that Zimmer, along with another member who had decided not to run for reelection, had become much more sympathetic toward teachers and understanding of the importance of good relations with them.

> Zimmer and one other board member made a 180-degree turn in relations with teachers during that period.

> Mr. Zimmer and Dr. Saxon came around 180 degrees while Dr. Miles was here.

While the search for Miles had included a committee of teachers and community members, their involvement was reported as a joke and a sham by the union leaders on the committee. However, the community/teacher committee during the 1984 search was given substantial responsibility for screening candidates, and their recommendations became the nine semifinalists.

One of the two finalists was a local man who had been in the district for many years. He had been a school administrator and a cabinet member, and was considered by most to be a good and faithful district employee. The small majority on the board, however, felt that he lacked the leadership and creativity for the job, especially because the atmosphere in the district was so highly charged. The other members wanted to reward an insider to give a message to employees in the district. As one commented, "Mr. Allari was capable and more experienced with Hill City. If you hire from within then others can hope to move up."

The second finalist, Robert Hardwick, was an outsider from a progressive, urban district in a neighboring state. Hardwick had an Ivy League doctorate and diverse experience. To the Hill City board, his most important credential was his history of good labor relations. A committee interviewed him on his own territory and came back very impressed, especially with his tendency to work within the schools and not in "the ivory tower." It was not surprising that labor relations skills and an interest in their concerns would be enticing to this embattled board.

Hardwick was called on a 5–4 vote in October 1984 to be the new superintendent of a financially troubled and strife-torn district. An explosive unresolved budget problem, five employee contracts expiring within six months, and a $2.5 million deficit greeted him at the central office door.

The New Superintendent Takes Office

Hardwick came in November 1984 and by January 1985 had devised a compromise to the driver education imbroglio. Classes would be reinstituted, but they would be held after school and in the summer, with parents paying for the course. He told an administrator when he presented his plan to the board, "I'm going to get a 9–0 vote on this." The administrator, knowing better than Hardwick the strife and acrimony that had gripped the board for so many months, was certain that Hardwick was wrong. But the vote was 9–0, and Hardwick won his first victory. No side was completely happy with the solution, but it was an escape from what had seemed an intractable dilemma.

Soon after the beginning of 1985, five contracts—those of teachers, bus drivers, maintenance workers, food service employees, and the clerical staff—came up for negotiation. Hardwick not only settled them all without strikes, he also restructured the contracts so they would come up in different years. He convinced the board to give each group a raise and a long-term contract that was staggered from the others. The unions signed.

During his first months in office Hardwick made sweeping changes in the central office routine. First he summoned teachers to his office, not to remonstrate with them but to ask their opinions and find out what was good and bad about their jobs. Some, he reported, were so nervous they hardly knew where to sit. No previous superintendents had consulted with them. At the same time, Hardwick began some meetings with DiLisi. They spent many lunchtimes together discussing board/association friction and conceiving some ideas for new relationships between the two groups.

On May 7 1985, the board ratified the first five-year contract in the history of the district. The teachers were given a 6.19 percent increase and a wage reopener clause.

Next came the budget. Unlike Miles, Hardwick had begun a discussion-and-negotiation process with the board in January. Collectively they decided what they could do, what they could not do, and how they would address the deficit. On June 10 1985, the budget was passed with all new contract raises included, an extra $1 million increase to begin to manage the deficit, and no angry crowds at the meeting. The vote was 6–2, a significant improvement over the year before.

By October 1985 a 9–0 board was passing a package of goals for the next year. In 1986 Hardwick was given a five-year contract. In 1987 and 1988 he received a 9-percent salary increase. Relationships among the board, the superintendent, and teachers had begun to improve, setting the stage for Mutual Governance.

BUILDING NEW RELATIONSHIPS

Previously, relationships among various school district groups had been conflictual and explosive. One of the first agreements that Hardwick got from the board, in personal discussions and intimate meetings, was not to address differences publicly, but rather to each give others an opportunity before a meeting to think about unexpected agenda items. "No surprises," he cautioned them. "No public bickering." He also asked them to stop responding individually to calls from constituents. He cautioned them to refer callers to the correct central office or building administrator.

In addition, while the board remained the fulcrum of power, leadership shifted from the board to the superintendent, as he both catered to their desires and led them, with their consent, in a direction he wanted the district to move.

Less than one year after Hardwick's appointment the board began to coalesce. This was the same group that had defeated driver education repeatedly 5–4, had barely passed the budget 5–4, and had hired a new superintendent 5–4. Not one seat had changed. The two strong women—one of them Border, the former President, were still on the board. Border's place as president was taken by the now more moderate Zimmer, who was now described as level-headed and concerned with teachers.

Hardwick's moves to solve the three most conflict-producing situations in the district were invaluable in establishing his reputation and leadership with the board. But he did not move very far without consulting them, nor did he offer any programs as one-only solutions. Board members told of his carefully written papers with at least three policy options for their consideration. He would inform them of his preference, but allow them without pressure to discuss all three. His choice obviously carried more weight, but they did not feel isolated from information, nor did they have to assume a defensive stance to protect their own position.

Within a short time, to be sure that every board member received the same information, Hardwick began publishing a board newsletter. Included were information about events in the schools, business and financial data, and articles from the local newspapers about the schools and from national publications about important educational issues. Pertinent communications between him and the administrators, or from outside people, would also be included. Board members described their inclusion in district business as a significant improvement.

Hardwick's discussions with DiLisi and with large numbers of individual teachers caused some uneasiness among the building administrators, who feared a loss of their authority in their buildings and possibly their status in the district. A new chairman of the local principals' association was named.

Teachers, on the other hand, were satisfied with the progress they made under Hardwick. They believed that communications and trust improved and that this superintendent took their concerns more seriously.

THE EVOLUTION OF MUTUAL GOVERNANCE

Hill City's Mutual Governance (MG) plan was developed as a remedy for the severe divisions between teachers and the district that had developed during the several years of conflict. Generated by discussions between Hardwick and DiLisi, the program was compatible with ideas that had been growing among various district staff members. It also benefited from Hardwick's previous experience in a city with a national reputation for restructuring. However, Hardwick tried to avoid some of the mistakes he had seen in that city. The program was adopted by the board, the central office, the principals, and the teachers to increase teacher participation in district and school decision making. The Hill City Education Association (HCEA) was seen as the organization that could most effectively represent Hill City teachers. Both HCEA and district officials felt that participation by teachers in the decision-making process would ameliorate previous divisions, and bring better information to the process.

During the development process, planners identified four pertinent constituencies: teachers as represented by the HCEA, principals, district administrators, and the board. All four constituencies would have to agree to any plans submitted to them for approval.

On May 9, 1988, the MG policy was adopted by the board, the principals' association, and the HCEA, with September 1, 1990, as the deadline for implementation. Members of the HCEA had received copies of the policy two days earlier and voted to endorse it. One important incentive in the plan was the coupling of administrator salary increases to the successful implementation of the program. A great deal of local and state publicity attended the adoption of the policy. Four state-level officials representing the four decision groups were at the board meeting when it was signed, and all the local newspapers carried the story.

On June 10 elections were held by the HCEA at each building to select the members of the new School Planning Councils (SPC) called for by the agreement. Fifty-two teachers ran for Council positions. The substantial discord that had previously occurred between teachers and the school board made attractive the opportunity to elect representatives who would materially address school- and district-level problems. Ninety percent of teachers cast their ballots for those representatives. In addition, an addendum to the contract extended that agreement for three more years, including salary increases and a contractual body to address transfer disputes.

The Mutual Governance Policy

MG created changes in decision making at three levels:

Board Level

• The presidents of the HCEA and the principals' association became formal, nonvoting participants at board meetings. They were given a place on the agenda of every meeting to report on association activities salient to district operations.

Central Administrative Level

- The presidents of the HCEA and the principals' association became permanent members of the superintendent's cabinet.
- A Faculty Senate was created, consisting of the building principal and one teacher elected to serve on the School Planning Council by the HCEA members of the building.
- A Joint Personnel Committee was created to review disputed transfers, assignments, and schedules. This committee became part of the contract between the bargaining unit and the school district.

School Level

- Each school created a School Planning Council, consisting of the building administrator and two teachers elected by the association members of the building, to review matters of building concern not covered by the bargaining unit contract. One of the two teachers became a member of the faculty senate.

Any teachers who were formal participants in district or school level mechanisms were to be provided with appropriate release time. A permanent substitute was assigned to each building to provide substantial release time.

The mission of these new bodies was to promote "demonstrably improved outcomes." To that end the following changes were also to be implemented:

1) The joint development of a professional evaluation program for teachers and administrators
2) A Master Teacher panel of outstanding practitioners, to be identified consensually by teachers, principals, and district administrators to serve as resources for curriculum and staff development
3) A Peer Assistance Council, to be identified consensually by teachers, principals, and district administrators to aid teachers who were experiencing problems in their instructional program
4) The collaboration of parents, teachers, administration and community in an At-Risk Support Team to support at-risk youth beyond the school day and school year
5) The movement of certain levels of decision making to the school

site, granting greater autonomy, initiative, and control of resources while maintaining a district level of standards and supervisory authority

Although "demonstrably improved outcomes" was not defined anywhere in the policy, nor explicitly defined by any interviewees, the central goal of MG was stated as: "Through higher standards of mutual accountability to achieve those superior outcomes so urgently required of American public education." The policy statement continued:

> Without those improved outcomes for our children and our nation, there really is no justification for our efforts. A spirit of accord was but a means to an end. The end is performance and it is by that standard alone that we must in the final analysis be judged.

While student outcomes were clearly central to the program, broader teacher participation and *accountability* were also an important part of the plan. Stipulation for development of a new teacher evaluation, and a matrix of "reciprocal changes" for administrators and teachers that charged teachers to "accept broader accountability" for program outcomes, teacher effectiveness, and implementation of regulations made that point clear.

All teachers received increases to base as part of the contract extension, but there were no differential financial awards for teacher participation as Master Teachers, Peer Assistants, or on any of the councils. All service was considered voluntary. No positions were added to schools or the district office that expanded either level. All new program positions were filled by teachers who continued to teach in their classrooms. Some additional time was bought from teachers with MG responsibilities, however, in the form of release time.

Preprogram Expectations

The groups constituent to Mutual Governance brought to it various perceptions, expectations, and goals. School board members uniformly perceived MG as a mechanism to obtain more accountability for building administrators and teachers:

> When we asked Dr. Hardwick to have evaluation be his goal, he came back to us with the plan.... How will it affect teachers and what they would get?... There are teachers who need to be

helped and should be helped and if they can't be helped they should take another job. We want accountability.

In fact, seven of the nine board members mentioned evaluation of teachers as an important component. No other factor was mentioned more than two or three times.

District administrators saw MG as a mechanism to improve the instruction of students and the morale of teachers. One building administrator saw many possibilities:

> The superintendent has given some excellent thought and directions. It gets teachers, through their representatives, involved in administering the school. We're looking at academic involvement, discipline, personal involvement with students, and character development.... Staff and administration who can feel free to address those issues will see outcomes for students.

But this same administrator saw some potential pitfalls.

> We're in the early stages. The number-one problem is that we have no book that says "step 1 do this, step 2 do that...." Sometimes the principals' group, because it's the smallest in number, may not be privy to initial information that unions and the administration know.

Principals were concerned about what their position might be within the new order. Publicly their conversations indicated support. One said, "I got enthusiastic. I saw the benefits if he could change board attitudes and teachers started trusting him, and he started talking to principals about his great visions." But privately there was suspicion and distress among some administrators. At one point early in the program, a journal article questioning the process and concept of shared decision making was distributed anonymously to building administrators. One building administrator perceived open communication as an opportunity for information that probably was not the main intention of the district as a whole: "If you sit down and listen to people, you have spies all over the building who can tell you things you need to know about things happening all over your building, if you just listen." Interestingly enough, this was the same administrator who remarked, in a conversation about how a previous administrator behaved and his reaction to it, "I sat with my back to the wall gripping my chair. You can't intimidate people and expect them to work with you. Nobody was talking to anybody. Factions were all over the place."

At every level, building administrators were often seen as those who would most resist the program, even though they were the first group to ratify the policy. One board member said:

> The principals do the most readjusting. In the past all wants, needs, desires, dreams, etc. were funneled through principals. Now the teachers have an equal and direct channel. Some people like to be administrators, some teachers, not subordinates and superiors.

A teacher saw it similarly:

> The administration, collectively—they had to deal with problems they used to be able to ignore. The new general feeling that their job is not to tell us what to do—they had to change that. There is more of a working feeling. Now they all have to work together.

Teachers hoped they could now solve many problems they had experienced before MG—typically concerning the absence of measures they thought would facilitate instruction. For example, many teachers were concerned about the length of the elementary school day; because there were insufficient buses to transport all students at the same time, the younger students were required to stay in classes until the high school students had been taken home. Many elementary school children had been up since very early and were beginning to fall asleep by 3:00. Teachers also experienced problems with poorly functioning building copiers and supplies. They complained about "cheap paper that can't be used. On half of it, the lines aren't straight, so kids can't write on it. We get cheap junk instead of quality. We throw it away."

Some teachers were cautious in their expectations, as this statement indicates:

> Nobody understands it. This is an effort so not all decisions will come from the top. Teachers will be involved in policy making. People will have a say and be a part of things. I'm not making any judgment on it yet.... Let's see how it develops. I want it to work. It's a great concept.

HCEA officials uniformly supported the concept. One official commented:

It protects the rights of each group. It takes nothing away. It's not threatening. The only way things can happen is if all four groups are for it.... A lot of decisions about school purposes will be made ultimately closer to where they are implemented. The greater the distance, the worse the decision.

Implementation of Mutual Governance

The first meeting of members of the School Planning Councils with HCEA representatives, district and building administrators, and board members took place at the community college in September 1988. Its most important function was clarification of the program. Hardwick was the main speaker, with his address and a dialogue between him and DiLisi providing the essential definitions and program purposes. At that meeting, discussion by teachers was tentative, infrequent, and not encouraged.

In October all the teacher members of the School Planning Councils met with Hardwick for a day and a half to discuss Mutual Governance further and clarify issues. During that meeting DiLisi separated problems into two categories: gripes and concerns. He challenged the district to take care of the gripes, which mainly consisted of money and supply problems, so that the councils and the faculty senate could address real educational concerns, such as curriculum, teacher evaluation, promotion criteria, grading procedures, testing procedures, at-risk programs, and so forth.

Hardwick was pressed for more concrete plans for schedules, procedures, criteria for selecting Master Teachers, and other implementation concerns. He resisted, saying he believed that such plans would lead to more bureaucracy and slow the process down. A portion of the discussion revolved around concerns that tension between elementary and secondary teachers might expand and create problems for teachers, the program, and the district.

The proposed Master Teacher panel was already beginning to create stress. Discussion about a change in name—from Master Teacher to Research Resource Articulator—later became a formulated plan that was submitted to central office. Discussions of the selection process created more consensus about the program, at least among meeting attendees.

Other problems were raised, such as building scheduling, which was later addressed with largely positive results. Several council members revealed that their colleagues were beginning to accept the program, and that they themselves were getting cooperation from their building administrators. Council members outlined their strategies for receiving communications from teachers about individual building problems.

Hardwick reiterated concepts he had presented in September, including the need for agreement among the four constituencies, a desire to maintain flexibility by not formalizing criteria, and the need for accurate and widespread communication. He also presented the concept of Mutual Governance as "supplementing and not supplanting" present organizational procedures. The group was told that the director of curriculum was designing the compliance plan for the state's staff development program, which would be submitted to the senate in December, in time to file it for the state deadline.

The Progress of Implementation

During the year, several incidents raised passions among the membership as a whole. The Master Teacher selection process created severe tensions. In one school, the unauthorized publication of the list of teachers who had been chosen by their colleagues for that building caused a significant protest. One supporter of the overall program expressed the fear that hostile forces were waiting at every turn, ready to scuttle it.

Many considered that the central office had failed the first test of the new district policy when it placed a breakfast program for at-risk students at one school without first discussing it with teachers. A teacher remarked, "They put the cart before the horse. They said, 'We have Mutual Governance. We're gonna have a breakfast program. How do you want to do it?'" The school faculty expressed displeasure, and the principal faced a confrontation with teachers and the HCEA.

In the spring of 1989 a meeting of the HCEA was held to discuss the entire situation. Those who participated explained:

> the meeting [was] to discuss problems and decide how to present the problems.... Three decisions have been made since September that didn't go through the Mutual Governance process. They were all fouled up, and if they had asked us, they would not have made the mistakes they did.

> The people feel that there has been too much publicity and that it has to stop. They feel it is too much window dressing.... No one is backing out or buying out, but it is discouraging. For [many] years it has been top down. Now they say, "You can have a say." But it is not a maximum say.

School Planning Councils. In October, the School Planning Councils began to meet with principals to try to iron out building problems. Most administrators set aside time every week so all members could meet together. Problems—situations that were not the primary responsibility and territory of the HCEA—ranged from inadequate copiers to poor playground schedules. In the spring council members in several schools participated in the classroom scheduling process. In one school the SPC got new menus for the cafeteria, and catalogued the school software holdings. In another school a student recognition program was instituted. Councils worked closely with principals to solve problems and smooth out the running of the school. Faculty members were encouraged to share their problems and suggestions with the council members for consideration and solution.

Master Teacher Panel. In late October 1988 selection of the master teachers began. This process required that teachers, principals, and district administrators generate lists of candidates. The teachers' list was synthesized from individual school lists that included everyone who had been nominated by teachers at each school. The principals' list was formulated from individual principals' lists. When all of the lists were consolidated, a panel of Master Teachers was announced. Those teachers named on all three lists were on the panel. The announcement of the panel in the district newsletter was accompanied by a list of "contemplated activities" that Master Teachers might be asked to do:

1) Advise the district on content of curriculum days or other staff development activities

2) Advise the district on text, material, or program selection

3) Advise the district on staff selection and liaison to community and other school districts

The description of duties continued by stating that the idea of a Master Teacher panel was to use the experience of teachers to strengthen instruction. All service on the panel was to be voluntary and optional. As of our final meeting with the district, however, the Master Teachers had not been assigned to any particular positions or asked to assume any specific responsibilities. The teachers who were on one or two of the three lists became part of a permanent Master Teacher pool. Some were invited to the central office to assist district administrators with various jobs.

The Master Teacher selection process created a great deal of tension and strife in the district. No specific selection criteria or guidelines were distributed to assist teachers in making choices. The one definition that was offered—"an outstanding teacher who periodically serves the district in the capacity of an educational consultant"—alluded to tasks and qualifications, but was not explicit. That ambiguity was very distressing to many. In addition, the concept troubled many who remembered an extremely divisive attempt to establish a merit-pay system years before:

> Master Teacher is the pea below the mattresses. Central administration wants teachers designated master teachers.... This building is high strung on this issue.... We tried to tell [them] to drop this and do other things.... Master Teacher conjures up images of the old merit-pay plan. Teachers feel slighted if they are not on the list.... We're trying to change the name of Master Teacher.

Another complaint was presented by teachers who had been transferred during the summer. Their new colleagues were not aware of their skills, and it seemed certain they would not make the lists in their new buildings. "I'm particularly bothered because I don't have any opportunity to be a Master Teacher because I just transferred in," said one such teacher. "I have as many qualifications as the rest." Even in the face of forceful protests, however, the superintendent held fast:

> Some people say "Let's get job descriptions and criteria." But I come from a place that did that. We would spend an afternoon deciding if someone with a master's plus 15 could be a Master Teacher.... The task of the Master Teacher is what you decide it is.... The board accepted the term Master Teacher.

The final formulation of the list was by Hardwick and the HCEA president-elect.

In addition to the distress created by the selection process, some stress was indicated when the panel was announced and teachers in one school wore T-shirts announcing that they were "un-Master Teachers." In the spring feelings were still mixed. Some had negative opinions about what had happened, others felt more comfort. One teacher said, "I feel that Master Teacher is not a closed issue. It has to be in writing how to get a new list without the controversy. We need to avoid controversy and hurt feelings." Another's teacher's opinion was more sanguine: "People were afraid that merit pay would follow. They were afraid of the unknown.... Now there is no more discomfort. We are extremely satisfied with the Master Teacher here. We think she is wonderful." Impressions of how Master Teachers would be used varied.

> She is a liaison for us with the administration. Someone we feel we can talk to about our concerns. We don't use her to assist us with our class, but if we felt the need, we could.

> They'll be resource people and will offer more. Master Teacher is one phase of continuing professional development.

The Master Teacher selection process created such divisiveness, however, that the administration decided not to publicize the list very widely. The Master Teachers were presented to the board and announced in the district newsletter, but little mention was made otherwise. The issue was kept low-key to avoid further inflammation of the situation.

Peer Assistance Council.   By March 1989 the appointment of 151 teachers to the Peer Assistance Council was announced. The disquiet accompanying the development of the Master Teacher panel became a referendum for the selection process for this new panel. Rather than developing formal criteria for selection or a consensus process, the PAC was made up of volunteers.

The announcement of the appointments to the council in the district newsletter included the description of the council as "teachers helping teachers." All schools, grade levels, and specialties were represented among those who volunteered to serve. Here again, service was to be unpaid and optional. By May principals of at least three schools had approached peer assistants to get help for teachers having classroom difficulties.

Everyone who wanted to serve was placed on the PAC. Nevertheless, teachers were reluctant to volunteer, some because they weren't sure about the program, and some because they weren't sure about themselves.

> We were slow to respond until we found out more about it. Then almost everybody got on board.... Not many volunteered at first. There was a lack of communication at first. People felt less willing to promote themselves. There weren't sure what

they'd be asked to do. Also they felt too pushy. They felt as if they were being arrogant if they said, "Yes, I'm good enough to help others."

There was less ambiguity about what Peer Assistants would do after they had been chosen: "It was devised solely for teachers helping other teachers. If a teacher has poor ratings, these people are there to help."

The nonevaluation premise of PAC assistance was important, especially to the HCEA, which by contract forbade peer evaluation. It was perceived as making peer assistance nonthreatening. Also, if teachers did not want anyone in their own building to know they were seeking help, they could approach someone in another building.

Evaluation Process. In December 1988 a working group of the faculty senate, chosen by consensus at the November meeting of the SPCs, was announced to address district concerns more efficiently. One of those tasks was the development of a newer, more comprehensive evaluation instrument for the district. The state-developed instrument then in use was perceived to be ineffective by both principals and teachers, with principals usually giving every teacher the highest rating, and little professional development resulting from its administration.

The working group consisted of the superintendent, a representative of the HCEA, another elementary teacher, two secondary teachers, and a principal. Each member had an "understudy" who could attend the meetings if he or she was unable to attend. The group communicated a summary of each meeting both with the rest of the Senate and with the whole district. It was announced that all decisions must be accepted by the entire Senate and each of the four constituencies.

The working group began meeting weekly in January 1989 to discuss the philosophy and the process of evaluation. They developed an instrument and a timetable for evaluating teachers and other staff, looking at many different types of instruments, and speaking with other experienced resources.

The final policy proposal of the working group, "Professional Personnel Performance Evaluation," was presented to the board and endorsed at its meeting on April 9 1990. The new policy made two important departures from the previous one: 1) a three-year evaluation cycle for all but first-year professionals, with most supervisors having about ten professionals to evaluate; and 2) the introduction of a dialogue-based process including self-assessment by the evaluatee, mutual goal setting, and the writing of a narrative that is developmental and mutual. The evaluation process was scheduled to be introduced to faculties in a series of in-service presentations.

Hill City District News.   While not an official part of MG, the district newsletter, *Hill City District News,* was an essential part of its operation. Developed several years earlier, the weekly newsletter carried articles about district affairs; issues and activities of board meetings, board decisions, announcements of upcoming meetings; highlights and summaries of meetings that had occurred; discussion of local, state, and national activities of general interest; county vocational-technical and community college issues; updates on continuing issues; athletic events and results; pertinent communications among district officials; announcements of student and teacher triumphs; district activities from previous years; and other useful and interesting insertions. By creating a body of shared and consistent information, the newsletter enhanced communication and reduced (but did not eliminate) the effects of rumors.

One point that teachers made about the newsletter, however, was that their input was not solicited. The newsletter was exclusively formulated by the superintendent and carried only his concerns and views.

Concurrent Programs.   During the implementation of MG, Hill City was involved in a number of other significant programs. The district applied for and received experimental status from the state, allowing the district to waive many state regulations in exchange for an expanded accountability. Some new programs featured collaboration among and with teachers. Previously, the district had explored participation in the Theodore Sizer Essential Schools Coalition, but that participation had not materialized. According to one board member, the board defeated affiliation with the Coalition by a 5–4 vote. Later its adoption by one single school was also rejected, that time by a vote of the faculty. Hardwick also supported the James Madison School concept to improve school curriculum and attract students from local private and parochial schools.

Hardwick in particular expressed his great interest in making the curriculum more stringent, and testing more relevant. In the *Hill City District News* he wrote:

> So much of the reform literature has focused on "process" issues such as who does what, who is on what committee, etc., while there has been much less attention given to the hard substance of what is actually being done inside the curriculum...

> Someone once observed that American school children are the "most tested and least examined" children to be found anywhere. What this epigram reflects is the inordinate amount of standardized testing done in American schools.

The newsletter regularly addressed curiculum topics, and often on the front page. International competitiveness was a common theme, and many issues of the newsletter carried articles and discussions of the need for attention to what was taught. A major revision of the high school English curriculum was reported to have involved a great deal of effort on the part of administrators and teachers. The high school English department sought to adapt the curriculum to make it the strongest possible. The essence of the change was a return to a more unitary curriculum from an eclectic approach that had ranged among various strands of communications and literature. Some electives were eliminated, but creative writing and communications were integrated into the unitary curriculum.

A revision of the middle school curriculum created a community disturbance. Hundreds of people (the number was estimated at 200 in the *Hill City District News*) came to the auditorium of the intermediate school to question the rumored elements, including Latin, five days of physical education, and the removal of study halls from the daily schedule, among other things. People in attendance wanted to be consulted before massive changes were implemented.

Reflecting the concern about standardized testing, the District announced its decision to cease administering the Stanford Achievement Tests. In addition, Hardwick opened the district to scholars and educators from all over the world, and compared the efforts of Hill City to the efforts of others. For example, Soviet students visited one of the elementary schools, and Japanese educators toured the district.

The district also assumed resource status in a similar cooperative labor/management state-wide program, sponsored jointly by the state Department of Education and the Department of Labor.

ASSESSMENTS OF MUTUAL GOVERNANCE

Initial enthusiasm for MG was quite high among all groups involved:

> People were enthused about the concept. This building had Mutual Governance more than others to begin with...teachers felt free to voice opinions to [the principal]. (teacher on the SPC)

Mutual Governance is to improve academic status of all kids in the district through cooperative work: a triad of the board, the teachers, and administrators. Staff morale is the most significant factor. (board member)

Mutual Governance is taking the best they have and the best I have and putting it all together. We're not here to make things comfortable for ourselves. Mutual Governance may give teachers the chance to feel more open to speak. (principal)

It gives linkages between the classroom teachers and the superintendent. It puts people face to face with the superintendent. It puts people together so they can hear each other and work together.... It allows people to manage the work they're responsible for.... It's a win-win situation. (board member)

Over time, however, some opinions changed. This section will discuss those changes among the four groups in the district whose goals were supposed to be addressed: teachers, principals, district administration, and the board.

Teachers

Teachers' views of MG varied with their positions. Most SPC members felt that they had benefited from their participation and that good things had been accomplished. HCEA officers were distressed by the problems, but confident that a new environment had been created in the district and that there should be no turning back. One SPC member was happy about personal experiences and felt personally enriched by them, but overall that the program had not worked:

We always had the proper rapport. We always had the basis of Mutual Governance. As far as the way it's supposed to work, I think it's failed. [A large number of faculty] came to us at [this school] with concerns. But responses were not forthcoming from the district. It's like Pavlov's dog. We've been trained not to expect anything.

Another SPC member in a different building was delighted: "Openness. People are not afraid to question us. Problems don't fester. People come to us that wouldn't have gone to [the principal]. Normally they wouldn't have an avenue. They would go around in circles."

During an interview with two SPC members, when a student

came on the PA system to make an announcement, the sound quality was poor, one remarked, "Next we'll work on the PA system." Another teacher observed that teachers' attitudes toward teaching were better. "It used to be that people were uptight and cranky toward the end of the year. That's not true now." In that school, many problems had been addressed and solved.

In another school, during a conversation between the SPC members, these positive things were said:

> There is more open communication.

> I agree. I can't think of any other way except a good feeling about school. But we always had that so that may not be a change.

> The lines of communication have opened. The teachers feel freer to come to us or [the principal]. They will send an anonymous letter or note to ask for help. The communication lines are really open, even teachers to teachers.

However, they talked about the serious cost of good feelings and participation:

> It takes time on our part. We have to take notes of our meetings and publish them in our so-called spare time.

> We've spent a lot of time on this. I type up our notes at home and put them on the computer. [We] use our breaks and planning time to work on this. It's getting hard.... We're running into time limits.

When asked if they resented the time spent doing the job, one Council member answered: "No, just the pressure. There's no deadline, but we feel we have a self-imposed one. We could have had a sub if we wanted but chose not to." Rank-and-file teachers were generally more tentative:

> I can't tell. It just started. We will have a share in the aspects that we have expertise in. We have the right or the ability to have input. There's a lot of talk, a lot of 'educatese.' I'd like to see what the results are.

> Being new it's cloudy. Teachers are encouraged to express their impressions and meet with principals to discuss their concerns.... Some people don't know.

I thought Mutual Governance means do it together. He means each of us four groups should do something separately and then put it together.

As time went on and the program developed, some teachers felt they had been rushed into a concept they did not understand. As one put it:

What has it done for me? I remember the larger salary I was taunted with so I would accept this new idea. "Give them a larger salary increase and they'll accept anything." It was evident then that the idea needed to be sold to us. We wanted more time, they wanted an early settlement.

Association leaders denied that they had offered salary increases as an incentive to accept Mutual Governance.

Some of the problems that teachers had expected MG to solve still had not been, creating a sense of frustration. When asked what problems still eluded the SPC, a teacher replied, "Budgetary. The paper continues to be bad, also the chalk and pencils. Those are handled in the business office and some things are beyond our control. We're stuck in the situation."

One important item that was perceived as essential but inadequately addressed was the length of the elementary day:

We were hoping Mutual Governance would make the elementary schools heard more. We wanted to do something about the length of the school day. So we still have that concern and we don't expect it will be solved. We wanted the day to end before 3:00. The kids are falling asleep because they have been on the buses or at day care since early in the day.... That's not administration's priority.... They don't understand that the kids can't manage.

While one teacher said that she had never thought the problem would be addressed, another said, "I thought they would listen."

Most agreed that communication had improved. As one teacher noted, "Having the association and the principals included in the cabinet meetings facilitates communication. There are no misinterpretations, no third party communications. That has to make it better." Both administrators and teachers saw the change in the quality of information they received from the meetings, even if sometimes they felt that not too much of what they wanted was accomplished. In addition, some thought that problems were handled more intelligently because the representatives were there.

When the principal of one school was promoted to director of personnel, the building's SPC helped choose his successor. This input into the process was a source of satisfaction to people in the building; they felt their voices and concerns had been heard. Central office people expressed their satisfaction with the process and the candidate that was chosen. This created a precedent in the district; it also caused some dissatisfaction among faculty members at another school where the selection process had not been collaborative and they disapproved of the principal who had recently been hired. During the feedback visit the following year, Hardwick said that a principalship that had recently opened up would be filled using the collaborative process.

At other points in the feedback sessions, teachers expressed their view that the negatives were still negatives. Gripes that had been presented at the meeting in October 1988 had still not been adequately addressed, and communication was selective. Though there was, indeed, more communication between teachers and the board, not every building was experiencing an environment of cooperation. One teacher said that Hardwick's process of "making it up as we go along" had raised expectations for teacher input into decisions that were not met.

Principals

Several principals were very pleased with the operation of MG in their own buildings. These two comments are typical of satisfied principals.

> Mutual Governance is still in a positive mode. Right now it's more "in process." Not as tangible as people want it to be. There is no product as yet.

> There is more communication. We took for granted that certain communication was taking place, but it didn't get through. Now we can talk to the proper person to get things corrected. My relationship with the SPC is positive. I can speak to them and they can speak to me in confidence—also teachers can speak to them in confidence—and we can come up with a solution.

On the other hand, some principals expressed their feeling that their building authority had eroded. During the feedback session, several principals stated that though they had been the first to ratify the program they had lost the most.

District Administrators

District administrators viewed the process from a more removed and global stance. They saw that whereas some principals had originally resisted the program, they were moving more in the direction originally intended:

> At the elementary level, it is positive. It has altered styles in a positive way. At first principals thought they were giving away too much. Now they see that input helps and there's no loss of managerial control.

> For those principals who thought they were the ultimate in power, this has been an awakening.... Principals now believe they have to talk to staff. They have to have input.

> The talents of people are opening up more.... The idea was to give people a feeling of worth. That's been accomplished. You can see it in their confidence and when they talk to administrators.

Teachers were seen as having grown in the process:

> The key is who is on the SPC. All those who are on it have shown growth.... They are not overjoyed, but it's working. It's satisfactory, but it still gets a watchful eye. Working relations in the district have never been better. That's unequivocal.

Good communication was perceived as almost universally positive. However, the opposite side to that coin was also presented: "More things are out in the open, so there are more things to wonder about."

Assessments of the Evaluation Process

Evaluation was a key concept to board members, one of whom commented, "With Mutual Governance, teachers know they will be more responsible for what they are doing every day. Evaluation will be the next step."

The actual content of the evaluation was anticipated to be such a charged issue that when the first draft was presented to the Senate in November, members were not allowed to remove copies from the room. The final form was released in the spring of 1990, to be implemented starting in September 1990.

Formal data collection was ended before the evaluation was released. However, communications from the working group allowed people in the district to understand what was being discussed and what the philosophy of the evaluation might be. Teachers' had formulated opinions of what might be coming by spring of 1989:

> If there is a need for improvement, now there will be an avenue for this to be accomplished. We want it not to be part of the record, but that is a disagreement between administrators and teachers. The teachers want it to be between teachers and principals.

> It's a better tool that they're talking about. But it will not help unless he picks up what we say. We've never had to look at ourselves. The self-evaluation will be good. Doing it together is the best part.

> It will be good for teachers and good for kids—if executed properly and with sincerity. It will be a complete change of attitude. The idea of them is for improvement of instruction, not job security.

It appears from these and other statements that the inclusion of teachers in the development and the ideas that the group communicated built trust among the teachers. The group pursued a course that was acceptable to teachers.

THE OUTCOMES OF MUTUAL GOVERNANCE

As stated in the Mutual Governance policy, the program was intended to develop a cooperative approach to decision making, extend authority and accountability, and raise productivity of teachers leading to increased student achievement. These objectives all are consistent with organizing structures that professionalize teaching. How well had MG achieved its objectives?

Our preliminary conclusions, based on our observations and the assessments by those we interviewed in the district were:

1) Communications among teachers within schools, between teachers and their building administrators, and between teachers and the central office had increased substantially.
2) Decisions were made much more cooperatively than previously in most schools, affording some teachers increased professional

opportunities and teachers more opportunities for input generally.

3) Increased decision making and communications opportunities had created a much more salutary climate in most schools.

4) While communications and decision-making opportunities had increased, the problems teachers put forward were not always addressed and sometimes their input was not sought, or was ignored.

5) Teacher satisfaction varied from school to school.

6) Final authority was still closely held at the central office.

7) Based on test scores, state incentive awards, and anecdotal reports, student achievement levels had increased although it is difficult to attribute these developments to MG.

In seeking explanations for these results, we concluded that:

1) The inclusion of Hill City Education Association and Principals' Association representatives in cabinet and board meetings had improved the quality of communication among those bodies and for the most part improved communications for the groups represented by the associations.

2) Some School Planning Councils were involved quite actively in working to achieve goals and solve problems within their own schools.

3) The Faculty Senate had developed as more of an authorizing body for policies put forward by the central office than as a policy-development group; the clear exception was the teacher-evaluation plan developed by the working group; no significant decisions were submitted to the Senate.

4) The structured communication procedures had facilitated wider dissemination of consistent information, but access to communication channels was very controlled.

The Approach to Decision Making

Hill City followed a model in which central-office control was supplemented by shared decision making. While the Mutual Governance policy promoted professionalism among teachers through teacher participation structures and inclusion in decision making, the actual implementation of the program was substantially bureaucratic, with significant impact on the outcomes. There was increased inclusion of the interests and concerns of each of the four groups identified in the MG policy, but for some key people in the process the continuing separation of those four groups was a cause for concern. Real cross-group collaboration happened in very specific instances—such as the inclusion of the principal and teacher representatives on the cabinet, the working group, and at particular schools—but few policies were developed in concert; feedback was mostly channeled through one central figure, the superintendent.

Many administrators wrestled with problems of both letting go of their central authority and understanding where they would fit in if the district really did develop MG. However, some had begun to grow with the program and were realizing its benefits.

This combination of centralized control and erratic teacher participation and empowerment created mixed results. For example, there were clear differences between the success level in the buildings, particularly those where SPC participation was significant and regular, and the success level at the central office, where the Senate had not been fully used. Mutual Governance—the professional approach—was followed in a number of buildings, in the selection of a school principal, and in the working group development of the evaluation, among others. Imposition of the breakfast program and the insistence on using the term "Master Teacher" were bureaucratic tactics that provoked serious resistance. Teachers' feelings that their influence did not increase, fueled by the failure to change the length of the elementary day and continuing problems with supplies, seriously undercut teacher acceptance.

> The "gripes" are still there, and if anything is going to drown Mutual Governance it's that. We look at the fact that our gripes have not been addressed, and we think it's not working.... If he does the small stuff it will help everybody's frame of mind. If not, anger will sink the ship.

The issue of "gripes" was important. The district office, and to some extent others in the district, saw the problems of supplies and equipment as inconsequential. They spoke as if the teachers were being petty in their insistence on dealing with those issues. From the teachers' viewpoint, however, the continuing problems with supplies and equipment seriously hampered their ability to perform effectively.

Collegiality. One side effect of shared decision making ought to be increased collegiality for teachers. While SPC members increased their interaction with colleagues in their buildings and with representatives from other buildings, it is not clear whether collegiality among the rank and file increased consistently. One collaboration that took place for the first time during data collection was a meeting of the high school and intermediate school department faculties to discuss integration of the curriculum for students so that the transition to high school would be smoother for new tenth graders. Representatives from both faculties found the meeting helpful. At one of the early release in-service days in November 1988, it was reported that for the first time in fifteen years all the art teachers were going to get together. These positive instances point to some increase in collegiality.

Overall, the real level of intradistrict communication, teacher input, and shared decision making had risen. One illustration was the third full meeting of the faculty senate. By that meeting, the group had become more comfortable with the format. Administrators and teachers conferred prior to the meeting; people asked questions during the meeting with more ease and less hesitation. Hardwick still dominated things and attempted to put his own spin on the topic, but others interpreted substance much more openly and discussed negative connotations with less reluctance. The HCEA president, who had been the only spokesperson for the group in previous meetings, was less visible than she had been in the past. DiLisi, who had attended every session of this group in the past, was not there. Two SPC members sat next to the superintendent. Several building administrators, most of whom had sat together during the first meeting, were interspersed with the teachers.

Incomplete Participation

"Incomplete participation" refers to the practice of asking people for their expert opinion and concerns, then disregarding their input in the final decisions. In a number of instances this phenomenon was apparent. According to one teacher:

> They keep saying, "We didn't do it right this time, but we'll do it right the next time." But they continue to avoid the [MG] process, and they don't get it right. So people are saying, "They share what they want to share. When do we move on our agenda?"

Incomplete participation also refers to the assignment of busywork that has little meaning for the work of the organization, and carries with it a paternalistic cast. A district administrator explained that:

> The teachers who worked with me on this in-service day were not elected to Master Teacher. They were unhappy about that.

> This gave them something to do. Their additions were minor.... We kept peace in the family.

In addition, the superintendent used the phrase "supplement and not supplant" to indicate that access to decision making was going to be limited. However, this approach threatened to increase incomplete participation. The use of the Faculty Senate to legitimate policies that had been developed centrally was a clear example of incomplete participation.

Researchers and practitioners have observed that incomplete participation creates frustration and alienation among people who come to believe that their invited participation will have an impact, only to find that in fact it was sought only for show. Though MG may not have been that hollow, at the feedback meeting many instances of incomplete participation and of resulting frustration and anger were expressed.

The Effect of Program Ambiguity

One side effect of Hardwick's decision not to develop initial guidelines was ambiguity. That uncertainty was unsettling for most teachers (and principals), particularly when their previous work atmosphere had precluded personal thinking and reflection. The Hill City School District administration had always operated prescriptively in the past, leaving little opportunity for teachers to practice problem solving and make decisions about how things should be done outside their rooms. Given that history, it is not surprising that suddenly having that opportunity thrust upon them created discomfort.

The superintendent exacerbated that discomfort by refusing to set guidelines and limits, stating regularly that all parties would "make it up as they go along," a situation that some found almost intolerable. However, that very ambiguity and refusal to unilaterally create another bureaucratic structure to replace the one that already existed created a potential for true empowerment. By not setting the terms and conditions, Hardwick had allowed the participants to negotiate terms and conditions that they were comfortable with, that worked for their situations and needs.

The Master Teacher selection process, entailing a certain amount of cooperation, also created ambiguity. Allowing each person to determine his or her own standards for what constituted a "Master Teacher," then merging those choices into a list of those who had met everyone's standards, resulted in a group that met the entire district's shared understanding of what constitutes good teaching, and once again avoided the institution of a bureaucratic structure. However, the refusal to change the name of the panel to one that did not offend the norms of equality that teachers held so fervently crippled the process and made impossible the effective use of the talent those teachers possessed. One year later their talents were still untapped.

Authority and Accountability

Authority had been irregularly extended, dependent on the building or the situation. Some teachers had realized a substantial expansion in the areas over which they had control. Others experienced none. Across the district there was a range of outcomes in this area. In those areas and buildings where real expansion had taken place, results were quite good, and it seems clear that those building administrators who had extended the circle had increased their own authority, as was promised by central office. In addition, many teachers and administrators had experienced substantial professional growth and confidence.

Central office administrators reported that one building administrator "gave away the store" or turned over too much authority for the process. The people in his building expressed unhappiness and frustration about their inability to realize success in resolving their problems. Probably the building administrator relinquished his leadership too completely, leaving the building without good connections to central office and without certain direction. It was important that the building administrators and their SPC representatives maintain some direction for the building, while allowing for increased consultation and participation.

The new evaluation held a great deal of promise for realizing the accountability the board and the district wanted while offering teachers beneficial developmental instructional support. Having teachers, an HCEA representative, and administrators involved in the development process protected the interests of the teachers, honored the language of the contract, and allowed a measure of confidence that both teachers' and administrators' needs would be met in the evaluation process. The self-assessment, goal-setting, and dialogue components of the evaluation cycle were designed to provide high standards and important feedback to the process. Both evaluator and evaluatee would be able to learn and reflect. The Peer Assistance Council and the Master Teacher panel would be meaningful resources.

In addition, as a developmental process the evaluation was professionalizing. It approached classroom instruction as a process of widely varying situations and solutions, not as a set of rigid and invariant behaviors.

Productivity and Student Achievement

The effects of MG on teacher productivity were seen as positive, as teachers were feeling more satisfied with their school life. In addition, the major advances realized in 1987–88 on the state basic skills test were not reversed. Given the turmoil caused by the Master Teacher selection, the ambiguity of the entire MG implementation, and the time required for participation, the ability of teachers to preserve those advances was notable. In addition, the newsletter reported a substantial number of important regional and state awards received by various schools, programs and students. Overall, however, it was too soon to make any authoritative judgment about increases in student achievement; and so many concurrent programs existed in the district during the implementation process that any or all of them might have been responsible for changes. Table 3–1 indicates no clear pattern in the percent of students who met criteria for adequate performance on the tests.

TABLE 3–1
Percent of Hill City Students
Meeting Performance Criteria on State Basic Skills

	1985	1986	1987	1988
3d Grade				
Reading	76	79	84	82
Math	85	90	96	96
5th Grade				
Reading	84	76	81	78
Math	82	85	90	87
8th Grade				
Reading	75	69	83	80
Math	74	68	87	86

The mobilization of Master Teachers and the PAC in conjunction with the effective use of the evaluation system should result in further improvement of classroom skills. Certainly the state awards received by various schools in the district pointed to increases in the quality of curriculum and instruction, although all the curricular changes were developed at central office and not in conjunction with any MG participants.

The Interests of the Four Groups

MG produced mostly successful results for two of the four groups, mixed results for one group, and unclear results for the fourth. The board desired better labor relations and an improved evaluation process leading to accountability for teachers. These goals were achieved, although labor relations had begun to deteriorate somewhat as frustration levels rose.

The superintendent wanted a showcase district, accountability, and changes in the curriculum. The district did receive considerable national and state attention, but many teachers believed that the attention was unwarranted. His desires for teacher accountability will be met through the new evaluation. The changes in the curriculum were developing, but not as a result of MG. New curricular decisions were made by a district administrator in consultation with Hardwick.

The teachers wanted some of their basic workplace concerns, such as equipment and supply improvement and a reorganization of the elementary day, to be addressed. Equipment goals were realized only partially. The supply situation continued to be a problem, and the elementary day reorganization did not happen. Teachers' concerns at specific buildings, however, met with more success. Where it was within the principal's ability to change things, change was often accomplished. The board's desire for an evaluation process was met in a way that minimized the threat to teachers. Because principals never clearly articulated their agenda, it was not possible to determine if it was achieved.

SUMMARY

Hill City's board invited Robert Hardwick into an intensely conflicted district to change the environment and to give more direction to the educational program. Hardwick set out to create more harmony by including teachers, through their association, in the governance of the schools and decision making at the district. He used the program to satisfy state requirements for teacher participation in staff development.

Hill City's Mutual Governance program was based on research into the issues of school governance, professionalization of teaching, and creating more positive relationships between districts and their labor forces. Teachers were asked to contribute more to some decisions, allowing some greater diversity of roles and opportunities for interaction with other teachers, along with the chance to inform the process more adequately; in other words, some professionalization had resulted. Administrators had been able to expand their leadership roles even as they included faculties in the process. The uniform distribution of rewards in the form of raises to all teachers was in concert with teachers' standards of equality. The program depended for incentives on differential intrinsic rewards of successful and meaningful participation. The program was considered a model for others around the state. This dramatic turnaround was initiated and guided originally by the superintendent, and had continued because of the committed participation of people in all areas of the district, including the teachers, the HCEA executives, principals, and district office staff. Board support had been substantial and consistent.

The SPC was an organizational governance body. The Master Teacher panel and the PAC were intended to be involved in instructional governance, but consistent involvement had not yet developed because of central office resistance to teacher dissatisfaction and input. Therefore, curricular change did not emanate from the MG structure. The new evaluation, developed collaboratively, promised a developmental—thus professional—assessment process for teachers.

Though a new environment of cooperation evolved in what was once an intensely conflicted district, as time went on tensions began to rise in response to unmet expectations and incomplete participation. The wider inclusion of teachers in decision-making structures and the professionalizing aspect of MG were obstructed by the district bureaucracy, which continued to make regular decisions without the input or participation of the new governance arrangements. On several occasions unilateral district decisions created serious problems and resistance. The tension between the stated policy intention to share influence with teachers and the actual central office tendency to control decision making was not resolved during the field period. As a result, as the deadline for full program implementation and reconsideration approached, teachers' support for Mutual Governance and commitment to the district were declining.

4. ACADEMY:
PROFESSIONAL REDESIGN

THE ACADEMY SCHOOL DISTRICT presents an example of professional redesign. The district's Career Enhancement Program (CEP) maximized distribution of funds to all teachers to buy more work, differentiated rewards through job enlargement, minimized merit pay, and used new positions for curriculum and instructional improvement. The effect of the program was to expand teacher participation in decision making, enrich the curriculum, advance the goals of the district, and increase teacher motivation, collaboration, and collegiality. The program also created a stubborn dilemma of whether to make permanent positions with increased responsibility and pay or to permit more participation and shared opportunity for salary increases by rotating them. Like Mossville's, Academy's program was initiated by a dynamic superintendent. However, when teachers opposed his initiatives, he (along with the board) sought a collaborative basis for resolving differences that took the program in a more professional direction.

To explain why the program worked as it did, this chapter will describe the district context that led to the CEP and shaped Academy's participation in it, summarize the state policy, examine the operation of the program in Academy, present information on its effects, and then assess the factors that contributed to the program's professional direction.

ACADEMY'S HISTORY

Background

Academy was a school district of about 13,000 students. Located in a moderately sized city, the school district was incorporated in the late nineteenth century and had a long history of growth and stability. The city was the site of a religious university, whose education department maintained close ties with the district, collaborating with the district office in planning and implementing many in-service projects for teachers and administrators. A majority of the district faculty had graduated from the university, and many young teachers supported their husbands, who were students there.

The state is one of only a few in the country that are experiencing student population growth. Class sizes in the state—and in Academy—are among the largest in the country. The district supports twelve elementary, two middle, and two regular high schools in addition to an alternative high school, a vocational high school, and a variety of special programs. One elementary principal, in response to the growing number of students, scarce educational dollars, and fiscally conservative community, initiated year-round schools as a way (among other things) to increase enrollments without adding plant.

The city was socioeconomically diverse but racially essentially homogeneous. Students ranged from poor to upper-middle-class. The presence of the university ensured a relatively well-educated population with a compelling interest in the schools and children's academic success. Yet the poverty rate was over 20 percent, reflected by the availability of free and reduced-price lunches. The fewer than 5 percent minorities were mainly Native American and Hispanic.

The district was among the better financed in the state, but still poor relative to other states. In fact, the area was listed as one of the ten urban areas with the lowest per-capita incomes in the country. Per pupil expenditure stood at less than $3,000. Comparatively, however, the district did moderately well. Facilities were well cared for, and the two high schools had relatively new plants and sophisticated computer equipment for students. The district owed its ability to maintain its facilities and remain technologically current to a low cost of living and innovative financing strategies.

The Academy environment placed high pressure on resources because of a low per-capita property base and low community resource commitment, but it did otherwise show high commitment to education. The state taxpayers' association actively fought tax increases no matter what the reason, creating a penurious financial situation. In addition, the state legislature was highly influenced by the same conservatism.

The university was a very visible influence on the schools. There was considerable interaction between the officials of the department of education and district officials. In addition to the university presence, many parents, especially the university faculty, had high expectations for their children and actively monitored the system. There was also a large contingent of poor families whose children required other kinds of special treatment and services from the schools.

The district worked hard to obtain the most benefits possible from every resource. Several staff members were knowledgeable about private funding resources. An informed teacher reported:

> We had very innovative and creative administrators who found extra money. [District administrator] got federal money. [District administrator] who is now a principal was in the central office.... They keep aware of what to write for.

The Insiders. From the middle of the 1940s until 1980, only two superintendents served the Academy district. One, Harold Greenly, was a widely respected educator who hired promising people and primed them for future upward mobility. One woman reported that he gave her free rein because she had been so highly recommended. He expressed confidence in her ability to succeed. Greenly surrounded himself with and mentored a cadre of promising male administrators. Several were still in the district at the time of the research and were very highly regarded. Teachers were pleased with Greenly because their needs were met and the climate was positive.

Greenly was an integrator. His philosophy was "we're all in this together." According to an administrator who had been one of Greenly's mentees, that philosophy began in the 1950s. Another principal said: "It's a trusting kind of thing. Greenly's idea was that schools ought to be different—professional to professional."

Greenly's successor, William Byrd, was less active but known for his ability to keep teachers and the public happy. He allowed principals and teachers substantial autonomy, and did not require strict accounting. The schools maintained a reputation around the state as being better than adequate, and test scores remained among the best in the state.

When Byrd retired, the five board members decided that the district administrators, most of whom had been hired and groomed by Greenly, might not be ready to lead the district in a new direction.

There was a widely held belief that the district was not moving forward. The board, three of whom were professors at the university, named a consulting committee of educators and community members; and, using the recommendations of the committee, conducted a national search to find someone who would lead the district forward and set a higher standard.

The Outsider. Their search located Brandon Crawford, who had grown up in the region but whose professional career had been out of state. Crawford, whose father had been a superintendent in one of the larger districts in the state, had other important family and cultural ties to it.

Crawford moved quickly and directly. He announced a philosophy of principal as instructional leader. While principals retained the authority they enjoyed under Byrd, they were also told that they must demonstrate a willingness to change and provide active leadership. They were to develop integrated in-service programs, institute clinical supervision, and work with their faculties to develop curriculum. Those who did not accommodate to the new expectations were encouraged to retire or resign. Crawford moved several principals to different buildings because his philosophy was that administrators who stay in the same place too long become stale and complacent. One board member reported that Crawford moved one resistant principal to a building where the faculty was more "with it" in a reverse attempt to get the faculty to socialize their principal. Another principal was sent back to the classroom, prompting adverse community and teacher reaction. Crawford also created tension by hiring new principals from outside the district.

The new superintendent also instituted clinical supervision. He established the Principles of Effective Teaching, a highly structured observation system that calls for specific components to be included in each lesson and specific teacher behavior in conducting the lessons, as the basis for observations and evaluations. The program structure includes a specialized vocabulary that is thought to facilitate teachers' communications among themselves and with administrators. Principals and others were trained to spend more time observing and conferring with their faculties about the improvement of teaching practices. In addition, administrators were directed to meet with their faculties to develop consistent curriculum for their schools. Crawford believed that though the curriculum, which was developed by teachers individually, resulted in interesting variations, it was counterproductive for students who needed continuous skill development.

Influencing the State. Crawford also began meeting with the deans of neighboring schools of education and key district superintendents to talk about improving education in the state. The group identified teaching as one area of concern: strengthening pre-service education, integrating pre-service and in-service, and adding variety to the career profile. Their discussions convinced Crawford that he wanted to institute a career enhancement program so teachers who wanted more responsibility and/or money could become leaders and mentors in their building and receive more pay without having to become administrators. They would be elected to special positions. A model for the CEP came from those talks. Crawford then went to the teachers and principals in the district, and they started talking.

The Superintendent, the Staff, and the Board

While the board was delighted with Crawford's energy, action-orientation, and forceful ideas, many teachers and principals became very distressed. They were not used to changes being implemented without their consultation or consent. Teachers were not accustomed to having principals observe and evaluate them at their work. They felt that this administration did not trust their competence. Pressure built up to a critical point.

The culture of the school district was nonconfrontational. However, at one teachers' association meeting with the superintendent in the room, a member asked for a vote of no confidence. The president of the Academy Education Association (AEA) avoided official action, but this series of events publicized the pressure felt by teachers and principals and placed the issue squarely on the table. However, it still gave the superintendent sufficient opportunity to change direction and operate in a less conflict-generating manner.

Greatly distressed, Crawford consulted a board member who directed him to show more concern and sensitivity and more closely to involve teachers and principals in his planning and implementation strategies. The same board member went to the schools to facilitate the new strategy by indicating that the superintendent knew of his errors and was making efforts to change. The board member asked the faculties for patience. This integrative rather than confrontational stance—that is, siding with the faculty by directing the superintendent to change, and siding with the superintendent by counseling patience—facilitated positive change in the district.

Crawford's desire for a career enhancement program offered an opportunity to follow the new directions of the board member. He convened a task force consisting of representatives of all buildings—teachers and administrators—to develop a CEP plan. The committee viewed his decision to chair their deliberations as a significant symbol of his commitment to the work and of their importance to the district. During the planning period, a disagreement about how to formulate the salary schedule arose. Crawford had one idea—to abolish the step and lane framework—but other members of the committee thought that CEP stipends could be meshed with regular salary scales. The committee asked to submit the ideas to teachers for their approval and Crawford agreed. Teachers sided with the dissenting committee members, and Crawford acquiesced. He said, "They thought I had become a new creature."

Nevertheless, while significant strides were made, Crawford remained legendary as a task-oriented, intellectual administrator. He appeared unable to create personal ties with even his closest staff, save one.

The Right-Hand Man.   Joseph Freeman, one of Greenly's mentees, had been a finalist for the superintendency when Crawford was selected. Afterward, Freeman immediately expressed his support for the new superintendent and worked hard to help Crawford implement district programs. The relationship that developed became famous. Even people in the state department of education spoke of the two. Respondents almost uniformly described Crawford's brilliance in developing innovative programs, pressing hard for changes, and strengthening curriculum and instruction; but they also told of his problematic implementation strategies and inability to relate to people. Crawford "didn't want people in his office," said a district administrator. "He didn't have time to listen to their concerns. He just didn't feel he could open up." And an AEA official explained:

> He had a lot of ideas he explored. He was like a tiger when he got an idea. He didn't turn it loose. He rubbed people the wrong way. Once a goal was set, there was no stopping until it was accomplished. Everyone had to assume responsibility for doing it.... He had definite ideas about things.... Some people got hurt.

Freeman, on the other hand, while strong in program areas, was more masterful at attracting people to work with him. He "is the opposite of Brandon," said a district administrator. "He has a people orientation. He talked to people in the halls.... He had a lot of support. People liked him. He works with them. He listened. He was more comfortable." Freeman's interpersonal skills were exceptional and he became the bridge in facilitating implementation. The team was held in high regard.

Soon after Crawford supervised the initiation of the Academy CEP, he took the superintendency of a larger district. Upon hearing that Crawford had applied, one board member had "mixed feelings. The district did, too. Some said it was good because he'd been pushing us too much. We need to settle. Others said that so many things were happening that are exciting. I was mixed."

Crawford told the board that he would like to take Freeman with him, but he thought it would be unfair to the district, and that others from the district might follow. According to one district respondent, when Crawford left he was given a standing ovation; many in the audience had registered a vote of no confidence in him just a few years earlier.

Some board members considered another national search; others now saw the wisdom of promoting Freeman to the post he had almost been given previously. Freeman helped them make their decision by stating that he had received other offers, subtly indicating that he would not serve as number two this time. Freeman's long service to the district, his skillful facilitation of Crawford's programs, and the expertise he had gained working with Crawford, along with his assurances that he would continue Crawford's programs, convinced the board that they would be losing too valuable a person if they did not appoint him this time. According to one board member:

> We decided Joe was runner up last time. He had good personnel skills and four years of tutelage from Brandon.... We decided we needed Joe. We needed settling. Joe was a good people person. He had ideas.... He developed a philosophical statement. He started with Brandon's. Each school worked on it. Then the principals worked on it. Then it went to the board. The board, administrators, and representative faculty met. Brandon took risks and Joe provided the buffering.

It would have been difficult for Freeman, with his close ties to people in the district, to make the drastic changes that Crawford had been able to. Crawford paved the way for him to continue and expand district reforms by drawing the lightning of discontent, then leaving Freeman the opportunity to carry them out with no loss of personal admiration.

The Board. In 1989 the board consisted of five members who had not been there at the time of Crawford's appointment, and four who had not voted on Freeman's succession. Two of the new members were women. No incumbents had lost elections in recent years. Most of the new members had been asked by their predecessors to join the board. One of the women had been troubled by the way that students—most important her children—had been assigned to the high schools when the newer one was built, and by her inability to communicate with the board members. She decided to run so that she could influence future decisions. All spoke of service on the board as a way to serve the community—almost as a religious duty.

The board practiced consensual decision making. Dissenting votes were rare, even over a period of many years. One new board member described the decision-making process as talking about a problem until a solution satisfactory to everyone was derived. Either they came to see the problem in the same way, or compromises were made until they were all satisfied. The process was not contentious or acrimonious.

The two women were more involved in the routine affairs of the district because they were available during the day. Both regularly accompanied the superintendent to schools for goal setting. Their visits were welcomed. Though board members were open to community input, they resisted community members' protests about individual situations and sent dissatisfied people to the appropriate district official.

Teachers. The AEA had an amicable relationship with the district. Crawford was an active member, and Freeman, also a member, expressed approval for and support of teachers' concerns. Although this state prohibited strikes, the AEA conducted collective bargaining with the district, and most teachers expressed confidence that the local chapter fairly represented teachers' concerns. Several respondents disagreed with the state organization but expressed their support for the local chapter.

AEA members were active at the state association. The local president during the year of the research was elected vice president of the state Council of Local Presidents. One Academy teacher represented the district on the state association board and represented the state association on the NEA board. That same person, because of a curriculum program she had developed, was recommended to us as someone to interview about the district CEP policy. Asked about Brandon Crawford's changes, she said, "In the first two years, he seemed radical. People said he did too much too fast. I never felt that. We needed direction. I like innovation."

Prior to the CEP task force, teacher influence had been largely confined to classroom autonomy, but substantial teacher influence and control over district processes came with the development and implementation of CEP. Principals asked teachers to interview candidates for positions, included teachers in school goal-setting deliberations, and allowed teachers the majority voice in curriculum development. Said one:

> There is a great deal of teacher influence on the curriculum as long as we follow the state core. How we teach, texts, etc. are determined by teachers.... We hired a new math teacher. Two of us [teachers] sat in on the interviews. We asked questions. When we got down to the one we wanted to hire, we observed him teach.

One teacher spoke about the lack of involvement in a district close to Academy. There teachers were not given keys to the building, or involved in curriculum planning; "I just got a book" was a typical teacher comment. By contrast, in Academy all teachers had keys to their buildings and the opportunity to be involved in curriculum planning. The representative to the NEA board said:

> Teachers can speak out. They do have ownership. Joe is a fine administrator. He's willing to let teachers own it.... People like him a lot and feel part of the whole.... In this state, with the limited money and number of kids, morale could be low. It's never been higher.

During the time of the research, the state legislature was negotiating possible distributions of a substantial surplus that had accrued after a tax increase. Teachers in the state wanted a significant portion to go for their salaries. When most of the surplus was directed towards other ends, the state education association was so inflamed it declared a one-day walkout. Academy teachers supported the walkout, and the district office openly supported their action.

The education association—state and local chapters—the state department, and the districts planned seriously for a strike in case the legislative session did not meet teachers' demands. The planning in Academy took place collaboratively; the president of the local AEA and the superintendent went together to schools and meetings to discuss plans and contingencies. Freeman determined that though the state would declare any strikes illegal and urge locals to fire teachers, those from Academy would not lose their jobs. However, the district would be legally required to keep schools open using substitutes. One beginning teacher expressed surprise that the superintendent met with teachers at all.

District Interactions. According to Freeman, openness between the board and the superintendent was not a trait in the district before Crawford: "Under the prior administration, we weren't to be present [at board meetings]. Under Brandon, it was open. I was at all of them and so were two others." This openness gave Freeman the opportunity to learn. Also, according to a board member,

> The faculty and the community got more involved than before. When I came on, the philosophy was "don't involve the public too much. You get dissidents." [After Crawford came] there began to be more the idea on the board and in the district to get more input.

The AEA president said that under "the old superintendent...it was a closed environment." The present board president spoke about the present administration:

> [Joe] has a very open administration. Incredibly open. Workshops, etc. More than [Brandon].... [Joe] tends to impose a lot on principals to inform us. They come to meetings and we have board meetings in the buildings.... [Joe] knows he works for the board, but he's loyal to the people under him.

And a PTA parent said, "I'm working on the city PTA and I get the feeling of what's happening around the city. There is an open administration, an open district office, and I think it's a result of CEP." The district office and the board buffered the organization from the community by maintaining good relationships and good outcomes. Because community acceptance of district outcomes was high, the district could keep the schools open to the community with little negative impact on the faculty.

THE STATE CAREER ENHANCEMENT PROGRAM

During the school year prior to the 1984 legislative session, Crawford worked with the Academy task force to develop a model for the district. The state superintendent then asked Crawford to chair a committee to develop a career enhancement program model to submit for legislative approval and funding. That design became the foundation from which the legislature developed its final bill. Crawford expressed pleasure that he could shape the state plan to be compatible with Academy's:

> By the time the legislature was in session, we had a model. Then the state superintendent asked me to head up a committee to develop legislative guidelines on [CEP]. It gave me the opportunity to promote concepts in the legislation that were consistent with the [Academy] effort.... Happily, [the state] took the route of allowing broad latitude, not a tight statewide model. In [Academy] we worked with the grassroots and really developed ownership that was not possible with the statewide model.... We were in front of most districts.... It was helpful to have a model to show the legislature an example.

A number of compromises were made during the legislative negotiations. Legislators were opposed to giving teachers more money without requiring more accountability. Even though teachers' salaries in the state were much lower than those in most other states, the conservative legislature believed that teachers were already well paid, and wanted to attach some conditions to more funds. According to Crawford,

> The strategy was to convince the legislature that this was not just an across-the-board increase. Incentives for outstanding professional teachers. A lot of legislators had a simpleminded notion from the private sector that you are rewarded for accomplishments only. That's not true anywhere except for salesmen.

Many legislators were anxious to impose what was largely a merit pay plan. According to a legislative analyst, some wanted 100 percent of the funds to go for merit pay, but that model cost the bill considerable support. The final package mandated a minimum of 10 percent for merit pay. Under this section teachers were to be paid solely on their ability to teach better than others. Another provision extended the contract for all teachers, allowing for planning days before the school year began or during the school year. However, a maximum allocation of 50 percent of program funds was set. The CEP plan provided money for teachers to assume some extra-class responsibilities. This job enlargement portion was extra pay for extra work.

There was also a master-teacher provision giving permanent, merit-based promotions as teachers' experience and skill increased. The language of the entire plan tied the package to the 1980s reforms, as described in *A Nation at Risk* (National Commission on Educational Excellence 1983).

The state teachers' association wanted more pay for all teachers. It was reluctant to accept or even to fail to oppose the new legislation. But with the inclusion of the extended contract and the provision of more pay for more work, its leadership decided that the money for teachers would not be available any other way, and agreed not to oppose the legislation. Since then the association has become more supportive. CEP was not negotiable in collective bargaining.

To convince reluctant districts to participate, legislators specified only guidelines and minimum/maximum expenditures. Within the guidelines, local districts could decide how much emphasis each component would receive and what the final plan would accomplish.

Although Crawford's committee had recommended full funding in the first year, the original legislation spread the funding over three years, with one-third of the funding added each year. The program was classified as categorical, with "sin taxes" such as liquor and cigarettes as a source of new dollars, but with no general tax increase. The legislature funded the next third the following year, but the final third was never appropriated.

ACADEMY'S CAREER ENHANCEMENT PROGRAM IN ACTION

The description of the CEP was developed from documents and interviews. The response data derive from a survey that was administered to Academy's teachers and administrators at the superintendent's suggestion. The questionnaire was parallel to one that had been administered statewide to determine teacher sentiment about the CEP. The Academy survey is printed in its entirety in Appendix C. Responses were chosen from a Likert scale continuum, with 1 indicating "strongly disagree," 3 indicating a neutral response, and 5 indicating "strongly agree."

Implementation

Although the legislation passed and Academy was prepared in advance with its own program, the failure of the legislature to fully fund it meant that Academy could not implement its design without additional local financial support.

Crawford had led previous campaigns to raise local dollars with voted leeways. He explained, "Being from the Midwest, I was shocked by the low level of school funding in the district." He felt strongly that he had to generate new money for operations and took his pleas to the voters. But twice the initiatives were defeated. In both cases the state taxpayers' association had opposed his proposal.

Crawford was anxious to implement the Academy plan, but felt strongly that it would not succeed partially funded. He decided to initiate a third voted leeway. To generate an acceptable plan, however, he took advantage of the year-round school concept implemented by one of his principals. This plan permitted each school to serve more students in the same space. Asking the town for permission to shift some capital dollars to operations, thus waiving funding for new facilities, Crawford committed the majority of the money to the CEP for teachers, and pledged that the district would not ask for a millage increase for five years. Thus, while the public voted to spend more on operations, there was no tax increase; the difference was made up by reducing capital expenditures. To make adequate the existing building space, Crawford promised to reorganize several more schools on year-round schedules. Unopposed by the taxpayers' association, this leeway passed; and Crawford began plans for local implementation.

Crawford presented his vision of using the skills and ideas of teachers to enrich the instructional and curricular life of the school, and his desire to keep teachers in the classroom by giving them the opportunity to earn more money without entering administration. This board member's response indicates the resonance of Crawford's idea:

> The idea was that we don't allow teachers to get status as teachers. Only as administrators. So we lose the best.... Part of it is to get teachers to feel more professional. How do you keep good ones in the classroom? Get them more money. The whole idea was that teachers could be leaders as teachers and not put them in an administrative role where they put fires out and are not curriculum leaders.

Fully funded, the Academy CEP was ready for implementation in September following the legislation. The largest implementation problem, initially, was to get some principals to grant teachers expanded responsibility—and therefore influence—in their buildings.

The Career Enhancement Program Task Force. Crawford had initially organized the task force to design the local program so that when the state funds became available the district would be ready to move. Each school[1] appointed a representative, and meetings began. During the planning process Crawford worked closely with the task force, and also kept his principals apprised of its progress. He presented principals' ideas to the task force. One administrator explained that Crawford asked them to develop the job descriptions for job enlargement positions, then submitted their descriptions to the task force for further formulation. During the year a rough model—quite close to the present one—was developed.

During a disagreement over the salary schedule, Crawford changed his position to reflect teachers' concerns expressed in the meetings. That fundamental and symbolic act began to build trust among the task-force teachers that their concerns would meet with positive responses.

Other factors institutionalized teacher participation in the process of CEP implementation. Crawford had been a top-down administrator in every other area. He worked only with board members and top administrators. However, he chaired the CEP task force even though most members were teachers. Said an AEA offficial:

> He came with ideas and gave us an overall view. Each week he'd have a part worked out. We'd change parts then. Other parts would get input and be changed later. Parts were adjusted. He was saying it was important enough to work with us on.

The task force soon realized that efficiency was being hampered by the group's size. One principal reported that it was difficult to get consensus on the task force because each principal "runs the program a little differently." In 1985 the task force created a steering committee of one elementary school administrator, one secondary school administrator, the president and president-elect of the AEA, four central office administrators, a PTA representative, and five teachers. The steering committee met monthly to evaluate the implementation and functions of the CEP model, hear disputes, and make recommendations to the task force for modifications and additions. In the spring the committee provided plans for the new year and solutions to problems. While the district and principals maintained substantial authority, conferences with teachers preceded most decisions.

One example of the task force's problem-solving activities was its continuing drive to fulfill the state requirement for merit pay without compromising the district aversion to the concept. It designed a "Writing Across the Curriculum" plan that included a performance bonus. The task force also thrashed out problems that had defied solution for years. The most obstinate of these was providing wide access to the high-paying teacher-leader positions without creating economic dislocation for people who were replaced.

Both task force and steering committee were paramount in planning for the CEP and solving problems. Members were directed to solicit input from their buildings and share input with the committee. Teachers reported:

> They involve teachers a lot. Money affects what can be offered. They take our ideas but it comes down to what they can support. They go to teachers first and then decide. They don't make decisions and tell us "this will happen."

> In Academy teachers have all the influence. Teachers made it through the CEP task force.... After six years the task force does a good job. Each year different teachers are on the task force.... They have involved so many more people in the decision making process. More people are responsible. Everyone feels involved.

Principals agreed:

> I like that teachers and administrators are involved. If administrators didn't like something, we could say our piece and be listened to. With teachers it's the same way. I've been on the steering committee. I saw the hammering out and give and take.

Most teachers and principals expressed their satisfaction with their inclusion in and their level of influence on district decision making. A high school principal said,

> CEP was suggested by Superintendent Crawford in administrator meetings. Literature was dispersed and discussed. Administrators talked about it. Teachers talked about it. The CEP task force was formed and beat out a program. They put it together. The board approved it.... The leadership started it. Administrators and teachers were involved.

The CEP task force was responsible for allocating CEP money, such as deciding how many nonteaching planning days would be available and how much stipends would be. It also communicated with the legislature, and influenced deliberations where possible.

The task force steering committee managed appeals by teachers who were refused CEP positions. When a teacher leader who had served since the beginning of CEP was passed over and appealed her case, she was asked to join the task force and help resolve the issue. The group employed consensus to reach decisions, much as the board and the school selection committees did.

Communications. The CEP plan stated that open communications among all parties was essential to successful function. Principals and task-force members were directed to hold open faculty meetings to explain the program, disseminate information through the staff newsletter and other resources, and provide time in faculty meetings to discuss the CEP, among other things. Job descriptions were to include communications activities, as were school plans. Teacher leaders and curriculum specialists were to hold annual meetings. New teachers were provided information in three ways: a mandatory faculty meeting at the beginning of the year, an in-service, and a brochure. Each school was directed to present an overview of the career enhancement program and explain positions available for the coming year. Even external communications mechanisms were outlined, including keeping the community, parents, legislators, and board members apprised of CEP activities and events.

The Extended Contract

The state limited expenditures on noninstructional, extended-contract days to half or less of state funds. The task force allotted the maximum, to be divided among all teachers for personal planning, school functions and district functions. During the 1989–90 school year, the district was able to fund eight days for extended contract. In this way everyone received some more money.

In regular nine-month schools, days were used prior to the instructional year. In year-round schools, days were distributed throughout the year. Guidelines were presented for use of the time. Employees were to be in the building. Teacher leaders and curriculum specialists were expected to meet with teachers and teachers were expected to plan curriculum for the upcoming year.

The most popular of the CEP programs, both in the district and in the state, the extended contract was credited with allowing teachers to be so ready to teach that "they are ready to give a test on the first day." As a secondary principal observed:

Professional staff say, "I now have time to get ready for school...to hit the road running." That's true. We used to change classes for three to four days after school started.... Now they'd shoot the counselor. There's too much important stuff early.

During this time the teachers can meet with teacher leaders, curriculum specialists, team members, counselors, and each other without having to cover their classes. They are also available to attend informational meetings. One teacher spoke of the time it allowed for concentrated thinking to prepare the curriculum.

The extended contract was especially useful for middle school teachers. "There's a lot of team teaching here," said one. "Part of the middle school philosophy...we have time through CEP. Prep days. Everyone has time to coordinate activities.... They can combine talents in three areas in humanities."

Teachers with full-year contracts in year-round schools also benefitted from the extended contract. During the year they were assigned to new students when their regular students went "off track." It was likely that they would say farewell to one group of thirty students on Friday, and greet a totally different group of students on Monday. The extra days allowed them to prepare for their new students.

There were also extended-contract days during the year. On those days, curriculum specialists and teacher leaders were often asked to conduct workshops for interested teachers. A teacher said, "I like the district meetings. The quality of people there rejuvenates me. The district has quality people. Because the district is small, they have a good handle on things. The people are committed." One parent also found CEP days beneficial: "Using the professional days, they spend time getting better. The teachers are not taking off as soon as school is out, and if we have a problem we can come to see them." This was not a universal sentiment. Many spoke about parent dissatisfaction that teachers were in the building but children were not. It was felt that some teachers wasted time. However, interviews indicated that teachers were heavily involved during their before-school CEP days developing curriculum and preparing for the year. During their school-year CEP days, they graded papers, entered grades on the computer, and attended workshops. Many administrators structured available school and district time to accomplish educational goals.

In the past, the kind of planning that could be accomplished during the extended contract days had depended on the commitment or availability of individual teachers, and therefore was erratic. With routinely available paid planning time, preparation became more consistent and the district could insist on teachers' participation.

Table 4–1 indicates that Academy teachers were not only very positive about this program element, they were more positive than their colleagues throughout the state.

TABLE 4–1
Teacher Assessments of Extended Contract

	Academy	State
The Extended Contract:		
increases teacher opportunities to plan for classroom instruction	4.23	4.35
increases teacher opportunities to develop curriculum	4.30	4.23
increases teacher opportunities to participate in professional development	4.26	3.95
increases teacher opportunities to do record keeping and paperwork	4.02	4.16
effectively allows the district to accomplish planning and management	4.01	3.39
should be continued	4.46	4.36

Merit Pay

The district decided from the beginning to deemphasize merit pay. Some on the task force had served on a similar committee in the 1950s, when the state had asked Academy to pilot a merit-pay plan. That group worked for days to operationalize what teachers do, then tried to develop an instrument to objectively assess total practice. They concluded there is no valid instrument to measure what a teacher really does, and that they could not precisely determine what is good teaching and what is not. They felt that such qualities as how a teacher affects a child's life and work in the future are not measurable. Because the plan was enormously complicated and too expensive to implement, they dropped it. The current board also opposed having different wages for the same job. The aversion to merit pay was reflected in the philosophy statement: "The [Academy] model has built in accountability for teaching effectiveness while avoiding some of the problems which are commonly associated with traditional merit plans."

Academy teachers also expressed fears of merit pay, believing that a competitive system would destroy their cohesiveness. They believed that under a merit system, teachers would begin to look out for their own territory and not share with others. However, the state plan mandated merit pay, and the department of education adamantly insisted that there be such a component. Academy avoided the issue for several years, but the state threatened not to certify their entire plan. To meet the requirement, Academy implemented a model in which teachers who had a successful clinical supervision and provided a satisfactory plan to comply with the district's Writing Across the Curriculum program would receive $200.[2] The central office liaison with the state explained:

> Last year the district's application was put on hold because of how they handled the performance bonus requirement. I wrote a letter to our liaison, giving our interpretation of the law and why we thought our approach was legal. He came down to meet with the task force and got ripped. That was a good thing. He thought I was being difficult, but after that he saw it wasn't just me.

The district always responded to pressure for merit programs with adroit avoidance, believing that such programs were divisive and counterproductive. That stance created a constant strain in district relations with the department of education, which believed that the district's compliance fulfilled the letter but avoided the spirit of the merit component. According to one university respondent, the state would not recognize the Academy model as one of the best in the state because of the district's stance on merit pay. One department person explained its objection to the Academy model:

> The law says don't discriminate about years of service on the performance bonus, but it's like pulling teeth. We want first-year teachers to be eligible. We want people to be able to get rewards for just doing a good job. We didn't want seniority to weigh so heavily.

She also said that merit pay was not working and was divisive. A legislative analyst stated that in "every district" there was resistance to merit pay because it was felt that there are no fair evaluation instruments.

Academy sentiment against traditional merit pay was consistent across roles. According to a board member, "The CEP was never looked at as a merit system. We'd reward for responsibility, not pay some more money because they were better. That's what teachers told us." A district administrator echoed his sentiments: "We get frustrated when we hear from the state that we need more merit, but we wanted to avoid merit and give more pay for more work. Merit is such an emotional concern and creates so many factions."

Numerous teachers offered their vision of what Academy's version of merit pay was trying to accomplish.

> I like the opportunity that anyone who wants to earn more money and likes added responsibility can. It's more fair. There is a lot better association.... There is more sharing here than if there was merit pay.

> The state says that CEP must be a form of merit pay. We have Writing Through the Curriculum. Also a couple of district workshops on English. She taught us how to implement Writing Across the Curriculum. To make it merit pay, they said, "Give us examples of what you do. Proof." We get $200 for that. That's the only form of merit pay in CEP which I like.

One woman was ambivalent about the Academy conception. Asked if she would rather get paid more just for teaching well, she responded, "Teachers at my mother's school [in another district] can get points for projects.... The extra programs [in Academy] are wonderful, but I'd like to get rewarded for good teaching also." This sentiment was unusual, however. Generally, teacher survey responses to the performance bonus were positive—far more so than in other districts (see Table 4–2).

TABLE 4–2
Perceptions of Performance Bonus

	Academy	State
The Performance Bonus:		
is an incentive for teachers to care more about the quality of teaching	3.52	3.05
incentive for teachers to remain in the teaching profession	3.18	2.69
allows the district to retain excellent teachers	3.09	2.72
allows the district to improve the morale of teachers	3.25	2.57
should be continued	3.86	3.20

Job Enlargement

The centerpiece of the Academy CEP was the system of special positions to be filled by those chosen to develop and implement the instructional program of the school and district. The task force emphasized job enlargement over merit pay and folded the differentiated staffing provision into the overall strategy. Officially the Academy CEP was developed to make teaching more attractive, offer opportunities for professional growth and advancement, reward outstanding teachers, allow them to contribute to the district's instructional work in a variety of ways, and improve the instructional program of the district by utilizing the skills and energy of its teachers.

An integral concept of Academy job enlargement was that these positions provided instructional support, not quasi-administrative services. The task was to expand the expertise and resources available to faculty members, relieving administrators of specific instructional support duties but not administrative duties. Administrators retained substantial influence in their buildings but were directed to use the energy and expertise of many of their faculty both in planning and implementing the curriculum. Two positions were assigned specifically to schools: curriculum specialists and teacher leaders. There were also district-level positions. Funding was available to select forty percent of the faculty as curriculum specialists. Teacher leaders received more remuneration. After some adjustment, the decision was made to allot two to each elementary school, three to each middle school, and five to each high school. Each school could determine how it wanted to utilize its CEP jobs within the framework of the state and district requirements.

Job enlargement became the most visible and active component of the CEP, with the extended contract organized to supplement and facilitate its operation. The performance bonus was also administered largely through job enlargement personnel. The board, the superintendent, and the teachers saw job enlargement as an important device to improve the instructional and curricular life of the district. As a previous board member explained, "Beginning teachers could get help. All teachers could provide input to the school. More seasoned teachers would get more responsibility. Some would be elected to special positions." District positions were used extensively. As one administrator explained, "The previous year they did literature. They used the twenty-three to twenty-six days to create and develop it. They worked it out jointly.... It's pretty well directed." Principals also used teacher leaders and specialists extensively to meet the needs of their schools as outlined in their schools' goals. Said one,

> My job with the CEP is to utilize it to its fullest extent. There are
> "worriers" that I can allow to worry about things I used to have
> to take care of. I used to have to plead with people to serve.
> Now we can select them.

There were sufficient funds so that, according to a district administrator, "Mostly any teacher who wants added work can get it. They can't
all be teacher leader, but not all want to be with twenty-six extra days."

Respondents believed that the job enlargement component provided many incentives and benefits. This middle school teacher
expressed the typical perception of the program:

> It gives teachers power and autonomy to have meaningful
> input. It gives variety to a static profession.... There are incen-
> tives to perform well. There is more money. There is more con-
> centration on what happens in the classroom and less on the dis-
> trict or the state.

While the Academy CEP was supposed to have integrated the
state differentiated staffing component with the job enlargement component, the Academy "career ladder" was not a true ladder. That is,
teachers did not proceed into successively more complex, prestigious,
and responsible positions and then stay there. Teachers "fell off" the
ladder if they were not reappointed, and they lost the job enlargement
compensation. It was not tied in to the regular contract salary.

The district administration and the task force were ambivalent
about the temporary nature of these positions. On the one hand, people could hope for appointment to the prestigious and rewarding
teacher-leader positions, even though others might hold them
presently. As one teacher explained, "The argument for making it
available to everyone is that more people will try if more get a chance
to serve. There's more experience and training for all. More get
involved in leadership roles." On the other hand, the temporariness
provided no security to people who wanted to remain in the classroom but to be paid well. According to the same teacher,

> The negative side is you're a teacher leader and then you're not.
> You get more money each year, and then you're a regular teach-
> er. It's a step stool. You step on and then you step off. I don't
> know which is better.

Others called it a perch or a pogo stick. One high school principal saw
it this way:

The teacher leader should be a career assignment. We should tighten up on selection even more. I don't like the trampoline effect. Teacher leaders have influence. They've got to have stability and respect.

The committee spent significant time and effort considering options. However, a study group of the task force concluded that it would cost the district at least an additional $2.5 million per year to fund a ladder that "wouldn't hurt anyone." Moreover, teachers clearly preferred the current system. In the survey teachers agreed strongly (4.01) that it should be maintained and disagreed that positions should be made permanent (1.50). Even present teacher leaders supported the current system (3.88).

Even with this disagreement about making the positions permanent, job enlargement was very popular in Academy (see Table 4–3).

TABLE 4–3
Teacher Assessments of Job Enlargement

	Academy	*State*
The Job Enlargement component:		
is an incentive for teachers to be paid for work they once did for no pay	4.25	3.99
is an incentive for teachers to share leadership responsibilities	4.02	3.43
is an incentive for teachers to use professional skills effectively	3.85	3.35
allows the district to retain excellent teachers	3.63	3.01
should be continued	4.13	3.55

The job enlargement component included two school positions—teacher leader, curriculum specialist—and two at the district level: secondary specialists and elementary grade leaders. After a description of these positions, the selection process is outlined.

Teacher Leaders. The task force developed a system of teacher leaders for each building. These teachers were to act as mentors for new teachers and model instructional practices for other faculty members. As well, teacher leaders conducted clinical supervision for provisional teachers and worked closely with college students who were full-time teaching interns. The program description defines teacher leaders as

> proficient teachers who also have outstanding skills for giving leadership in the improvement of teaching. Their appointment as teacher leader is based on their excellent teaching skills and their ability to help other teachers improve.... The primary focus of the work of teacher leaders is to teach on a regular basis.... It is not intended that they become involved in administrative work unrelated to instructional leadership.

Appointments were for two years, at an annual stipend of about $1,100, and included pay for twenty-seven additional days each year at the teacher's daily rate. The appointments were to the school and not to the district, so that appointees would not be transferred. Teachers were assessed at the end of the first year to determine whether they were meeting their goals and satisfying school requirements.

Release time was at the discretion of the principal with a guideline of 10 to 20 percent stated in the district plan. Some schools hired two college seniors majoring in education as interns. The interns assumed full classroom duties at half salary in one school so one teacher leader could be released full time. Teacher leaders and a student teaching supervisor from the university closely supervised the interns, who had completed their course requirements but not student teaching.

Teacher leaders' responsibilities varied within and among schools. In one elementary school, where one teacher leader was released full time and one spent more time in the classroom, the full-time teacher leader assumed more responsibilities, including some that were administrative.

One important function of teacher leaders was to work with interns, new teachers, and provisional teachers who had not done well in their principal evaluations. Provisional teachers who performed poorly during evaluation were referred to the teacher leader for special help.

Teacher leaders became integral to the fabric of schools, even acting as unofficial assistants to the principals. Although they were to improve the instructional program of the school and not to report what they saw during clinical supervision to the principal, in fact some did just about anything the principal asked. One teacher leader reported doing a cleanup in the hall, and several said they were usually asked how an evaluation or clinical supervision went. One teacher felt that the message, which had been loud and clear when the CEP was developed, had not been adequately conveyed to newer principals. However, teacher leaders at one high school stated that they reported their observations only to the teacher unless it was necessary to speak to the principal. One said,

> My job isn't to report to the principal. It's to work with the teacher. It's important not to be a spy for the administration.... [If there were a problem] I'd work with the teacher first before bringing the administrator in. If I felt the administrator needed to be involved, I'd ask the teacher's permission.... My job is improving teacher's skills.

Other teacher leaders reported a similar philosophy. clearly the understanding of the role of teacher leaders in clinical supervision varied from school to school.

One problem that the teacher-leader position carried was the requirement for more than a month's work in the summer. Although this was the biggest addition to the teacher leaders' yearly income, it was reported that some teachers valued their summer time with their families and would not apply for jobs that required summer commitment. Other teachers had alternative summer plans that gave variety to their lives. The high school principal told of a teacher who had a forest-service job, and another who took her children to France for the summer. The extra prestige and money were not sufficient to lure those teachers to abandon their alternative plans.

Curriculum Specialists. Curriculum specialists worked in one curriculum or school-designated area in individual schools developing programs and lesson plans, obtaining materials, and conducting in-service at the administrator's request. The official description of these positions describes specialists as

> teachers who are willing and qualified to take on additional responsibilities directly related to the improvement of teaching. The additional responsibilities are not to be administrative. Examples of additional responsibilities are modeling for and coaching student teachers and beginning teachers, curriculum development and refinement, curriculum implementation, conducting staff development workshops for other teachers, and developing better instruments for assessing student learning.

School administrators determined their curricular goals, often in consultation with faculty members, formalized them during goal setting, then decided how best to use their curriculum specialist positions to meet goals.

According to the CEP plan, the curriculum specialist positions could vary from year to year, depending on a needs assessment completed in March of the previous year. Once the positions were announced, teachers indicated their interest to the principal. Curriculum specialists could be appointed by the principal acting alone after conferences with the selection committee, but committees in at least two buildings reviewed applications for both curriculum specialists and teacher leaders.

Curriculum specialists were appointed for one year with a stipend of about $1,100 but no additional paid days. According to a high school teacher,

> Specialists coordinate the curriculum. All teachers know what they should be teaching. The specialists also coordinate with the core [state curriculum]. In the summer, specialists write up the curriculum for the year.

Although this statement implies a routine position, variation in specialist job descriptions was even greater than for teacher leaders. Specialists had a range of capabilities and commitment. Some put in a minimum of time and showed little inclination toward working in the classroom with teachers. Others felt that they contributed many hours beyond the formal requirements of the position. Specialists exhibited a range of competencies in their curricular areas. Some were experts, others were learning as they worked. Nevertheless, respondents from administration, faculties, and the outside agree the curriculum was far richer with the specialists than it would have been without them. The district's extremely tight financial situation did not allow for full-time specialists in any curricular areas. However, the curriculum specialist position provided part-time specialists in many areas.

One school implemented a gifted and talented program using specialist talents. The program allowed the entire school to experience enrichment, and allowed students who had specialized gifts but not necessarily academic superiority to develop those gifts. That same school had an art program that featured one famous artist for several months, allowing all students to learn about the artist's life, work, and style. The specialist, who was an artist herself, invited leather workers, a stained-glass worker, potters, and others to visit with teachers' classes. Another specialist developed a cooperative learning model that she shared with her own faculty and other schools.

In other schools, theater and music programs were developed that were unique to the person who created them. Students from two schools took a trip to Russia as a final activity for a history unit cooperatively developed by several curriculum specialists. One specialist reported that the school's musical instruments had been in a box in a closet for years until she found them and shared them with the teachers. A high school specialist developed the AP Spanish curriculum, attending workshops at the university and collecting materials.

The high school principal initiated a program for at-risk students that guaranteed academic success if they stayed with the program. The students did not fail, but worked until they had mastered a particular subject. The principal used a curriculum specialist to develop and implement the program. That same specialist was preparing to submit a specialist proposal for the following year for hermeneutics in literature. One teacher was asked by the department chair to coordinate tutoring for the ACT and SAT tests and to coordinate placements when middle school students come to the high school.

Specialists usually saw themselves as responders and not as initiators. They did not force themselves on the faculty. "Some say they don't want to teach art. I don't worry if they don't want to," said an elementary specialist. Another way to interpret their orientation to staff was given by this teacher:

> Teacher leaders helped me on instruction. It hasn't come without asking. I had to go ask. Some people are not aware that that's what they're there for. I don't see them as that's their main role. They just take it as understood that's what they're there for. I haven't seen them in a lot of classes.

However, if the principal wanted the specialist to perform workshops, in-service at faculty meetings, or to work with new classroom teachers, the specialist would do that. They were also expected to go outside the district for ideas.

What magnified the effects of particularly good specialist programs was the sharing that went on among schools. Specialists met with those from other schools to exchange ideas. Many stated that they would probably have done the work anyway, but having the extended contract time and getting the extra pay facilitated their work and made it more rewarding. When someone has specific responsibility for particular programs, "so many things can happen," said one teacher.

Things they've provided are immeasurable. The art specialist did a presentation to my first graders on Monet. They understood it. We have a discipline-based art program that focuses on two to three artists in each grade. I can get the kit with prints on Monet or whoever. We developed this with Getty money.

One task force member, an elementary teacher, summarized the role of specialists particularly well:

[CEP] is wonderful. I'm the PE specialist in my school. I get a chance to generate ideas. I make plans to get time to help teachers learn how to integrate PE into their curriculum. It's an incentive. I'm a new teacher in the district. It's my first year as a specialist, and I have been both recipient and contributor.... We work together.

District Positions. In addition to specialists in the schools, elementary grade leaders and curriculum developers were selected to work with the district elementary director in program and curriculum development. According to the CEP plan, developers worked on curriculum and special projects on a specific grade level during the summer, then presented the new materials to teachers in the grade-level meetings before school opened. The curriculum developer received twenty-three additional days at her or his daily rate. Grade leaders conducted meetings with teachers, developed new teacher in-service, and coordinated opportunities for teachers to share ideas and materials. These people worked with both teacher leaders and curriculum specialists. The stipend was about $1,100, and three additional days at their per diem. Both positions reported to the elementary director.

A somewhat different arrangement emerged to address the difference in organization of the middle and high schools. Secondary specialists worked only with teachers in areas designated by the CEP guide—for example, art, language arts, math. The four specialists—one from each school—in a subject-area cluster would develop long-range curriculum plans to guide activities in that area. Appointed for one year, cluster specialists received eight additional days at their per diem.

The Selection Process. Selection procedures were carefully laid out in the CEP plan, and included combinations of teaching evaluations, peer evaluations, self-evaluations, statements of qualifications and experience, proposals for goals and activities, assessments of student progress, and committee-selection processes.

A panel consisting of the principal and two teachers selected teacher leaders. Two teachers who opted in advance not to apply for the position were elected by their peers from the faculty. The selection process included two successful clinical supervisions, a peer evaluation by the entire faculty (or in the case of high schools, those with whom the teacher leader would be working), a program proposal of goals for the school, a resume listing skills and experience, and evidence of student success. To select a candidate, at least two of the three committee members, including the principal, had to agree. Theoretically, the two faculty members could block a principal's choice but not appoint a candidate over the principal's objection. In some schools the principals protected their right to block a selection. In others the principal would defer to the teachers if both insisted on a candidate. Several respondents in different schools stated that their experience on the selection committee was that the principal had the final say.

Curriculum specialists and secondary specialists were selected by the principal alone, after conferences with the selection committee. The process included one successful formal evaluation by the principal, a post-observation conference, and an application process in which the candidate proposed a program of goals for the school, explained pertinent skills and experience, completed a self-evaluation, and presented evidence that students had experienced success in the candidate's class.

District positions were filled by a committee of the district elementary or secondary director and two teacher leaders elected by the group of teacher leaders. Information similar to that collected for teacher leaders and curriculum specialists was collected for the district positions.

In all cases, if the applicant did not agree with the decision there were provisions for appeal to the district CEP task force, and if the decision of the task force was unacceptable, the teacher could bring a grievance.

The selection process began when the job descriptions were posted in the spring, and concluded once all the positions had been filled. Although the selection of the teacher leader was fairly standard throughout the schools, the selection process for specialists varied from school to school. In one elementary school, the selection committee used a list of twelve selection criteria to make their determination, including ability as a classroom teacher, ability to teach adults, ability to relate to other teachers, the information they offered about themselves, and their experience and training as shown on their dossiers.

Administrators carried a heavy load in the CEP. The process consumed a good deal of administrative time each spring in goal setting and selection, yet principals were not reimbursed. During the time of the research, there was considerable discussion about getting CEP funds for principals, even though the legislature had expressly forbidden it.

The selection process was painful when more teachers applied than could be named. Principals talked about people feeling "sore" after the selection process was concluded. Administrators and committees were often the targets of bad will from people who were not selected. One elementary teacher said, "When the selection process takes place in the spring they are tense. It is tooth and nail.... There is a two-month period of building tension." However, when the fall came most people were able to work together. A number of people stated that they had no bad feelings if another applicant was chosen.

Several teachers stated that the confidential peer review was the most difficult part of the process. "Peer review is hard to handle. Some abuse it and their responses are not in the right spirit," said one. That sentiment was supported by survey results. People were more afraid of the peer evaluation than of the principal evaluation. The mean response to the statement "The Career Ladder creates a fear of principal evaluation" was 2.12 and the mean response to the statement "The Career Ladder creates a fear of peer evaluation" was 2.59. Although both scores indicate disagreement with the statement, there is less disagreement with the one about fear of peers. And while only about 12 percent feared the principal evaluation, 27.5 percent feared the peer evaluation.

Selecting appropriate people was sometimes difficult. Balancing between continuity and wide opportunity was especially challenging, the AEA president explained:

> We recognize that good teachers aren't always good leaders. We need to have some information about teachers' qualities of leadership of peers.... Taking turns is not official. We need to change the document.

Clinical Supervision and Evaluation

Clinical supervision was not an official part of the CEP, but a continuing part of the larger changes that Crawford instituted. It is described here because of its integral place in the functioning of Job Enlargement generally, and the selection process specifically.

Initially teachers were not fond of clinical supervision. They had not been supervised before Crawford, and they saw the practice not only as an intrusion but also as lack of faith in their competence. However, Crawford believed that use of a standard observational instrument would give a common structure and language for communication about teaching. As he put it, "It made sense in developing a common conceptual framework. We had a vocabulary so we could converse."

Although the observation instrument was based on Madeline Hunter's concepts and was similar to others already in the field, it did not quantify teaching skill as Mossville's program did. It was based on observations against certain criteria, some subjective and some objective.

Every teacher was required to undergo clinical supervision. In addition, candidates had to complete clinical supervision to apply for CEP positions. State legislation in 1988 mandated that new and provisional teachers be evaluated at least twice each year until they became tenured, although choice of the instrument was left to the individual districts.

Academy came to view clinical supervision and evaluation as a formative process to help teachers, not evaluate them. Crawford fully expected that his principals would become highly skilled, visible, and interactive: "I wanted fairly intensive training of principals. Instructional observation and analysis. Stimulating feedback from principals to teachers. That struck a responsive chord" with the board. When Freeman replaced Crawford, he announced to the district that clinical supervision would be continued. The conception of clinical supervision as assistance was strengthened.

Several years ago, a number of Academy teachers availed themselves of an opportunity to retire early and the district hired a substantial number of new teachers. District policy was changed so that all new teachers would be trained in the Principles of Effective Teaching. They could not move on the salary scale unless they had completed the course. Since then all teachers have been trained in PET. According to one board member,

> The climate for innovation started.... A whole lot of teachers caught on to learning about teaching. Everyone went through the teaching learning course. At first there was a lot of heartburn—"We know about teaching." They began to see that they were learning through the course...
>
> Peer review was started for assistance not evaluation. Some began to ask for it. The attitude that this is a good district and we can make it better caught on.... Test scores went up. People began to stand taller.

Statements from teachers supported the positive relationship stated by the board member. One elementary teacher said:

> I taught seventeen years before I had an official evaluation as a teacher. At first that was very scary for the older teachers.... Unless a teacher is in great difficulty, it's hard to do an evaluation without praising the teacher for a few things. Teaching is so complicated that you can find things to praise. I always get compliments and a few suggestions. All but one of the suggestions made I wasn't aware of so I was grateful.... As a teacher you can spend a lifetime not knowing if you made a difference. PET provides a vehicle for the principal sitting down and saying you're doing this well and I appreciate this.

One parent testified to the effectiveness of the process in one specific case:

> Instruction has improved dramatically because they have to take PET and be evaluated by administrators. Now they are accountable. My second grader has a teacher I wouldn't have wanted a child of mine to have two years ago, but now she is doing well.

However, teacher support was not uniform. Said one, "It all boils down to whether the teachers follow through. There is another factor in the school that says, 'I don't need any more.'"

Teacher leaders employed observations extensively to assist new teachers in their adjustment to the classroom, and several principals indicated their endorsement of clinical supervision as an integral part of their interactions with their teachers. A teacher leader told of one experience:

> I went to work with him. I gave him a negative evaluation. He responded well.... It mostly came from within the guy. He started growing. I came close to putting him on probation, but he improved and improved. He became a specialist. He took more math classes. This year he applied for teacher leader. It was hard to imagine he'd ever do that.... It amazed me. I'm in the realm of saying to struggling teachers, "change is possible."

One board member conceptualized its usefulness in planning in-service around faculty weaknesses.

PET was not the only instrument that people in the district were experienced in using. The Teacher Expectations for Student Achievement (TESA), an assessment of teacher-pupil interactions, was also widely used. Some teachers reported that they asked either the principal or the teacher leader to administer it in their classrooms so that they could determine if interactions were positive. Several teachers stated that they requested supervision or were pleased to have the principal do an evaluation.

PERCEIVED OUTCOMES OF THE
CAREER ENHANCEMENT PROGRAM

This discussion of the outcomes of CEP relies on interviews, documents, and the survey. The profusion of district activities and the unique district culture make it impossible to attribute improvements to the CEP with total confidence. The district was certainly considered adequate prior to the CEP. However, many within the district believed that not only teaching practice and personnel relations had improved, but also that student achievement and total district function were better. This section examines changes in student achievement, curriculum, and teacher motivation, with special attention to new teachers, and administrator-faculty relations.

Student Achievement

District data indicated that student achievement improved after the implementation of the CEP. Both standardized test scores and ACT scores had risen since 1982—CTBS test scores by 10 to 15 percentile points and ACT from 20 to 20.8 points on a 36-point scale. ACT scores were the highest in the state. However, one district administrator doubted that he could link achievement gains to the CEP: "I can't pin achievement to a block grant or just the CEP, or clinical supervision and PET, or in-service. It's a combination of all of them."

Some respondents had more student-centered criteria for their assessment of improvements for students:

The students are getting a more diverse education. The whole school is like a Gifted and Talented program.

Students learn better. They don't get stagnant. CEP makes it more fun.

Bringing in new ideas helps kids.... [The science specialist] does a science olympics. It will enhance the kids' excitement.

My school climate thrust helped kids' self-image.

Whatever the criteria, both achievement and classroom life had improved. Teachers believed the CEP encouraged them to improve teaching in ways that would help students. They agreed that "the performance bonus is an incentive for teachers to care more about the quality of teaching" (3.52) and that "job enlargement is an effective incentive for teachers to use professional skills more effectively" (3.85).

Curriculum Improvement

Curriculum improvement was the most visible benefit of the CEP. Examples of enrichment abounded in the interviews. One teacher mentioned that the curriculum work of the specialist for cooperative learning had helped her to improve her curriculum and her teaching. One cluster leader met with a social studies teacher from the other high school. One had a psychology orientation, the other a sociology orientation. They collaborated to integrate both into their curricula.

According to teachers, their involvement in curriculum improved resource management. As teachers acquired more influence over how funds were allocated for curricular resources, they could direct funds to areas of greatest need.

A whole new way of thinking about constructing curriculum developed in the district. Brandon Crawford talked about the variation and lack of coordination and continuity that he found when teachers were totally autonomous. There was still a great deal of variation because school goals were different and faculties had different skills and interests. However, official recognition of faculty interests allowed principals and the district to coordinate those interests with school goals. The intra- and interschool sharing broadened the impact of particularly good programs. Consistency was maintained by the collaboration of district and school planners working on district-wide curriculum. A core was maintained ensuring that broad district curricular goals were met while individual and group skills and gifts were maintained.

Teachers appreciated these changes. They agreed that the CEP "is effective in providing comprehensive curricula" (3.42) and "results in better curriculum materials and training" (3.77). The Extended Contract was believed to "effectively increase teacher opportunities to develop curriculum" (4.30), and the multiple positions of the job enlargement component were credited with "effectively allow[ing] the district to carry out curriculum planning" (3.95). Several people expressed the concern that if the state curtailed CEP funding, curriculum development in the district would be seriously compromised.

Teacher Morale and Motivation

Many Academy teachers said that although the stipend wasn't enough, it was better to get paid something for extra work than nothing. Moreover, they said their participation gave them feelings of professionalism.

The economic incentive, while important, was not central to teachers' overall opinions of the CEP. Teachers' were not as sure about its ability to retain teachers or to act as an incentive to remain in the profession as they were about the desirability of continuing it. They agreed that the CEP was "effective in providing incentives for good teachers to remain in teaching" (3.58) and that the job enlargement component in particular "retains excellent teachers" (3.63). Not only did they want to maintain specific components of the CEP, they also strongly endorsed the continuing overall program (4.30).

In interviews, principals generally emphasized the program's benefits for teachers:

> The teachers are given planning time and it boosts their morale.... It really is teachers helping teachers.... It has boosted morale so much.

> Departments are more cohesive. Morale is up in most respects. It trickles down to the kids too. Happy teachers do a good job with kids.

So did the teachers themselves:

> The teachers who are actually on the ladder benefit the most. It's really made me stretch.... Applying for curriculum specialist and teacher leader is a good training session.

> I get more interactions with people.

> I'd like to be a teacher leader. I'd like to facilitate teaching new teachers.... As I think about my own problems less and less, I want to help teachers teach better.

> This has been the best thing for morale, ownership, and participation. And, teachers are finally getting extra pay for their extra work.

Assessments by Beginning Teachers

Beginning teachers were most positive about the benefits of the CEP. They were less enthusiastic than regular teachers about its specific provisions for them. However, beginners agreed more strongly than regular teachers that the CEP helped them, would keep them in teaching, and should be continued (see Table 4–4).

TABLE 4–4
Assessments of the CEP by Beginning and Experienced Teachers

Statement	Beginning Teachers	Experienced Teachers*
The CEP:		
results in better training and support for beginning teachers	3.75	3.97
provides a cooperative work environment	3.91	3.60
gives me support so I can teach my students	3.81	3.67
gives me the chance to interact with other teachers	3.98	3.77
provides incentives for good teachers to stay in teaching	3.80	3.56
should be continued	4.30	4.25

*n = 97 respondents with three or fewer years' experience and 396 respondents with more than three years' experience.

The interviews support the survey data. According to an experienced teacher:

I've seen teachers start who didn't make it through the year. Several years ago I had a lady. It was like going to war. She was near a nervous breakdown. That was before [CEP]. There is no reason for problems like that if [CEP] works like it's supposed to.

New teachers also stated that having teacher leaders benefited them. "It goes easier. They assist you," said one. "I've had people come and help me. It helps in your weaknesses." Teachers pointed to specific activities, like the PET, that helped raise the level of teaching *and* the functional level of principals. Said one:

We are required to go through PET and that has improved the teaching. There is a requirement to go through clinical supervision. The principals have to be on their toes. They can't slide any more. You can't be a bad teacher and stay in the system.

Teaching Practice

CEP was integrated into the district agenda of curricular and instructional improvement. Each became interwoven into the fabric of the other. Teacher leaders modeled good instruction while curriculum specialists enriched the curriculum. Extended contract days provided opportunities for in-service and mentoring. Teachers with job enlargement positions were resources for experienced staff, and especially for new teachers, whom they could orient to the classroom and ease into the job. The curriculum and instructional improvement was expected to prepare teachers for the CEP positions. How well did CEP succeed in meeting the goals?

The CEP was seen as valuable in offering support for new teachers. Both administrators and teachers spoke positively about the CEPs impact on the level of teaching; teachers, for instance, agreed with a survey item that "The CEP has improved the overall instructional program" (3.49).

Even those farther away from the instructional process saw the benefits. According to the district administrator in charge of facilities:

> [CEP] is a pain in the neck for maintenance people. The teachers are in the building when they are trying to get them fixed and cleaned.... I see a positive part though. Now since they come in early they are prepared for their students. That also creates a positive attitude for teachers because they have a chance to get more money. I run the printing. The stuff I had to do as a teacher during the first week are ready two weeks early. When school starts, they teach.

The president-elect of the AEA summarized the benefits of the CEP this way:

> Professional growth. Greater gain in student achievement. It's measurable. Morale is greater. It has helped teachers to be more accountable. If you apply, you must have clinical supervision. You have to upgrade what you do. Everyone gets better. They [teachers] are more accountable because they look at what they do.

The clinical supervision cycle was subjective and conditional on variation in administrator preference, but it did not inspire continuing opposition. The principals' observation was often welcomed and clinical supervision is credited by many as having created an environment for instructional improvement.

Administrator/Faculty Relations

Administrator-teacher relationships, which had been positive under previous administrations, were strained by Brandon Crawford's efforts at rapid reform. By the time of our research, however, after several years of CEP implementation, positive relations had reached a new high. Strong leadership coexisted with unusually cooperative relationships between teachers and administrators. During the research period, the AEA president reported that the association was trying to get money for principals for their participation in the CEP. Association leaders also complimented district leadership. Two long-time AEA activists, one a teacher leader, the other a specialist, summarized many of their colleagues' feelings in these descriptions of the relationships between faculty and the central office. The first was from an interview. The second was part of a letter submitted for publication in support of Freeman:

> People have the freedom to go about their work thinking they have value. That also says you don't have to be an administrator to contribute. You can contribute as a teacher. There's not an administrator in the district that is respected any more for the job they do or the person they are than I am for the job I do or the person I am. That's not true here all the time, but it is a lot. (past AEA president)

> It is a rare person who has the talents to make people feel good about what they do and inspire them to want to do more. We have had such leadership from Superintendent [Joseph Freeman] and our board of education. The well-being of this or any other district should never be taken for granted. The direction and efficiency of this district is no accident. All too often we forget these are rare people who truly are friends and advocates of children and teachers. During the difficult times we are experiencing in education, it takes great courage to support teachers and programs when there is little funding from the legislature.... Newspapers are good place [sic] to read facts and news but somehow cannot express feelings of love, loyalty, dedication, unity, and unselfish service. (NEA board member)

Newcomers to the district had similar views, as this comment from a beginning elementary teacher illustrates:

> I was interested in working here. I loved the school from the beginning. I knew [refers to principal—by first name] well enough from student teaching that I could approach her often.... The interview team was the principal, the assistant principal, and four teachers.... The teachers probably had considerable influence because [principal] realizes how closely they work together.

While expressions of positive administrator-teacher relations were not universal, they were very frequent. It is particularly notable that such positive statements came from active teachers' association representatives who represented the district also at the state and national level.

At the same time, administrators cooperated with teachers. Freeman and Crawford were both loyal members of the AEA. Teachers said that they felt like peers of their principals, and looked forward to their appearance in the classroom for clinical supervision. It did not appear that this was because evaluations were social events or lacking in rigor. In difficult times principals and teachers worked together, as this principal's comment illustrates:

> When teachers were contemplating a strike [statewide in response to the legislative package] and we met as principals, the teachers' organization leader was always there to discuss it. The teachers' organization understands that if there is a strike, the principals would have to be in school. We made plans for a strike at a meeting where a member of the board, district office, and the teachers' organization came. They all went to the schools to talk to faculty, and said, "Here's what we have to be responsible for if there's a strike."

FACTORS AFFECTING CEP SUCCESS

The success of the CEP was contigent on the strength of board and administrative leadership, teacher assertiveness, and relations with the state.

The Function of Leadership

Leadership from the board, the district administration, and principals was fundamental to the transition to more professionalized teaching.

Because the superintendent who preceded Crawford had been unwell late in his administration, the district's principals had operated autonomously in their own buildings. The board's decision to search outside the district opened Academy to new ideas and influences. Board members' continuing support of the reform allowed district leaders the latitude they needed to develop the program adequately.

Brandon Crawford's vision of reform was essential to both the district's and the state's adoption of the CEP. His efforts to energize principals and make them accountable set the stage for the necessary building change. His acceptance of teachers' responses to his ideas set the stage for cooperative development of the CEP. His establishment of an open environment further facilitated the development process within the district.

Freeman's aptitude for personal relations—both as assistant superintendent and then as superintendent after Crawford—also advanced the changes; and his decision to continue Crawford's reforms ensured that they would be institutionalized. His continuing leadership, management of difficult state and local relationships, and contact with outside professional and funding organizations maintained the energy and infusion of ideas necessary for ongoing success.

Crawford and Freeman had wonderfully contrasting leadership styles and practices. Weaker in social skills, Crawford was very definitely a mobile, cosmopolitan administrator. He had been in Northeast and Midwest states before he came to Academy and left there for a larger city. His network was with outsiders for the most part, and he showed strong but situational loyalty to the district. His orientation was to his job, to his professional life.

On balance Freeman, one of Greenley's mentees, was more locally oriented and less mobile. He worked his way up through the system and retired there at the end of the research period. Yet he was cosmopolitan as well. He had an out-of-state doctorate, kept contact with the legislature, joined an academic consortium, and was chosen for a national organization's exceptional district program. Moreover, he had the social skills to build support for the CEP that Crawford lacked.

Principals' acceptance was also important to implementation. Some were originally less than enthusiastic about the changes. Commenting on her principal, one elementary teacher said he

> had a negative attitude in the beginning. He might have felt intimidated and might have thought he'd be overrun. He learned that it's there for teachers to help teachers. He hates the

interview and selection process. He just wants to choose who to work with. He sees the tension build.

However, most of the principals, this one included, had accepted the program as important for the district and the school, and useful in helping to get the day's work done. The same principal mentioned above spoke this way about his role in the CEP:

> My role is directing, giving leadership, making sure it happens, supervision, conveying to the public what it is. Using it as a vehicle to strengthen the curriculum.... I have extra evaluations to do, but I can save some time by having specialists do things. And it lowers the mail load. I can send things to the teacher leaders and specialists when it is in their area.

As in most districts, Academy principals originally believed they had the most to lose, but their developing acceptance created a supportive atmosphere in the schools.

Teacher Assertiveness

Although relationships between teachers and administrators were generally positive, teachers stood up for their rights when they thought a violation was occurring. Teachers confronted Crawford first at the AEA meeting, where they complained about the innovations he initiated before planning for the CEP began. Later, in the first task-force meetings, they opposed his plans to link merit assessment to teachers' salaries. Without that opposition Academy's reforms would probably have been more bureaucratic. After the basic program format was established, teachers contributed time, energy, experience, resolve, and ideas to the development, implementation, and institutionalization processes, which permitted the program to mature and flourish. The AEA supported and cooperated with the process while protecting the interests of the teachers they represented.

Relations with the State

If local conditions facilitated the development of the CEP, state vacillation after the initial provision of funds undermined district planning. The state continued to fund the CEP, but the last one-third of the funding was never authorized. The program was continued as a categorical rather than a general fund program. Over the years, the district was forced to cut back two extended-contract days because the state raised salaries but did not add funds to the CEP.

The continuing need to let the state know how the district felt about the CEP was expressed by a number of people, including these two principals:

> With the lack of money and the number of students in the state, we have to lobby the legislature all the time. It's enough to make you tired.

> There is a fear it could be taken. They could take the money for the program and use it elsewhere.... The majority of districts don't care if they lose it because it is administrator imposed.

One administrator acted as legislative liaison to inform that body about Academy's interest in maintaining and stabilizing the CEP, but each year changes were made. At the end of each legislative session in February, the task force had to make plans for the next fall. State discussions about block grants and continuing dissatisfaction with the Academy performance bonus created uncertainty. While the task force did not want to wait until the last minute to make their plans because the uncertainty caused stress among the teachers, it could not plan for the next year's program without knowing what the legislature would decide.

SUMMARY

Teacher redesign as developed by the state allowed significant local discretion and judgment in complying with state requirements, even though merit pay was a clear and important priority with the legislature and the department.

Prior to the state program, Academy's board had invited Brandon Crawford to create a more energetic atmosphere. At first his methods caused severe discomfort, anxiety, and resistance; but as Crawford began bona fide involvement of teachers in planning and continued to open district operations to ever-wider view, and as his programs began to generate improvements, support began to grow. His influence on the state program significantly helped Academy shape a response that met local concerns. Joseph Freeman, Crawford's assistant and successor, was vital to the growing success and acceptance of the program. His exceptional ability to work with people created an environment of openness and professionalism. Freeman's decision to maintain Crawford's changes facilitated their institutionalization. The teachers' association, a strong force in the district, supported the changes and cooperated fully in all aspects of adoption and implementation.

As implemented in Academy, the CEP professionalized teaching by promoting a system of curriculum and instruction leaders who worked to improve the district's instructional program and supporting coherent and widespread changes to district curriculum. The CEP, by permitting significant and sustained teacher influence over the structure, implementation, and administration, increased the quantity and quality of professional contributions. And it allowed the expansion of an existing but less well-defined and well-realized cooperative and collegial atmosphere within the district. Teachers' commitment was increased.

While the CEP created some problems for the district—such as the financial uncertainty, disagreements about whether new positions should be permanent or temporary, and hurt feelings during the selection process—it was widely viewed as valuable and desirable. Its professional design and implementation has been responsible for strengthening curriculum, and for meaningful involvement and leadership opportunities for teachers.

5. THE DYNAMICS OF BUREAUCRACY AND PROFESSIONALISM

THE MOSSVILLE, Hill City, and Academy cases provide useful illustrations of the bureaucratic and professional designs in practice and of how they can become blurred when the differences between them are not well understood. The remainder of this book provides more detailed answers to two of our original questions. This chapter will examine how bureaucratic and professional designs affect teacher motivation and behavior. Chapter 6 will explore how specific districts come to adopt particular designs.

To address the consequences of redesign, we first summarize outcomes from the three districts. Mossville implemented the bureaucratic theory; Academy's practice closely followed the professional theory; Hill City did not clearly adopt either theory, and its outcomes reflect that confusion.

We then examine the enactment of the bureaucratic and professional theories of organizational design through two key means—job differentiation and governance—by looking at the concrete manifestations of those theories in the districts. This analysis suggests that selecting people for differentiated positions will be difficult using either the bureaucratic or the professional approach. Teachers distrust bureaucratic procedures, no matter how elaborately codified, but they may mistreat their colleagues if they make the selection themselves. On the other hand, teachers do not take personal characteristics into account when selecting peers for positions, suggesting a relatively fair selection process. They are relatively gender-blind, and though older teachers are somewhat more likely to get positions of greater responsibility than younger colleagues, there is not enough differentiation to create a truly staged career pattern.

Finally, we focus on the question of teacher motivation and find that the crucial link between design elements and that outcome is the incentives provided. As past theories suggest, bureaucratic designs emphasize merit pay and reduce teacher autonomy; they rely on extrinsic rewards and external controls, which effectively standardize performance but lead to a work-to-rule mentality rather than an interest in improving as teachers. Professional designs, which emphasize job enlargement and increased teacher influence over strategic decisions, provide intrinsic incentives, which encourage greater teacher reflection and improved practice in many directions while building teacher motivation. As structural changes, these affect teacher motivation indirectly. Teacher empowerment is directly rewarding for some, but for many its importance is as a means to improve instruction. Financial remuneration appears to be more important than past studies of intrinsic rewards have suggested, but not as a reward in its own right; money is essential to buy the time necessary to create the intrinsic incentives that truly motivate teachers.

DISTRICT OUTCOMES

Table 5–1 summarizes the outcomes identified in the three districts. Mossville illustrates the likely outcomes of the bureaucratic design. Higher test scores, although modest, were central to the district's effort, which was clearly focused on improving student achievement. The TDP's contribution to improved test scores was to standardize instructional practice around the principles of direct instruction. This outcome was viewed more positively by administrators than teachers. The price of standardization was noticeable, as was, in the early stages, active opposition to administrative proposals and some general discouragement and loss of interest in their working among teachers.

Academy is an equally clear example of the professional design. Test scores increased, but district staff made fewer claims about the direct link between the reforms implemented and achievement as operationalized in those tests. They were also less willing to treat test scores as the ultimate criterion of success. The program there substantially enriched the curriculum by diversifying and enriching offerings in several areas, including those where knowledge was not tested

TABLE 5–1
Educational Outcomes in Three Districts

	Mossville	*Hill City*	*Academy*
Student Achievement	Modest improvement at third, sixth, and eighth grades on CAT.	Stable scores on state minimum-skills test.	Modest improvement on ACT and locally administered standardized test.
Curriculum Change	No discernible change.	Substantial discussion but no change.	Extensive diversification and enrichment in art, science, and other areas.
Teacher Skills	Extensive standardization of teaching approach around the principles of direct instruction. Improved use of those principles.	No discernible change.	Introduction to and selective use of several instructional approaches including direct instruction, discipline methods, and changing expectations of students.
Teacher Motivation	Noticeable opposition to administration and to redesign program. Slight loss of overall interest in teaching.	Enthusiasm turning to ambivalence and then discontent as supposed influence sharing did not materialize.	Substantial support for administration and program and slight increase in commitment to teaching.

directly. Moreover, teachers were introduced to a variety of approaches to instructional improvement and given more leeway to select directions for improvement. Teachers did report skills enhancement. They were very enthusiastic about the program and viewed it as a reason to stay in the field.

Hill City presents a mixed case. Test scores remained stable. Two kinds of curriculum changes were proposed: the superintendent's efforts to implement something like Ted Sizer's Essential Schools idea and teachers' efforts to get better supplies and schedules. Neither one materialized. Although arrangements were made to facilitate teachers helping teachers, it was hard to identify real changes in instructional skills. Teachers' sentiments about the program crystallized slowly because it was difficult to discern what exactly it was; after early enthusiasm, teachers became more pessimistic.

JOB DIFFERENTIATION

The two districts that clearly articulated well-recognized theories of redesigning teaching had outcomes that reflected those theories. Where the district's own theory was less clear, so were the outcomes. To understand how those outcomes were achieved, we turn next to the formal design elements implemented in each district to illustrate how they reflect the underlying theories of teaching. The design changes that were made either increased job differentiation or changed internal governance patterns.

Three kinds of changes were made to differentiate jobs: the introduction of new principles for differentiating positions among teachers, the use of new procedures for selecting people for positions, and the actual distribution of positions. The changes made reflect not only bureaucratic and professional conceptions of teaching but also two pervasive themes in the culture of teaching: teachers' norms of equity—the idea that all teachers should be treated equally—and feelings of vulnerability (Lortie 1975; Johnson 1989).

Principles for Job Differentiation

Earlier we identified four approaches to job differentiation—merit pay, master-teacher plans, project add-ons, and career ladders—to be adopted depending on whether the programs featured pay for performance or job enlargement and whether they were permanent or temporary job changes. None of the three districts implemented pure cases of any of these job redesigns; but in the two cases where jobs really changed, the tendencies were quite clear. Mossville's TDP was largely a master-teacher program. CS I and CS II teachers were not required to take on added responsibilities, though CS II teachers had the option to accept project add-ons. They were paid for conforming to the state's conception of direct instruction. While positions were essentially permanent, there was a provision to demote teachers whose performance declined. Thus, the CS II position was not akin to associate and full professorships in higher education, which provide permanent recognition for a teacher's performance to date.

The anomalous position in Mossville was that of Observer-Evaluator. In one sense, OEs did experience job enlargement. As evaluators of teachers, coaches for and helpers of principals, and designers and deliverers of teacher training, they gained expanded variety of work, control over their own time, and opportunities to influence others. However, they gave up all teaching responsibility when they took on their new job. The position was also difficult to place on a time perspective. It was typically held for several years. Incumbents were expected to become teachers again, but several became administrators shortly after giving up these special assignments. Thus, while the positions were supposed to be temporary, they were of quite long duration and also had an unexpected transitional character not easily accommodated by the original typology.

Academy's teacher-leader and specialist positions featured job enlargement. The teachers had increased responsibility; this included summer work for all teacher leaders and some cluster and grade-level leaders. The new responsibility increased work variety and influence opportunities, although it also increased the time required for district work. In most buildings, these positions approximated a career ladder because they were not temporary projects, but real jobs. One high school did turn the specialist position into projects by asking candidates to submit proposals for the work they would do and selecting the best ones. However, all positions had one- or two-year terms. Teachers could be reappointed, but they had to reapply for the job periodically.

Hill City's experiment with job differentiation never came to fruition. There was never any plan to pay the master teachers or peer assistance council members. Although the former were selected, they were never active; and the latter group maintained a very low profile.

The culture of teaching created a preference for job enlargement. Academy and Hill City had earlier experienced merit-pay programs. Those who remembered that far back were unimpressed; selection on the basis of merit was believed to have increased vulnerability to potentially unfair evaluations. Teachers in Mossville also worried about administrative misuse of their system to reward friends and punish enemies. In addition they thought merit selection made them more vulnerable to students and unfairly constrained opportunities. As one Academy teacher said,

They shouldn't base extra money on merit pay or how students test.... [Teachers shouldn't be judged by tests because] students are students. I like the opportunity that anyone who wants to earn more money and likes added responsibility can get it. It's more fair. There's more sharing.

In Academy, where job enlargement was clearly present, teachers were adamant about making positions temporary. A small minority who had been teacher leaders for several years and resented having to be repeatedly reselected said the district did not have a career ladder but a "career pogo stick" or a "career yo-yo." This was not the dominant feeling, however. The survey asked teachers if they preferred rotating positions or making them permanent. Seventy-six percent of the teachers agreed that the current system of periodic selection should be continued. Even teachers who were or had been teacher, cluster, or grade-level leaders accepted the idea that there should be turnover among positions. Seventy-one percent of them agreed with the current system, as did 83 percent of those who had never held any position—not a great difference. In fact, only 11 percent of the current or former leaders agreed with the suggestion to make CEP positions permanent.

Moreover, in both districts with job differentiation, the pattern noted elsewhere to reduce distinctions between teachers and allocate rewards equally to all (Malen and Hart 1987) was apparent. The most popular part of the Academy program was the one that gave all teachers additional days for preparation. In both Academy and Mossville, some teachers suggested they would prefer an across-the-board salary increase to job differentiation.

Selection Procedures

Selection has been a major reason why efforts at job differentiation have foundered. Yet only a limited range of options, all linked to the bureaucratic conception of teaching, has been considered. In the bureaucratic approach, objective criteria for advancement are specified. Someone, typically one or more administrators, collects information to see if teachers meet these criteria; and positions are distributed accordingly. Usually the objectives have to do with teaching practice, but student achievement data can also be used (Southern Regional Education Board 1990). Models for designing such systems have been carefully specified; there is a fair amount of literature on how to develop valid, reliable systems for assessing teacher behavior (Millman and Darling-Hammond 1990). Such models both standardize and centralize the selection process.

This approach is so pervasive that it has even been adopted by those interested in professionalizing teaching. Even the Carnegie Forum (1986) suggests that people other than teachers should decide who gets positions: "The Task Force encourages experimentation and additional research to explore ways that school staffs which produce outstanding gains in student performance can receive substantial benefit from that increase in productivity—including increased compensation" (91). Yet such procedures can undermine attempts to professionalize. Popkewitz and Lind (1988) describe projects intended to give teachers more autonomy and professional responsibility. Where selection was done by principals using formalized criteria of teaching quality, the effect was to shift power to administrators and encourage teachers to ritualize their compliance, thereby undermining the major purpose of the change.

The professional ideal suggests that responsibility for selection ought to rest with teachers rather than administrators. This conclusion is a simple extension of the idea that teachers should control licensing, or who enters the field (Wise 1989). The bureaucratic selection approach assumes that criteria for good teaching can be based fairly strictly on scientific research and are known best by experts who are not teachers themselves. Moreover, teaching is routine enough that effective teaching strategies can be easily standardized. The professional conception suggests not only that teaching requires expert judgment for execution but that the same kind of judgment is required to identify excellence. Moreover, that judgment rests with teachers.

Not only has the professional approach rarely been considered by reformers; it is not popular with teachers themselves, especially their associations. Teachers associations developed on an industrial union model, which views the work to be performed as largely unskilled (Mitchell 1989). As a result, control over who is assigned which jobs is ceded to management. In fact, the industrial union model treats all workers as the same in order to facilitate the unity needed for strikes. This philosophy works against allowing teachers to select their peers for special positions. Moreover, given the uncertainty that affects teaching and the fragile colleagueship found in the field, teachers may not want to make selections from among their own.

Among these districts, Mossville adopted a rigorous bureaucratic approach to selection, whereas Academy used a modified professional one. Both proved troublesome. Mossville's evaluation system was carefully crafted. Major parts of the system were designed at a state university for statewide use. The evaluation criteria were based on the direct instruction research. Evaluators were systematically trained, and the training was made available to all teachers so they would understand the system. Each teacher was assessed by two individuals during the course of the year; this practice provided both a technical reliability test and a political check-and-balance on any administrative arbitrariness. The time of one expert was reserved to provide assistance in case of disagreements between the principal and the OE. Moreover, district staff agree that it achieved its purpose of increasing the amount of direct instruction in the district. Even teachers agreed that "it has increased time-on-task."

Academy's selection process was a modified professional approach over which teachers had a great deal of influence, although not total control. The system did not rest so much on standardization as on consensus among informed people. The teacher-leader selection procedure was the archetype on which all others were based. That decision was made by a committee of the principal and two teachers elected by their peers. The actual criteria were allowed to vary somewhat from building to building to reflect local preferences. However, they typically included some mix of principal observation of classroom practice, peer assessments, and a statement of a project to be completed. The district's teacher evaluation system lost the high-stakes character found in Mossville because it was just one factor among several to be considered. It should be noted further that this was not a merit system for selection. Teaching quality was important, but so were such other factors as leadership skills and the value of the project proposed. The deemphasis on teaching merit fits a system to select people to fill particular jobs.

Both Mossville and Academy systems dealt with three problems. First, they had to establish their legitimacy, or fairness, among teachers. Legitimacy was never established in Mossville. Some of the concern may have arisen because this was a high-stakes evaluation; one's total chance for increased income (and among younger teachers for receiving tenure) depended upon the results. Hence teachers were very sensitive to flaws in the system. They were well aware of even minor discrepancies between evaluators. They questioned the expertise of evaluators who were not familiar with their grade or subject areas, and they argued that the three or four hours of observation each year were an inadequate sample for making judgments on how money would be distributed. These problems were exacerbated by worries that principals would misuse their authority to reward friends or punish enemies. Finally, some questioned the model of instruction on which the evaluation system was based, arguing that it made teaching more rigid and inflexible. This was a point on which teachers and program advocates seriously disagreed.

The legitimacy of Academy's selection system was also questioned, although not to the same extent. The Mossville survey asked if the district had "fair and reasonable procedures for the TDP" and if the "evaluation process [was] fair and objective." Responses averaged 3.24 on the first item and 2.71 on the second. Academy teachers were asked if the district followed "fair and reasonable procedures in administering its job enlargement component": the average response was 3.94 on the same 5-point scale. While the Academy teachers were more convinced that the selection process there was fair, the interviews suggested a lingering concern that the principal could overrule the teachers on a committee.

Second, both systems had operating costs (Murnane and Cohen 1986). Mossville's proved extremely expensive and time consuming, even with what teachers considered to be too limited samples of classroom performance. The most obvious cost was for the new roles required to complete the evaluations and provide related training: the OEs and the program director. If one assumes that the twelve OEs had an average salary of $30,000, this element of the program alone would have cost $360,000. In addition, even with the presence of OEs, classroom observation, the pre- and postobservation conferences, and the development of end-of-year summative evaluations took a great deal of principal time.

Academy's process was not as time-consuming as Mossville's. Principals were responsible for classroom observation, although that activity had been initiated before the CEP began and served other purposes as well. They also chaired the selection committee meetings. While some teacher time was required for the selection committees, the demands were not as great as those made on Mossville's OEs.

Finally, both programs created stress among teachers. A major concern about merit-pay programs is that in order to gain advantage in evaluations, teachers will hide ideas from each other. The fragile collegiality that now exists among teachers and provides some opportunity for learning and improvement will be impeded (Rosenholtz 1985). There is evidence from both surveys and interviews that competition did reduce communication among Mossville teachers, but the change was not great.

If anything, Academy's selection process was more divisive because of the teachers' role in the selection process. The problem was not discontent with the teachers who served on the committee so much as the "peer evaluation" survey of candidate capacity filled out by teachers who knew the person. The survey data showed that teachers were more afraid of that peer review than of principals' review. According to teachers familiar with the process:

> The only bad thing is the peer review.... Teachers don't sign their name. Some accountability is needed. Last year some people felt inadequate for the teacher leader job because one person gave them a negative peer review.

> We've had people call in sick for days because of the shots taken at them through the peer reviews. Applicants tried to withdraw from the position.

Most of this stress, however, was limited to a short period of time during the spring while selection was taking place.

This comparison suggests that there is no easy way to select teachers for differentiated positions. The professional option of giving teachers substantial influence has not received great attention, but in any case it does not eliminate tensions. The advantage of the professional option is that teachers see it as more fair—even than bureaucratic procedures with substantial formal safeguards such as those used in Mossville. The disadvantage is that it can be more divisive than competition for merit positions when teachers evaluate their peers harshly and candidates are sensitive. Both options can be time-consuming, although the edge in this case goes to the bureaucratic procedure, in part because its careful design adds to its elaborateness.

Distribution of Positions

There are at least two questions about how positions are distributed: how many people get them and which people get them? The questions raise concerns about motivation and teacher culture. People will work for a reward that they have high probability of receiving; the probability must be low enough so there is a real challenge but high enough so receiving it is not automatic (Ryan et al. 1985). Not everyone should be able to receive positions that are used as rewards. While there has been some concern that job differentiation schemes would make special positions too scarce to be realistically achievable (Newcombe 1983), in practice the problem has been to make them rare enough to be rewarding. Teachers strive to redefine programs so positions are open to the highest number of people or to rotate positions so everyone has a chance (Malen and Hart 1987). These changes avoid divisiveness, but they also reduce motivational potential.

In this regard, administrative tone and actual practice were at odds in Mossville. The district emphasized the challenge of obtaining positions. The tone of discussion in the district emphasized the difficulty in obtaining promotions. In comparison with the other pilot program, Mossville was more conservative in awarding positions, especially at the CS II level. In absolute terms, however, 76 percent of the teachers who applied for the CS II position received it. About 80 percent of the teachers in the system achieved the CS I rating or higher, and over 40 percent achieved the CS II. Many of those who had not achieved the higher rating had too few years of service to be eligible.

Academy emphasized equal distribution of rewards in its use of the extended-year and mandatory merit-pay components of the state program. Funds were available to allow 40 percent of all teachers to become specialists, 10 percent to become teacher leaders, and additional teachers to become grade-level or cluster leaders. If one focuses on the teacher leaders—as many did—rewards are scarce. A broader view suggests that something was available for everyone and that at any given time differential rewards were available for more than half the staff. The rotation of positions meant that even more people shared in the top positions. The survey data shows that after four years of operation, only 37 percent of all teachers had held no special CEP position. Twenty-nine percent currently were or had been only specialists, 34 percent either teacher leaders or cluster or grade-level leaders.[1] Although neither statistics nor positions are strictly comparable, one's general impression is that positions were broadly distributed in both districts. In fact, more teachers had received some remuneration in Mossville than in Academy.

The second question is what factors affect the distribution of special positions. The tension is generally between merit and seniority. If special rewards go to the most skilled regardless of experience, selection is most fair in the sense that it is most performance-based. Yet there is an extremely important argument for incorporating seniority. A career-ladder system that strives to create incentives for continued growth and development should save some rewards and challenges for more experienced individuals (Carnegie Forum 1986). If all the prizes the occupation has to offer are made available in the first few years, there are few incentives for continued growth or even staying in the field.

Moreover, true merit pay is almost as scarce in the private sector as in the public (Lawler 1981). Pay for performance occurs only in the rare situation where there are clear criteria for assessment that all can agree on. In the absence of those conditions, rewards are often distributed using less judgmental criteria such as seniority. This is especially likely when members of an occupational group must make decisions about their colleagues and are uncomfortable doing so. Given the concerns raised in both districts, it is worth exploring the extent to which seniority was reflected in selection processes.

Seniority was built into the Mossville system; four years of experience were required before applying for the CS II position. This is a rather mild constraint; two years after receiving tenure, one could achieve the highest teaching rank in the district.

Still, a few younger teachers objected to the seniority requirements built into the Mossville system. There was also an undercurrent of concern in Academy where a few younger teachers found it "irksome...that a starting teacher is just as qualified as older teachers. By your third year you can do just as well as a fifteen-year veteran, but you're not allowed to because other teachers are more familiar to administrators." State officials also viewed the Academy program as a way to hand out special plums to older teachers.

The teacher survey shows a real but weak relationship between seniority and position achieved in Academy. Half (52 percent) the teachers who never had any position had less than five years' experience while 24 percent had more than ten years'. Ten percent of the teacher, grade-level, and cluster leaders had less than five years' experience while two-thirds (65 percent) had more than ten years'. In addition, 24 percent of the specialist positions went to those with less than five years' experience. Thus, a preference was shown for experienced teachers, but there was certainly room for younger teachers to get CEP positions, especially as specialists.

Another issue raised in interviews was an apparent tendency for men to receive more positions than women. Two reasons were suggested for this. First, the selection committees may have favored men who were seen as the primary breadwinners in their families. Second, women may have wanted to be home with their families in the summer and so may not have sought the jobs as aggressively as their male peers. In fact, 81 percent of those with no CEP positions were women, as opposed to 73 percent of those who were specialists and 62 percent of those who were at the time or had been leaders.

The apparent preference for men was somewhat misleading because gender and experience were correlated. Men stayed in teaching longer. Many female teachers stayed for only a few years to put their husbands through the large university in the district. Table 5–2 shows that when one controls for experience, gender is only modestly associated with position at the elementary level; and there is no association between the two in the middle and high schools. In both cases, experience has a stronger relationship with position. Moreover, these factors explain almost none of the variance in who has positions at the secondary level and are only minor explanatory factors in the lower grades.

TABLE 5–2
Positions Held in Academy's Career Enhancement Program
Regressed on Experience and Gender

| | Standardized Beta | |
	Elementary	Secondary
Experience	.44**	.25**
Gender	−.13*	.03
Adjusted R^2	.23	.05

* p < .05
** p < .01

These data illustrate the limited impact of the most notable demographic criteria for selecting teachers to special CEP positions. Under these circumstances, routinely staged careers along career-ladder lines would be difficult to accomplish. On the other hand, fairness appears to have been an important issue to teachers, although these data alone do not demonstrate directly how important were teaching performance, leadership, or similar criteria.

GOVERNANCE

Changes in governance affected how both operational decisions (those affecting the classroom) and strategic decisions related to the whole school or district were made. In both areas, the bureaucratic strategy emphasized centralization while the professional one was more inclusive and interactive.

Operational Decisions

Teachers have substantial influence over operational decisions as to what happens in the classroom (Bacharach et al. 1986). This is in fact the essence of the loose coupling (Weick 1976) of schools. Many of the failures of American education are attributed to this structural loose-ness (Rowan 1990). A fundamental distinction between the bureau-cratic and professional designs is how they address this issue. The bureaucratic design centralizes control. One way to control instruc-tion is through increased supervision and evaluation and standard-ized criteria for effective instruction. While developing such controls over teaching was not a major focus of the 1980s reforms, some statewide teacher evaluation and certification systems did include measures of in-class performance (Firestone et al. 1989). The bureau-cratic apparatus that links merit-based pay to in-class evaluation is a way to control teachers' work. Merit pay is not only an incentive but a sanction that can be applied and withheld to induce compliance with centrally determined criteria of good instruction.

The professional design is less coercive. It seeks to shape profes-sional behavior through increased collegial interaction. According to this view, extreme teacher autonomy stems from isolation. Teachers are seen as the most effective trainers and developers of other teach-ers. Frequent sharing in nonthreatening ways will allow all teachers to get help in areas where they feel it is needed. It should also provide special assistance to beginning teachers and those who are especially ineffective. Opportunities to help others and receive recognition for their expertise should motivate better teachers, and all teachers will benefit from the exchange of new ideas (Little 1982; Rosenholtz 1985 1989).

The most obvious change in operational decision making in these three districts occurred in Mossville, where the TDP and the new evaluation system created notable constraints. Teaching was standardized around the principles of direct instruction. Teachers found that this standardization limited their judgment and opportu-nities to experiment. As one said, "a teacher may shy away from a creative lesson because it doesn't follow the 6-point lesson plan." At times they felt pressed to adopt classroom tactics more because they conformed to evaluator expectations than because they were appro-priate to the situation.

Academy made a more subtle change that was not experienced as constraint. Instead, teachers spoke of "more sharing of ideas" so "the teachers are up-to-date and know what is happening" and "there is more implementation of curriculum." Operational autonomy was preserved because there were few specific requirements about what teachers should do. On the other hand, more ideas about what to teach and how were shared by teacher leaders, specialists, and others so more common elements worked their way into the classroom.

In contrast to both these districts, the changes in Hill City had very little impact on operational decisions in spite of all the attention given to strategic decision making.

Strategic Decisions

There has been considerably more ferment around strategic decision making than around operations, with most attention given to the professional viewpoint that argues for "teacher empowerment." According to the professional theory, teachers bring critical knowledge to the strategic decision-making process so the decisions made will be more appropriate to the setting (Firestone and Corbett 1988). An extension of this view is that as carriers of special values, teachers can be advocates for their students in ways that others are not (Weick and McDaniel 1989). To ensure that their unique voice is heard, they should contribute to strategic decision making. Lanier and Sedlak (1989) extend this position to argue that teachers should become leaders in the formation of state and federal policy. In addition, teachers will be more committed to decisions they help make, although the evidence on this point is mixed (Firestone and Corbett 1988). Finally, participation in decision making is said to help teachers develop the knowledge and skills needed to change their behavior (McLaughlin and Marsh 1978); it has an educative function. Even if it does not lead to changed behavior, it at least helps teachers understand the constraints under which administrators operate.

The bureaucratic theory emphasizes the need for centralized control over strategic decisions for two reasons. First, it emphasizes the limits to teacher knowledge stemming from poor training and lack of content expertise in various fields and the need for technical expertise in designing curriculum and identifying effective instructional strategies (Smith and O'Day 1990). Second, it recognizes that as governmental agencies in a democratic society, schools must be responsible to the public (McDonnell 1989). Thus the public and its representatives, the legislature and school boards, should set goals for educators to achieve. If constructively done, this goal setting can reduce much of the confusion and overload teachers now experience over what they should accomplish (Porter 1989). In this view, administrative controls over teachers both ensure public accountability and reduce confusion for teachers.

There is a growing concern that neither the bureaucratic nor the professional design in their pure form provide sufficient guidance for strategic decision making in schools. This has led analysts like

Bacharach and Conley (1989) and Smith and O'Day (1990) to try to differentiate decision areas more finely in order to identify what the balance of teacher, administrator, and public input should be in separate spheres.

The complexity of the issue, lack of clear analysis, and strong advocacy by those favoring more teacher influence or protecting administrative prerogatives creates considerable confusion for those working in schools. This leads to a kind of false sharing of influence that Firestone (1977) called "mock participation." This label implies an intentional effort to use participatory forms to manipulate teachers to accept administrative decisions. While such conscious cooptation of teachers does go on, there is also a great deal of confusion about the consequences of sharing influence. Sirotnik and Clark (1988) give examples of superintendents who initiate site-based management programs yet still insist on making key building decisions themselves. In these cases, administrators set up the forms for participation without actually sharing influence.

Among these three districts, Academy reflects the professional extreme. Teachers' increased influence was most marked in the operation of the CEP itself and in the development of district curriculum. The major formal mechanism for influence was the CEP task force, made up primarily of teachers from the district's buildings and association representatives along with two principals and the superintendent. The group's authority was established early in its history when it became the means for communicating massive teacher discontent with efforts to modify the district's salary structure to include a merit component. It made decisions annually about how to modify the CEP to reflect legislative changes and district developments. During the authors' field visits, it addressed the disagreement among teachers about whether to make CEP positions more permanent.

Teacher influence showed up in several other areas as well. First, teachers played a major role in selecting their colleagues for CEP positions. Second, there was considerable diversity in the way the CEP was administered from building to building, reflecting an openness to local conditions and preferences. Finally, the CEP became a means to delegate considerable responsibility for curriculum development to teachers. Specialists became "worriers" for particular content areas and were given considerable leeway in developing those areas. Cluster and grade-level leaders had similar autonomy to identify areas for development and work with other teachers to ensure that useful work took place. They also controlled a budget for buying summer work to address the needs they identified. This strategy of curriculum development released considerable energy and led to a great deal of work. How coordinated this work was is not clear. On the one hand, teachers from different schools worked with each other and communicated about their buildings' concerns more than ever before. On the other, central office staff did not play a strong directive role, so there was very little overall coordination of the direction in which the district moved. Individual grade-level leaders and specialists and groups of cluster leaders who shared a content area made decisions in their own areas with no sense of what the district's overall goals were.

Mossville represented the bureaucratic extreme in public schools even though it had two bodies for teacher deliberation: the TDP Steering Committee and the TDP Council. While these bodies provided some input to district decision makers, most district decisions about the TDP were made by central administrators. In fact, the district had less authority to design its own program than Academy because many issues dealt with by the latter's task force were made for Mossville by the statewide program steering committee which consisted almost exclusively of administrators. The curriculum development that characterized Academy was simply not possible in Mossville because it used merit differentiation rather than job enlargement. The OEs did play a role similar to teacher specialists and leaders by designing and delivering the training that teachers received. However, they were not regarded as colleagues by most other teachers, and, in fact, many never did return to the teaching ranks.

Hill City is an example of administrative confusion about teacher influence. Despite the superintendent's extensive consultation with union leadership in designing Mutual Governance, teacher influence was not extended at the district level. Addition of the presidents of the teachers' union and principals' association facilitated communication between these groups and the superintendent, but the key mechanism for teacher influence should have been the Faculty Senate. The superintendent controlled the agenda of the early meetings, so the Senate never developed a habit of shared discussion. In fact, most of the teachers' key concerns about issues like bus schedules and supplies were never dealt with. The one major issue the Senate addressed was the development of an evaluation policy, a priority of the board. There, teachers used their influence to avoid unwanted provisions. A number of crucial decisions were made outside the Senate framework, most notably the one to initiate a breakfast program at one school. This program was actively resisted by teachers in that building; and when another building initiated its own program for dealing with at-risk students, it intentionally avoided cooperating with or seeking support from the district office. By the end of the research period, teachers were notably discontented with their lack of influence, and it can be argued that both teachers and the superintendent had been vetoed in efforts to achieve their major agendas.

The situation was more diverse at the school level. Some School Planning Councils actively instituted desired changes within their own buildings; one even helped select a new principal for its building. Others, however, appeared to have no more than token influence and serve only as communications mechanisms.

These efforts did not reflect conscious attempts at manipulation by Hill City administrators. When we shared preliminary interpretations of district events with top district administrators, we raised several examples of failure to include teachers fully in decision making and indicated what we thought were the consequences of doing so. The administrators generally agreed with this interpretation, provided additional instances of the same phenomenon, and indicated that we had identified a problem they had not fully considered in the past.

INCENTIVES AND MOTIVATION

Changes in job differentiation and decision making will affect what teachers do and how they feel about it by modifying the mix of incentives available to them. Typically, job differentiation and decision making changes are treated separately. The debate over job differentiation focuses on the relative value of extrinsic and intrinsic rewards, with most researchers emphasizing the motivational power of the latter (Johnson 1989; Lortie 1975). The question about decision making is whether more control over strategic decisions will enhance commitment (Firestone and Corbett 1988). As we unpack these issues, we suggest that:

1) Though money does not buy commitment or increased motivation directly, it can buy certain concrete behaviors like compliance or time.
2) Sharing power over strategic decisions is associated with increased teacher commitment, but it is difficult to separate the direct effects of power sharing itself from its results.
3) Under appropriate conditions, money and power sharing can create conditions that increase teachers' intrinsic incentives and thereby increase teacher motivation.

Money

Two extrinsic rewards were potentially available in these districts: money and prestige. Prestige could have been linked to the differentiated positions in all three districts, but they were not. Mossville teachers said the TDP positions caused "a lot of envy and unfriendliness. People get jealous. There's friction." Much the same thing happened in Hill City when master teachers were selected. Not only were unselected teachers bitter about the process, but some of those selected questioned the procedure. One came close to resigning from the position. In Academy, some teacher leaders described a backlash from their new position. One described "a little negativism. Teachers perceive that the teacher leaders are like administrators almost. I've lost a little credibility or trust among a few. A minority. Some see us as pushing administrative programs." This is not surprising. Studies of merit-pay plans in education (Malen, Murphy, and Hart 1988; Murnane and Cohen 1986) and industry (Lawler 1973) suggest that differential rewards often cause resentment rather than increased esteem and are often kept secret.

In effect, then, the primary extrinsic reward was money. For all the discussion of intrinsic rewards, it is clear that teachers are motivated by the opportunity to earn more. Teachers who were asked why they participated in Mossville's TDP said they did so "for the money":

> It's a big thing. I am struggling to make a living; there was a sense of inevitability of implementation, so I figured I might as well get in on the ground floor.

> To raise teachers salaries. I'm making what would take an additional four years in experience right now.

Academy teachers too said that "the most important thing is the money," and agreed strongly (4.25) with the survey item that the CEP "gives me additional income." Nevertheless, a somewhat different flavor pervades their comments from those in Mossville. Teachers appreciated being reimbursed for the added days at the beginning of the school year, saying,

> before the CEP a lot of teachers came in early to prepare for school and never got paid for it. We wanted to be ready. Now there are so many days we're paid for. It's made it seem worthwhile.

> We're paid to do what we tried to do before. There's less pressure than when you had to prepare on your own time.

These and other comments suggested two interpretations. First, the distinction between strictly financial and other rewards was difficult to make. In particular, teachers felt appreciated when they were paid. Second, while teachers talked about getting paid for what one did anyway, they were more likely to do additional work when remuneration was available, as the last comment indicates. Furthermore, it was quite clear that they appreciated the days for their own preparation more than those for school- or districtwide training and would not have tolerated as much staff development without remuneration.

The importance of getting paid was also apparent in discussions of the leader and specialist positions. Even some of the tasks that might have intrinsic appeal, like developing new programs, were valued in substantial measure because they were money-making opportunities. When asked who benefits most from the CEP, two teachers replied:

> Teachers who are innovative, willing to develop things, and help with new courses. It's nice to know you can get paid for what you do. Before the CEP, we weren't paid for new ideas. It was expected. The bottom line is financial.

> Teachers who want to spend time in curriculum development can apply for special jobs at the secondary level. They get paid to update and make professional curricula. The things some of us would do anyway but for nothing, others wouldn't. It provides the option to do something professional and be paid a professional stipend.

Yet, as Etzioni (1961) points out, financial rewards are associated with a calculative involvement that is based on profit. Teachers looked carefully at what they were asked to do for the additional money they got and tried to measure their work accordingly. Mossville teachers were required to submit to the state's new evaluation system, but teachers hired before the TDP was adopted had a choice about whether to compete for CS I and CS II positions. Under the circumstances it usually made sense to compete for the additional funds. A few teachers disagreed, however, believing that the time or stress were not worth the money. One teacher said, "Yes the money is important, but CS II doesn't make a lot of difference to teachers, especially if they feel they have to go through pressure and heartache to get those steps."

Most Academy teachers arranged what they considered a fair exchange, as this comment from a teacher specialist indicates: "This year I spent eighty-five hours on curriculum development.... They pay us $1,125. If I work at my professional hourly rate, it should come out to that many hours." Others, however, felt the exchange pushed the limits of what was reasonable, saying,

> the down side is it keeps you awfully busy. You overwork yourself. Getting paid for work is stressful. (A teacher leader)

> [The specialist job] takes so much extra time. This year has been so much time that I may not reapply. [Specialist work] has taken away from my personal planning time.

Moreover, Academy's CEP operated in a free market where teachers had other options to make money. For instance, secondary teachers in that district usually had two preparation periods. One school, however, paid teachers about the same amount of money to teach during one of those preparation periods as they would make as a teacher leader. Teachers reported that some of their colleagues preferred that option to being a teacher leader.

More important than alternative income sources was the teacher's commitment to regular teaching. According to one teacher,

> There are really good teachers who don't apply because they are so busy with their own departments that they have no time or they have a summer job. The first reason is more important. The CEP is more work for more money.... I finally had to say there are no more hours in a day. I can't do any more.

The trade-off between costs and financial rewards, the availability of alternative sources of income, and availability of alternative sources of income, and involvement in regular teaching all created a situation where some schools had problems filling the more time-consuming positions like teacher leader. Said one administrator, "We're filling four [teacher leader] positions, and we have five applicants. We have two good ones. They are repeating. Three are not as strong. It's hard to choose."

In sum, for all the value of intrinsic incentives, paying teachers was critical to the changes brought about in both Mossville and Academy. Teachers would have been less likely to comply with the new evaluation system in the first district and to put in the time required in the second. However, some teachers were calculating in their involvement.

They looked at the work required for the money, and in some cases decided that it was too much or that they could get a better deal elsewhere. Others in both districts took the money available but did not feel adequately rewarded. Moreover, money alone did not buy attitudinal change or commitment. Teachers who did it "for the money," especially in Mossville, reserved the right to be critical of the program.

Strategic Power

The clearest argument for the effects of power sharing on teacher motivation comes from a comparison of the three districts. Essentially, where teachers had more influence, they were more supportive of the program and more enthusiastic about their work. In Mossville, the administration and state together made decisions about the TDP design, with only the weakest forms of input from teachers. While decisions about what training to offer were made in response to teacher feedback, they were essentially made by the central office staff. Promotion decisions were made by principals with OE input. Program implementation took on a notably adversarial quality, with open conflict expressed at board meetings. The program generated a disproportionate number of appeals of promotion decisions, some of which had to be settled in court. Teachers said TDP had "become an instrument to intimidate some teachers" and "another means of control." Not surprisingly, this was also the program about which teachers were the least enthusiastic. Teachers did not believe the program would attract more people into the field or retain good teachers and did not see it as increasing their satisfaction with their career.

Hill City's administrators were confused in their approach to sharing power. Teachers gained very little influence at the district level; they got substantially more in some buildings, but little or none in others. This confusion is reflected in teacher interviews that show considerable tentativeness about the program in the beginning and growing discontent toward the end of the field period.

Academy went the farthest in sharing power over such issues as design of the CEP, selection of teachers for positions in the program, curriculum development, and content of training. For all the friction over teacher selection and position rotation, this was also the program about which teachers were most enthusiastic. They believed it retained good teachers, agreeing that the "CEP provides incentives for good teachers to stay in teaching" (3.58), whereas Mossville teachers disagreed that "TDP provides incentives for good teachers to remain" (2.64). Academy teachers overwhelmingly wanted to maintain the program (4.23); even the least-desired component received a strong endorsement on the survey (3.86). Finally, they said that it improved teacher morale (3.50).

The directness of the connection between shared influence and teacher enthusiasm varied. Not surprisingly, association leaders believed that sharing power was motivating. One such person in Mossville said

> [The evaluation instrument] started from the ground up. Now it's coming from the state to us. We thought we developed the plan. When you buy into it, it's yours. But when people say you've got to do it this way, it's harder to sell.

A person in a similar position in Academy explained that a major reason for the program's success was that "the teachers actually developed the plan. We made the decisions."

Rank-and-file teachers were not as sensitive to these issues as were the leadership. Mossville teachers generally did not discuss their role in decision making. Academy's rank-and-file teachers rarely volunteered observations on their influence over decisions, but we specifically asked twelve of them about their influence over the CEP. Seven indicated that they had substantial influence and four disagreed. One said the program had been designed by the superintendent, and he did not know how influence was distributed at the moment. When giving evidence of teacher influence, three referred to the CEP task force and four to decisions they could make in their own school. Some of these did not understand the larger district context for decision making. As one explained, "Teachers make up the [teacher-leader] selection committee. The faculty votes on who is on the committee. Beyond that, I don't think they have much input." In effect, teachers disagreed about how much influence they had, and many were not well informed about what happened at the district level. Those who were better informed suggested that having power was not important as an end in itself so much as for its results:

> What I like best is that we got to spend money in the district instead of the administrators. We spent it better than they would have thought. They have no idea of what the classroom needs are.

> Teacher involvement helps in implementation. It keeps programs responsive to classroom needs. The teachers have an opportunity to lead. It keeps administrators involved with the classroom.

In sum, a cross-district comparison highlights the motivational effect of sharing influence. However, a more fine-grained examination of teachers' sentiments suggests that only the more militant teachers found increased influence directly rewarding. Many other teachers were poorly informed about how much influence they had while others saw influence as a means to other ends rather than motivating in its own right.

Intrinsic Rewards: The Effects of Money and Influence

Intrinsic rewards depend on both the assumed probability that the task can be accomplished and the value attached to accomplishment. The probability of succeeding depends on how the work is structured and the skills of the individual. Anything that improves skills and structures facilitates task accomplishment and thereby increases intrinsic rewards (Staw 1980). Paying teachers for extra work gives them time to develop the skills, and materials that facilitate task accomplishment. More influence over strategic decisions gives teachers the opportunity to modify structural arrangements to facilitate task accomplishment. Academy made changes that helped teachers accomplish what they valued as educators, but Mossville used money more as a reward for compliance and did not increase teacher influence.

Academy. Academy did a great deal to facilitate teachers' success in three ways. The most pervasive was the opportunity to prepare for teaching provided by the extended-contract days. Teachers agreed almost unanimously that with those days,

> teachers are better prepared to start school in the fall. Teaching is more effective because of those days in the fall.

> We are more organized as a department, plus you are ready to start. You have the room ready, the back-to-school stuff ready.

In effect, buying extra days—an option the CEP law allowed and teachers pushed for—gave them time to do their regular work better.

The second way was to enrich the curriculum with a wide range of materials and activities to use in class. Some teachers thought these materials were more useful or accessible because they had been developed by their colleagues:

> [Specialists and leaders] give us materials and ideas. They run things off for us. They share neat ideas about how they feel it

should be implemented and say "if you like it, see me, and I'll share it."

> The CEP improved [the curriculum] immensely. The different specialists have different times to present their lessons. The art specialist is good about challenging us to do the lessons.

Finally, most teachers saw the CEP as a way to improve their own skills. "Teachers are in charge of helping us use computers," said one teacher. "They help us learn so we're not as scared to use it. There's district things like assertive discipline and PET that have been assigned to teacher leaders." Both curriculum and skills development resulted from the early decision to stress job enlargement rather than merit and could not have happened without the resources to pay leaders and specialists for their work.

Teachers looked at these facilitators from two perspectives. Personally, the availability of materials and learning opportunities provided opportunities for "professional growth." Professional growth reflects an increased capacity for the individual but it also raises task variety, making the process itself more interesting (Oldham and Hackman 1980). As a teacher reported, "For me as a person, I've grown by leaps and bounds. It's wonderful." In addition, teachers believed that these new opportunities benefited students—in other words, that through these opportunities they accomplished their major objective (Lortie 1975). Though one teacher talked about "measurable" increases in achievement, most spoke about changes in environment that were more subtle. One commented that "students learn better. They don't get stagnant. The CEP makes it more fun," and another remarked that "bringing in new ideas helps kids."

Although most attention was given to facilitators as regards instruction, one additional benefit was mentioned—increased social interaction. Most people find the work process more interesting when they are not alone but working with others (Staw 1980). That was certainly the case with the Academy teachers, one of whom said, "There's a unity knowing we all work together. It's a plus. It's wonderful for teachers because they have a support system. They are not totally solo." While the tensions surrounding the selection of people for CEP positions worked against such increased interaction, other factors helped. Most teachers appreciated the assistance they received from leaders and specialists after the selection process tension had dissipated. In addition, the extra CEP days provided opportunities for teachers to work together that had not existed before. Overall, these factors tended to overcome the problems created by selection. In the interviews, however, the rewards of social interaction were mentioned more in the elementary than in the secondary schools.

Mossville. Mossville teachers mentioned fewer intrinsic rewards. References to facilitators of accomplishment were less frequent than in Academy. Neither increased preparation time nor improved curriculum were mentioned. In fact, a minor theme in the interviews was that the TDP took away from preparation time. One teacher said that "lots of times we are pulled in to do little things, and lots of it is decoration," and one of the teacher association leaders complained that much of the documentation required to be considered for CS II was unnecessary paperwork.

Most discussion of facilitating accomplishment focused on increased skills. Teachers reported that the TDP "increased the instructional methods of teachers," and that "it helps me because I can look at what I need to focus on. I haven't been teaching long." Teachers recognized learning opportunities within the TDP, but were not as enthusiastic as Academy's teachers about those provided through its program:

> [The program has increased] teacher awareness of what they're doing.

> There were lots of things you couldn't explain before, but this has given us a language to do it. It's nice to find out that things you were doing already are recognized as good.

> It's a tool. When a kid fails a test, you don't look at the test. You look at your evaluation and try to see what's wrong. It's something to help you grow.

As a result, while some teachers did believe that "student achievement is bound to have increased," as one of them put it, there were also doubts. Comments about students, especially at the secondary level, often focused on how students responded to the evaluation of teachers:

> Kids don't like it.... They get angry when they are rehearsed for three days. I don't know how widespread that is.... The students feel the same stress the teachers feel.

> The kids enjoy it. They have a big time when the OEs come in. They are watching the game unfold.... I don't think it has helped the scores.

They acknowledged some learning of new skills but doubted the overall effect of the program.

On the other hand, teachers noted the loss of what is supposed to be one of the traditional intrinsic benefits of teaching: classroom autonomy (Lortie 1975; Johnson 1989). Autonomy is an important intrinsic motivator first because it is a desired task characteristic in its own right (Oldham and Hackman 1980), and second because autonomy is necessary for one to attribute the results of an endeavor to one's own effort. Without autonomy, the individual has no sense of accomplishment (Ryan et al. 1985). Yet Mossville teachers reported that the program had "become an instrument to intimidate teachers" and that "in spite of its supposed objectivity, we don't control everything we're accountable for.... It's insidiously and gradually stifling individual style." From the teachers' perspective then, Mossville's TDP, while reducing their autonomy, provided very few of the intrinsic benefits offered in Academy.

CONCLUSION

A comparison of the three districts illustrates both the outcomes of the bureaucratic and professional redesigns and how they are achieved. The bureaucratic design relies on external knowledge. It uses external controls and extrinsic incentives to induce compliance. These may reduce teacher motivation, but that is a secondary concern. Mossville illustrates that within its own framework the bureaucratic design can be successful. The district adopted the direct-instruction framework, and the TDP clearly changed teachers' behavior in the preferred direction. From the bureaucratic perspective, the opposition and declining motivation that resulted was acceptable because compliance with what were deemed ideal standards increased.

Whereas Mossville benefited from a clarity of focus and a well-executed bureaucratic design, Hill City did not manage notable improvement in teaching practice or curriculum during the course of this study. The Mutual Governance program created a lot of dialogue and helped to improve communication, but it did not resolve fundamental differences between teachers and the superintendent about how to improve education. On the positive side, however, Hill City managed to avoid some of the demotivating aspects of Mossville's program.

Consistent application of the professional design was also successful in its own terms. Here the emphasis was not so much on compliance as on teacher initiative, which was enhanced by a combination of teacher empowerment in specific areas and the purchase of additional time. Paying teachers did not change their work motivation directly, but it did buy effort. That effort facilitated the accomplishment of instructional tasks that provided the intrinsic rewards necessary for teacher motivation.

The professional design also had its problems. While it contributed to collegiality and professional development through the use of teachers helping teachers, including teachers in the leadership selection process—a central element of any truly professional strategy—proved divisive. The program did not always offer adequate rewards to recruit the best teachers to leadership positions. Finally, the coordination achieved was not as coherent as it might have been. This was balanced, however, by multiple sources of initiative. On balance then, it was quite successful.

A comparison of Mossville and Academy suggests that the professional design offers opportunities not available through the bureaucratic one. The professional design led to comparable achievement gains and teacher learning with the added benefits of increased curricular development and improved teacher motivation. These differences can be attributed in large part to the investment approach inherent in each strategy. Essentially, the bureaucratic design buys compliance. Teachers teach the way administrators want them to, but they expend no greater effort. The professional design buys time and effort. That effort can be used to facilitate student learning both directly and indirectly through its effect on teacher motivation.

6. THE POLITICS OF REDESIGN

THE PREVIOUS CHAPTER examined how bureaucratic and professional designs affected teacher motivation and behavior. We will now explore how districts decide what designs to adopt and implement. The cases themselves provide strong support for the political theories of organizational design presented in the introduction. In none of these districts was the final redesign developed through a consensual process where all parties shared common goals. Instead, designs were negotiated, often with a certain amount of conflict, among parties with differing—and sometimes at least partly contradictory—interests. The central administration initiated the reform, sometimes within parameters established by the state. However, the administrators' vision was challenged by teachers. The final design reflected the outcome of the contest between those two groups but was shaped by the action of the school board.

The cases suggest two other implications of the selection process. First, the more influence teachers exercise in the development process, the more professional will the final design be. Second, administrators may win the battle and lose the war. Involving teachers in the design process can be frustrating for administrators. Particular program features that are important to them may be vetoed and elements of which they disapprove may be substituted. The process may take longer. Yet a less administratively controlled planning effort can lead to more successful implementation. That is, more may be accomplished with less conflict.

This chapter first describes the process by which each district decided which redesign it would adopt. This process had numerous players but centered on a conflict between teachers and administrators. While the players in all three districts were similar, the results were quite different. The second section identifies several factors that contributed to those different outcomes. Finally, the implications of the political aspects of the redesign of teaching are elaborated upon.

THE DYNAMICS OF DEVELOPMENT

The development process was a four-way interaction in which (in two cases) the state provided a framework for development, the central administration (usually the superintendent) initiated the process, teachers resisted, and the board played a role that affected the outcome.

The State Contribution

The states' contribution to these redesign efforts was to provide money and a framework. The two state programs (Mossville's TDP and Academy's CEP) provided funds to reward teachers and create new formal positions within the district. Without similar support, Hill City simply lacked the money to put in place the more extensive operations found in the other two districts.

With money comes constraints, however. The state TDP and CEP regulations shaped the local political process. For instance, it established the limits on local discretion and teacher influence. Mossville responded to highly restrictive legislation that limited the district's choice in how to proceed. By contrast, the state legislation that initiated Academy's program was much more open-ended, giving districts broad guidelines within which to operate and requiring teacher and parent participation on the local program design. While some districts in that state did not include teachers actively in the planning, the legislation gave teachers license to participate in Academy.

Legislation also set the basic direction for reform. This was especially clear in Mossville where state legislation specified:

1) The promotion steps in the TDP
2) Criteria for advancement in the form of an evaluation scheme

3) Who would do the evaluation (including the number of observer-evaluators, since the state supported these positions).
4) The rough shape of the appeals procedure.

Academy's legislation did not encourage the professional direction the district took but did permit it. That legislation specified four categories for expenditure. It set maximums and minimums for expenditures in each category but allowed the district to determine its own emphasis by deciding how funds were allocated to categories. Academy had the option to stress job enlargement at the expense of merit pay (although state monitors believed that the district deemphasized merit pay more than the law permitted). The district was also allowed to develop its own evaluation scheme.

State policy can also be shaped by the political work of local actors (Fuhrman, Clune, and Elmore 1988), and these districts did influence the legislation to which they responded. In Mossville's state, Joan Dark, the assistant superintendent in charge of TDP, was quite active on the state steering committee that set policy. A state department employee said she was

> very influential on a technical level. Very smart, hard working, articulate. Within the state career-development organization, she was looked up to as a leader. She had prestige among the superintendents that no other assistant superintendent had because she was...willing to stand up and make her point.

The state language on the appeals procedure reflected her interest because appeals were so frequent in Mossville.

Brandon Crawford, the innovative superintendent in Academy, also had a strong reputation at the state level. According to a legislative aide, "Everything Crawford does is pretty first class.... He sat down with [some legislators] and spent time getting it to look the way he wanted. He put together a model that has been copied a lot." More generally, Crawford was credited by many as the person who shaped the original CEP legislation. Although he worked with a group of other superintendents and deans, he was the point person. Later, when Joseph Freeman became superintendent, he and other members of the central administration fought the holding action to circumvent the state's merit-pay requirement. When state officials thought the district administration unilaterally initiated opposition, those administrators set up a meeting between those officials and the task force to clarify the depth of local opposition to merit pay.

The Central Office

In all three districts, redesign was initiated by a new superintendent. In Mossville, Jack O'Brien took a number of steps to respond to board-identified problems. One concern was personnel, so O'Brien systematized the evaluation of principals and teachers and used that new system to motivate principals and avoid giving tenure to incompetent teachers. Unlike his predecessor, O'Brien also encouraged his administrators to take advantage of state initiatives. The district volunteered to pilot the new state teacher evaluation system and later the pilot TDP. While the proposals for these efforts were written by Dark, the assistant superintendent for personnel, O'Brien encouraged efforts that fit his agenda to develop more "data-based" approaches to evaluation.

Early in his tenure, Academy's Crawford initiated several changes in curriculum and instruction. One was a new personnel evaluation system. To make principals instructional leaders, he introduced Principles of Effective Teaching and otherwise changed how instruction took place. The CEP idea came out of discussions Crawford had with deans of schools of education and superintendents of other districts. He was instrumental in designing the CEP bill, and he devised the scheme to get local financial support by moving to year-round schools and redirecting funds that would have been needed for new buildings to support teachers.

Hill City's Mutual Governance program came out of discussions between the new superintendent, Robert Hardwick, and teachers. As part of an effort to bring groups together after the conflict that preceded him, Hardwick began inviting teachers into his office for long, open-ended interviews on their view of the district and its history. He also began private conversations with local association leaders and the regional NEA representative. These helped both sides get to know each other and their agendas better. At the same time, he initiated a five-year contract with teachers to promote financial stability. Near the middle of that contract, he started discussions with the NEA representative that led to Mutual Governance. Gradually, as consensus began to emerge, local association leaders and the board were brought into the conversations. The process was highly consultative among a limited number of people. By the time the agreement was worked out, both groups were committed to it.

Teacher Responses

The results of these superintendent initiatives, even when teacher leaders helped with their development as in Hill City, depended on rank-and-file teacher response. Mossville teachers were involved in the early planning of the TDP, but as the program moved toward implementation, their formal input through the Teacher Development Council and Steering Committee was reduced. Dark believed that the Council became "a bitch session" after the first year and controlled its deliberations more carefully. She also felt that the local steering committee had "so broad a spectrum that the committee is unworkable." To the extent that it made decisions, teachers complained that they were underrepresented. They also believed that she really made the important decisions.

Teachers had one more outlet, but not to influence collective decisions. They could appeal promotion decisions and did so at a much higher rate than any other pilot district. In two cases where teachers were denied promotions at all stages and believed they were being penalized for their teachers' association activities, they sued the district.

Relations with teachers in Academy began in a similar manner to Mossville's, but took an important turn. Crawford pushed program development and instructional improvement so hard that teachers objected and communicated their concern to the board. Matters came to a head at a teachers' association where a no-confidence vote was almost passed with Crawford in the room. The motion alone made the point so strongly that when Crawford began planning the CEP, he developed the steering committee, which is still in place. Moreover, teachers were listened to. Crawford's original plan to replace the conventional salary schedule with a merit-based promotion system was deleted because of teacher opposition and a job enlargement scheme based on joint teacher-administrator selection was substituted.

As Hill City began implementing its new plan, the association leaders helped introduce it to the membership. Teachers were generally suspicious of the new procedures, partly because of a past history of poor labor relations but also because the agreement was complicated. One said:

> Nobody understands it. This is an effort so not all decisions will come from the top. Teachers will be involved in policy making.... I'm not making any judgment on it yet. It's too early. People have said it's great and that it won't work.

The association leaders found themselves trying to sell the new plan to teachers without appearing to be too close to the administration. For example, at a Mutual Governance meeting of the teachers who were on individual School Planning Councils, the regional NEA representative sorted people's comments into "gripes" like equipment problems and dusty chalk, and "concerns"—the more significant issues that MG was designed to meet. The representative challenged every one of Hardwick's people to take care of the gripes so that MG could deal with the concerns. His presence at many of the discussion meetings served both to protect teachers and to support the program.

The thrust of Mutual Governance was to make district decision making more open to teachers and principals. This was done partly by the new decision-making bodies—most notably the Joint Professional Senate and the School Planning Councils—but in other ways as well. For instance, when the presidents of the teachers' and principals' association joined the superintendent's cabinet, they talked more than the assistant superintendents.

The Board Role

The teacher-administration interaction was shaped by board actions. In Mossville and Academy, where conflict was more apparent, the boards served to varying degrees as mediators. In Mossville this mediation was not particularly effective. The board's handling of individual appeals appeared inconsistent. Neither teachers nor administrators could predict how it would act. Early in the project's history, teachers also appealed to the board as a group although they did so with considerable trepidation. The board listened and even discussed what it was hearing with the superintendent, but no substantial change resulted from these actions. This created some frustration among board members, one of whom said "educational administration isn't accountable," even though the board had the option to fire the superintendent.

Teacher opposition to the program did undermine the board's support for the superintendent. After the 1989 election, three of the seven board members were former teachers with numerous personal ties to current ones. Shortly after that election, the board decided not to renew O'Brien's contract. Other factors, notably concerns about bussing, were more important to the final decision, but the friction surrounding the TDP contributed. Even during the remainder of his contract, however, the program was not substantially changed.

In Academy at least one board member was in the schools talking to teachers before the near no-confidence vote. Crawford spoke to this member individually and to the whole board afterward. The board directed him to listen to staff concerns more closely and incorporate them into his plans. At the same time, this member went to teachers in the schools, told them that Crawford had changed his approach, and urged them to cooperate. As a result of this interchange, Crawford created the CEP task force, which began planning the program and substantially influenced program design.

The Hill City board was not as active. Without public conflict the board did not have to mediate between teachers and the superintendent. Moreover, Hardwick believed that maintenance of positive relations with the board was among his most important tasks and tried to anticipate their concerns. This contributed to certain constraints on the process. Because the board was very sensitive to any increase in expenditures, Hardwick did not put additional local funds into Mutual Governance. Unlike his opposite numbers in Mossville and Academy, however, he did not search for outside income either. Moreover, one of the most important issues addressed through the Joint Professional Senate was teacher evaluation, a prime concern of the board.

EXPLANATORY FACTORS

The common thread among all three designs is that the central office initiated them. What differentiates them is the subsequent influence of teachers. This was highest in Academy, where teachers substantially shifted the design's direction. Teacher influence was moderate in Hill City, where the teachers' association helped develop the original design and teachers and administrators appeared to check each other on a variety of issues throughout the project's history. Finally, teacher influence was insignificant in Mossville, where the initial program design reflected administrative interests and, with the exception of the elimination of the 6-point lesson plan, was not adjusted to reflect teacher concerns. One factor that helped the central office initiate redesign efforts and contributed to its influence later on was its responsibility for managing the interface with the environment. Factors that affected how much teachers would become involved later included the superintendent's vision for the district, the role of the second administrator, the board's initial sense of crisis, its support for the program, and the role of the teachers' association in the district.

Environmental Interface

A major source of central office influence was its work with the outside environment. All three sought to obtain maximum resources

with minimal constraint. In two districts the central office aggressively sought financial assistance. Academy had a long tradition of
entrepreneurial fund seeking outside the district. Before he became
Crawford's assistant superintendent, Freeman and another district
administrator were respected within the district for their work in
tracking state and federal programs and looking for ways to fund
local ideas. This other administrator continued that effort under Freeman. In addition, Crawford's work with the legislature helped get
state money for the CEP. Later, when the state enforced the merit-pay
provisions of the act more strictly, Freeman and one of his district
office staff worked for a more locally acceptable interpretation.

Local fund seeking had no precedent in Academy. Crawford
broke that tradition by trying to get the community to accept voted
tax leeways. When these efforts were unsuccessful, he used a different strategy to gain local support for the CEP. He engineered a trade-
off that allowed the district to shift capital funds to program operations. In return the district agreed not to respond to growth with new
buildings but to increase the number of year-round schools. This
strategy was ultimately successful and increased financial support for
the program. It is worth noting that Crawford's ability to sell this
trade-off depended on a principal's initiative in experimenting with
year-round schooling. On the other hand, the principal could not
have sold the voted leeway to the community. This successful strategy depended on complementary efforts.

Similarly, there was no tradition of outside fund-seeking in
Mossville before O'Brien. Indeed, his predecessor discouraged the
cosmopolitan orientation that would facilitate such a search. O'Brien
changed that. One of his strengths was in public relations, both locally and at the state level. He and a board member worked with the
county commissioners to get support for the building program he
started. Later, he encouraged Joan Dark to follow up when the state
initiated pilot programs both for the training of beginning teachers
and for the TDP. Although Dark did much of the actual work, he created a supportive context.

In contrast, Hill City did not aggressively seek outside funding.
At about the time Mutual Governance started, a joint effort of the
state's education and labor departments provided support to a small
number of districts that wanted to pilot new strategies to develop
more cooperative relationships between teachers and administrators.
Hill City developed an advisory relationship to that effort but did not
seek money from it. At the same time, the district's recent history of
financial problems discouraged any effort to generate additional local

funds for the program. Moreover, Hardwick believed that money was not the answer to the problems the district faced. As a result, this district proceeded with less financial support than the other two.

On the other hand, Hardwick did seek out another external resource: publicity. As a result of his work, the signing of the agreements that initiated Mutual Governance was attended by the chief state school officer and the directors of the teachers', administrators', and school boards' associations in the state. This publicity built support for the new endeavor among the board in particular, helping to convince it of the importance of this locally initiated action. Hardwick also reached an agreement with the state that would facilitate the waiver of certain regulations in order to reform curriculum. At the end of the research period, however, little use had been made of the agreement.

Even before this time, however, Hardwick's handling of external relationships gave him internal credibility. His ability to resolve the major disputes around district financing and driver education, as well as his ability to bring together a conflict-ridden school board, substantially increased his credibility with teachers and administrators and set the stage for what would follow.

Superintendent's Vision

All three superintendents had both substantive beliefs about what should be changed and process beliefs about how to change it. In Mossville, Jack O'Brien's strong substantive vision stressed "accountability." At various times, he explained how the board that hired him or the state were strongly interested in accountability. His vision of accountability incorporated the use of formal, objective measures of performance. He was proud—"Hell, yes, I look at data!"—that he elaborated the district's testing program with his own basic facts tests. Another part of this vision was an emphasis on technical competence strictly defined. That emphasis motivated him to seek out principals from outside the district, to try to avoid hiring or giving tenure to incompetent beginning teachers, and to give great authority to administrators he thought were performing well and seek the dismissal of those who were not.

O'Brien's process belief was in strong, centralized leadership. His view emphasized the kind of central direction by experts associated with reformist superintendents at the turn of the century (Tyack 1974). He said, "My attitude is, you hired me to run this railroad. I know how. If you don't like it, get rid of me." This attitude led him to delegate tasks (sometimes broad ones) to specific individuals—as he delegated the TDP operation to Dark—and give them considerable leeway as long as those individuals met his expectations. He was also a strong believer in the use of "pressure" or negative sanctions. Examples include his publication of school test scores to force principals of poorly performing schools to improve and his use of cluster groups, where more effective principals could be used to motivate less effective ones to improve. Finally, he did not work on building support among separate constituencies. He "put people into two categories: strong and weak.... I don't like to mess around too long with the weak ones." Because he did not build support, board members complained that he was uncommunicative and teachers said he was unresponsive and hard to reach. Thus his tactical approach contributed to the exclusion of teachers from the planning and management of the TDP.

The emphasis on accountability and centralized leadership did not encourage O'Brien to try to sell the TDP broadly to teachers. While he did encourage the cooperation of the subset of principals who performed to his satisfaction and adopted his view, he did not try to persuade others. It was enough to set up a system to monitor and reward performance and let it do its work.

In Hill City, Hardwick had thought carefully about the need to work with different constituency groups within the district. His frequently repeated admonition about Mutual Governance was that "there are four groups in the district with veto power. They all have to like something to make it work. These groups are the board, the principals, the teachers, and the superintendent." He was especially sensitive to the needs of the board: "The care and feeding of the board is the superintendent's most important task. My leverage in the district stems from their belief that 'he has control of the board.'" This does not mean that he was subservient to the board. In his first months in office, he took on the drivers' education challenge which had polarized the community for six months. Much like Babe Ruth pointing past the right field fence before he hit a home run, Hardwick told his administrators he would get a 9–0 vote on this issue where the board had been split 5–4. His success raised his internal credibility considerably.

If Hardwick was sensitive to the board, he also reached out in other directions. He described how he "brought...teachers into the district here to sit on that couch" to ask about what should be improved. While responding to board needs, a teachers' association militant said, "his stress is cooperation with the union." Similarly, a building administrator said: "Dr. Hardwick changed the whole atmosphere. There was terrible strife before. Dr. Hardwick has involved everybody. He shared power with us. He has used suggestions and examples to change things." Thus, he appeared to reach out and consult with all groups.

At certain points, however, Hardwick ceased to listen and build compromises. Instead he became more controlling. Sometimes this was to avoid certain pitfalls that he anticipated:

> I saw [the first meeting of the senate] as an exercise in atmospherics. I was embarrassed that it was me talking for ninety minutes.... I had no alternative because these people only talk through their union. If I'd asked the eighteen [elected teachers] what was on their mind, they'd have frozen. They met before and planned what they'd say. [A teachers' association official's] questions were scripted. It's pragmatic. Also there are historic memories of reprisals.... I knew it wouldn't be a free-flowing discussion. I know the danger of having twenty minutes left and then asking for questions.

Sometimes, however, he became more directive to achieve his own content vision. He had his own curricular agenda that he wanted endorsed and new roles he wanted teachers to play. In the early days of Mutual Governance, this vision centered on the proposals for master teachers and a peer assistance council. He also showed more interest in the kind of narrowed curriculum and emphasis on higher-order thinking reflected in Theodore Sizer's (1984) ideas about Essential Schools. On two occasions he tried unsuccessfully to get the district to cooperate with essential schools programs. Later he initiated changes to simplify the district's middle school curriculum to concentrate more on academic content, but these met substantial teacher resistance. Similarly, at one school he encouraged the development of an at-risk program for the district.

Hardwick was unsuccessful in selling these ideas to his staff, and somehow he refused to endorse certain ideas that were key to teachers, like changing the elementary schedule and responding to certain supplies issues. The result was a series of reverses on the master-teacher program, the curriculum changes, and the breakfast program for at-risk youth. When a different school began its own at-risk youth program, its staff avoided seeking the help and support of the central office, even though it was a program which Hardwick would approve. In effect, Hardwick's specific educational approach (which was not adequately implemented) created a situation where he needed but could not get staff acceptance of his vision of education, nor would he accept theirs.

Crawford's process approach was not as self-conscious as that of the other superintendents. Instead it appeared underdeveloped. As he recalled his early years in the district, "I should have done more interpersonal things. I get into ideas and don't give enough recognition and nurturing." In fact he felt some sympathy for the people to whom he applied pressure: "It's not easy. In some ways I feel bad. You come in as a superintendent with different expectations. Some principals have been at it for twenty years and are five years away from retirement." With that orientation, he could be convinced to respond to strong opposition. For instance, he tempered his vision about merit pay to reflect teacher concerns.

Freeman, Crawford's successor, was extremely sensitive to process and tactical issues. As numerous staff members pointed out, his contribution was to create an environment in which teachers felt comfortable trying new things. Said one, "Freeman didn't bring things on, but he made them work. He said there were good ways to make them work. Crawford brought the ideas. Freeman facilitated them. He helped with the process so they grew." Even when he became superintendent, his interest was in curriculum development in general and in helping schools develop their own goals rather than specific innovations.

Crawford's substantive vision was dynamic and motivating in its context but, for the staff who came to accept it, it had a diffuseness about what should be done that gave them considerable opportunity to initiate their own changes with the hope that they would be supported centrally. While Crawford was known as the idea person, his vision for improvement allowed considerable room for middle management to initiate changes:

> My interests were in curriculum and instruction.... I'm interested in leadership of principals as instructional catalysts. I wanted fairly intensive training of principals: instructional observation and analysis; stimulating feedback from principals to teachers.

Although he focused on training principals in the principles of effective teaching, the idea of instructional catalyst was broad enough to permit a variety of changes. When he changed his process approach to incorporate more teacher input, this breadth of vision allowed him to be open to more teacher ideas. Freeman's innovations emphasized process so much more than content that they gave staff considerable room to initiate their own ideas.

In sum, there appears to be a complex interaction among the superintendent's educational vision, his process approach, and the redesign strategy underway. The bureaucratic strategy is congruent with a directive process vision and a specific content vision. Then the superintendent generates his own ideas and supports those who share his vision but doesn't try to sell it extensively to staff. The professional strategy is congruent with a more inclusive process vision and a more general content agenda that permits the incorporation of the ideas of others. It is useful to sell this vision but in a general form that encourages people to innovate along that theme. There are probably a variety of noncongruent alternatives. The one observed here includes a specific educational vision and a persuasive process vision. This can create a situation where teachers do not accept the superintendent's vision while the superintendent will aggressively override the interests of teachers. The result can be a situation where relatively little is accomplished.

The superintendent's vision was crucial because the superintendent himself was crucial, at least in the eyes of teachers and board members. They attributed much of the direction and dynamism of these programs to the chief executive officer:

> Dr. Freeman has been the most influential. Because he's committed, the principals are committed. Because the principals are committed the teachers are committed.

> It's now beyond rhetoric and into real tangible action. Guided by the superintendent who is enlightened. The person most responsible is Dr. Hardwick. The concept of Mutual Governance is a decided strength. I can't think that any of it would have happened without Dr. Hardwick.

> The supertendent [O'Brien] is the chief administrator, the educational leader of the district.... As far as the system is concerned, it was the superintendent.... He wanted to get in on the ground floor and shape the program the way he thought it should be.

The Consiglieres

The two larger districts had a consigliere (Hord, Hall, and Stiegelbauer 1983), a second administrator who helped administer the change programs. In Mossville the consigliere was Joan Dark, who took charge of the local TDP and ensured that it would work. She shared O'Brien's tactical vision and fundamental suspicion of faculty motives. Moreover, when the Council raised too many concerns, she controlled the direction those meetings took.

Academy's consigliere was Joe Freeman, who later became superintendent in his own right. Both teachers and board members agreed that he helped Crawford build better relationships with the staff. The consensus was that, as one board member put it:

> Dr. Crawford wouldn't have survived without Joe. Dr. Craw-
> ford...had important directions to move us in, but he went too
> fast.... Joe is a touching, warm guy. People feel he's on their
> side. His nurturing and massaging kept it viable.

The Board's Sense of Crisis

Superintendent selection illustrates the level of crisis in each school board. Hill City's history most approximated a crisis. When the state first legalized collective bargaining for teachers in the early 1970s, the board tried to break its new union. Negotiations were acrimonious and strikes common. By the early 1980s, attention shifted to financial problems. The district's industrial base was crumbling, expenses were climbing, and the board had to make several large, unpopular millage increases. Program cuts were equally unacceptable. When the board began the search that selected Hardwick, it had two objectives: to reduce labor-management conflict and to control the fiscal problem.

Mossville's story begins with the desegregation suit that led to riots in the early 1970s. Bussing problems and plant deterioration created a need for a new building program that O'Brien's predecessor could not manage. Meanwhile, the instructional program was deteriorating. Somewhat earlier, when the community lost its single largest employer, it began bringing in new businesses. The outsiders arriving with these new companies created a demand for a more rigorous program, especially one for more academically talented students. In 1981, when the board recruited O'Brien, its first concern was to find someone who could carry out a building program, but it also wanted a person who could modernize the district's general approach. This included improving student learning and tightening up personnel procedures.

The disruption and discontent apparent in Hill City and Mossville was much less present in Academy. That district had two superintendents in thirty-five years, both promoted from within. Teachers were left on their own to teach as they saw fit without the benefit of more than minimal curricular guidance or staff development. Most board members in the early 1980s were employees of the large university in the city. The consensus was that the district was stagnating and could do better. To that end, that board too sought an outside superintendent.

The three boards hired superintendents who initiated redesign efforts because they were unhappy with the current situation, but the extent of unhappiness varied. Only Hill City faced a true crisis. Academy, the district that moved farthest in the direction of professionalization, experienced no crisis or deep discontent. Moreover, the sources of discontent were not always addressed by redesign. Mossville's board was most concerned about its plant, although rationalizing personnel management was a concern. Hill City's financial crisis was more important than labor-management harmony.

Board Support for Redesign

Board members generally understood the main points of the redesign programs. Mossville's board members grasped the main features of the TDP but evaluated them somewhat differently from district leaders:

> As a teacher, there were some things I liked. It gave us training to show us different ways to teach.... But we all had to do the same thing.... If I were a student going through something like that six times it would be boring for the kids.

In Academy, even though the board members interviewed were mostly new, they knew the district's position on the CEP and had an opinion of its success. Said one, "Academy's is successful. It is designed to reward teachers who go the extra mile—not for what you've always been doing. It's an opportunity to expand teaching skills." Academy board members also knew more details about the program.

Hill City's board members knew the philosophy of Mutual Governance:

> It is nothing in and of itself, but with leadership there is more sharing, a sharing of the decision level. The last discussion and policy remain at the board. We have overall responsibility, but day-to-day decisions are more appropriately made back at the building.... It gives linkage between the classroom teachers and [the superintendent].

Moreover, the program was always handled to ensure that the board's interests—for staff evaluation, for instance—were attended to.

In two of the districts the board's understanding was translated into concrete support. In Hill City the board agreed to every contract and the salary increases contained in them that Hardwick brought to them. There were no public conflicts over annual budgets, and board members repeatedly stated their satisfaction with both the Mutual Governance program and the labor peace that had resulted. Their agreement to open up the five-year contract to consider salary increases two years before the contract expired indicated their support for their superintendent's programs. In Academy, because the state did not fund the CEP fully, Crawford developed the proposal to save capital costs with year-round schools and use the money saved to fund the CEP. The board allowed Crawford to take his initiative to the public, and it passed. When Crawford had problems with teachers, the board intervened to mediate. In Mossville the state provided funding for the pilot TDP so the board did not have to provide financial support. The board was unable to effectively mediate between the administration and the staff, and questioned what the program was doing.

In all three districts, the board's support for the local effort depended on more than its understanding of that program. General confidence in the superintendent was also an issue. Hardwick was careful to maintain the Hill City board's support. He did so partly by moving slowly with Mutual Governance and handling it so the district (including the board) received a great deal of good publicity. Perhaps more important, he got the budget situation under control and reduced millage increases from five and six to one per year. This was partly because several new homebuilding projects raised the tax base, but also because he changed the budget planning cycle to start it earlier and get more board input into early formative stages.

By contrast, O'Brien alienated Mossville's board over an eight-year period. In the beginning, the board supported the new superintendent, but the TDP created difficult situations for the board to deal with. Still, the board faced more heated conflicts related to bussing plans and gifted programs, both of which provided settings to air disagreements about desegregation. Between 1981 and 1989, six of the seven members who hired O'Brien left the board, most in 1989. Over that time several became increasingly disenchanted with him but found themselves unable to modify policy. The board's support for the TDP waned, but it did not abolish the program. Instead, in the fall of 1989, it chose not to renew Dr. O'Brien's contract. These examples suggest that the board's support is often as much for an administration in general as for specific programs.

The Teachers' Association

Teachers' associations differ in their access to district decision-making processes depending on both the legal arrangements for collective bargaining and historical and cultural factors. Mossville's associations were least included in decision making. That state had a statewide salary structure determined by the legislature. Raising teachers' salaries depended more on statewide action in general and lobbying in particular than anything the local association did. As a result, the local branch of the state NEA association was relatively weak. Moreover, there were still vestiges of the preunion orientation in the local association. Both teachers and administrators belonged. What could have been a sign of teacher-management cooperation instead seemed to signal more of a passive association. The NEA president said, "We're not like a union. We don't bargain. If I want something, I go to Dr. O'Brien and Dr. Dark. Not a lot is refused." On the other hand, in most specific instances she mentioned—for instance, an effort to move up the date for starting school—the association was unable to get what it wanted.

The passive role of the NEA affiliate frustrated a small number of teachers, who joined the AFT. However, the majority of teachers stayed with the NEA. At board meetings the AFT president regularly made a point of appearing and speaking on issues, but neither unit was part of the regular decision-making apparatus.

Academy's teachers' association bargained with the local board for salaries. Collective bargaining in the state is optional, and there is no right to strike. Still, the existence of a local association with a regular, effective line of communication to administrators provided a basis for discussion. At the same time, Academy was more open than Mossville to allowing administrators to join the association. Freeman continued to belong even after he became superintendent, and he was sympathetic to the teachers' desire to strike if the state did not give them a salary increase. In effect, the association was part of the decision-making apparatus through formal arrangements and local norms that called for consulting with it as decisions were made.

Hill City negotiated with its association in a state that allowed teachers' strikes. In contrast to Academy, the district had a history of extremely acrimonious labor relations. When Hardwick arrived in Hill City, relations between the board and the association were polarized, but both sides wanted peace. Moreover, the association was a strong entity, well organized to advance its own interests. It had in effect forced itself into the decision-making apparatus, and the superintendent had to deal with it. However, Hardwick elected to use an inclusive rather than a confrontational strategy, thereby changing the nature of association inclusion in the decision-making process. On the other side, association leaders welcomed this change and worked with Hardwick in a manner appropriate to their role. The regional NEA UniServ representative exhibited clear leadership, walking a thin line between working with and supporting Hardwick and the district, and protecting the interests of the teachers. The local association executives worked closely with Hardwick but were not coopted by the district. Where there were problems, the executives presented them clearly and fairly to the superintendent and the district.

Summary

In all three districts, the central office—usually the superintendent personally—was the catalyst for redesign. The central office has the access to outside sources of ideas and money as well as the opportunity to shape state initiatives. It also has the internal authority to initiate such changes. However, teachers also contested the central office initiative in various ways in all three districts. Only Mossville's central administration was able to control the subsequent development of the program. In the other two districts, the ultimate design and much that followed from it resulted from an ongoing give-and-take between teachers and administrators, sometimes mediated or constrained by the board and the state. Teachers' influence over the new design stemmed from a combination of the orientation of the superintendent and the consigliere, the role played by the board, and their own role in district decision making.

IMPLICATIONS

The political nature of the redesign process suggests that professional redesigns are most likely when teachers play a substantial role in that process. Certainly in these three districts the most professional design came about in Academy, where teachers opposed the superintendent most successfully and were incorporated into the design process. Teachers were sufficiently active in Hill City to avoid serious loss of autonomy. They were not strong enough to achieve their own objectives, and there was very little real change in either design or teaching. In Mossville, where the administration most clearly dominated, the result was the most bureaucratic.

Such behavior makes a certain amount of sense, at least in the short run. Whatever administrators believe about the nature of teaching and the motivational value of teacher empowerment, including teachers in decision making entails a loss of administrators' authority that may limit their control over specific decisions. One has to take a very long-range view and strongly accept a professional view of teaching to accept the potential advantages of voluntarily sharing control. Such a view may be difficult to sustain for administrators who have specific reform agendas of their own or who are under fire from external constituencies and may want to maximize their control to deal with those threats. There is in fact considerable evidence that administrators do not understand the implications of including teachers when decisions are made and that even those with the best of intentions balk at doing so when there are no countervailing powers (e.g., Firestone,1977; Sirotnik and Clark 1988).

Clearly, there are trade-offs involved in sharing influence with teachers. Maintaining control has the advantage that the administrators' vision of what the program will be is more likely to be realized. This advantage will be especially appealing to those who hold the bureaucratic view because they believe they have the knowledge teachers lack as well as the responsibility for making key decisions. However, there is a price to pay. Part of the price in Mossville was continuing teacher opposition. When compared to other districts in the same state that piloted the same program, Mossville is notable for the acrimony the program caused. The number of promotion appeals was unusually high, even when one allows for the district's size. These appeals cannot be explained by the district's promotion rates which were well within the range of other pilot districts. Instead, they appear to be a manifestation of resistance to the centralizing, controlling style with which the program was administered. The two court cases reflect the same tendency. The other price, of course, is shortened administrative tenure. While the major reason that O'Brien's contract was not renewed was his handling of bussing, the gifted and talented program, and other issues related to desegregation, opposition to the administration of the TDP had to be a contributing factor.

Being more open to teacher influence has the opposite advantages and disadvantages from maintaining control. Administrators will not be able to dictate the program's design to the same extent. In Academy, for instance, Crawford made substantial compromises when he began working with the CEP task force. Moreover, many of the detail decisions about what training to offer and how to schedule it and deliver it were made by teachers within the framework established by the program. Administrators do not have to abrogate their content vision entirely. Academy administrators did gain acceptance for some specific ideas, like writing across the curriculum. They were successful partly because the redesign framework gave teachers considerable opportunity to initiate their pet projects as well. A major advantage to including teachers is that it builds support for the program and minimizes the ongoing struggles that characterized Mossville. This was certainly true in Academy, where most teachers were extremely enthusiastic about the local program.

Where key administrators neither clearly control the design process nor clearly include teachers, the result is likely to be confusion and limited progress. In Hill City, Hardwick appeared willing to share influence with teachers; he established the apparatus for such sharing to take place. Yet when specific decisions had to be made—how to select master teachers, what the middle school curriculum should be—he consistently insisted on particular positions. The result was a governance structure that delivered less than it promised. Hill City teachers did not oppose the program to the extent of those in Mossville, but their enthusiasm was far from high. Moreover, both teachers and administrators found that they could not achieve their major objectives.

Substantial advantages seem to accrue to central administrators who share control over the design process with teachers. While they may lose on specific points, they will win a great many. Moreover, such a process is more likely to lead to a redesign that motivates teachers, takes advantage of their ideas, and to avoid generating ongoing antagonism that distracts from the central business of schooling.

Accepting the inclusion of teachers is facilitated not only by a professional perspective on organizational design but also by a new view of managerial responsibilities. Peters and Waterman (1982) differentiate between product champions and executive champions. Product champions come up with specific ideas or programs. The inventors of Scotch tape, lap-top computers, Principles of Effective Teaching, and a new way to teach art to third graders are all product champions. Yet product champions require a hospitable environment. Part of such an environment is undoubtedly a professional work design. However, such a design is facilitated, Peters and Waterman argue, by executive champions, who encourage product champions to pursue their own ideas even at the expense of considerable loss of time and money. The executive champion creates the environment that allows product champions to develop. Crawford and Freeman were executive champions for all staff. O'Brien played such a role with Joan Dark and a few administrators who accepted his content vision, and Hardwick did not play it at all.

Accepting the role of executive champion requires rethinking managerial responsibilities. Often the manager's task is not so much to decide on specific innovations but to set the organization's general direction and then decide how much invention and change are compatible with that direction. The executive champion role has the advantage of encouraging new ideas from many sources. Moreover, when combined with the successful exercise of teacher influence, administrators' willingness to be executive champions contributes to the development and maintenance of the professional redesign of schools.

7. CONCLUSION

OVER THE LAST DECADE substantial efforts have been made to reform teaching. Much has been written and much has been tried, but it remains difficult to know where we are and how we ought to proceed. One reason is that ambiguous rhetoric has hidden real differences in what people imagine the nature of a redesigned teaching profession to be and how to achieve it. We have tried to reduce this confusion by analyzing key differences in reform beliefs and theories, but even more by analyzing real cases where people have tried to redesign teaching. In this final chapter, we place our cases in a larger perspective by analyzing how much change we have actually seen. We then summarize our own case for professional reform in teaching and identify some challenges that must be met if a professional design is to flourish.

THE THREE CASES IN PERSPECTIVE

In light of the dramatic rhetoric about restructuring, it is important to put these three cases in perspective. The restructuring literature argued that the design of American schools was simply incompatible with the improvement of the education of our children, that radical reform in school organization was needed to help this country become more competitive again (Elmore 1990). Some instances of serious changes in governance arrangements have been documented (e.g., David 1989), but more careful analysis suggests that many of these changes have actually been less revolutionary than they first seemed (Timar 1990).

Another line of reasoning holds that whatever the educational consequences of the organizational forms of American schools, they serve a different purpose by providing legitimation to those institutions (Meyer and Rowan 1977). That is, organizational forms in and of themselves provide a sort of comfort to the public and "proof" that education is going on. Metz (1990) speaks of the myth of "real school," the need to maintain certain patterns and procedures—forms and rituals—for the public to believe that the organization in question is a school and deserves support. Even where these forms prove dysfunctional, they are maintained because that is what people think schools are supposed to be like.

These three districts were selected because of their reputations as leaders within their own states. Two were known as pace setters in implementing state policies intended to redesign teaching. The third had received extensive publicity for its new approach to governance. As we got to know them, it became clear that they varied in the amount of change they made. Mossville and Academy made the biggest structural changes. Both incorporated modest but notable job differentiation features. Academy also took some steps to incorporate teachers into the internal governance of the district. Hill City's changes in governance turned out to be smaller than the changes made by the two other districts. Structural changes led to or were accompanied by other developments. Mossville's job differentiation was accompanied by a modest increase in accountability through student testing. The involvement of Academy's teachers in curriculum enriched the district's offerings and strengthened its training functions. Hill City seemed always on the verge of instructional changes.

As far as we can tell, Academy and Mossville compare favorably with some of the better-documented restructuring programs around the country in the amount of actual change that resulted. Still, all three districts maintained the myth of the real school. The basic governance structure with a school board, superintendent and administrative staff, principals, and teachers was maintained even where teachers were given somewhat more voice in decision making. The egg-crate architecture, the daily and annual schedules, the curriculum, and systems for teacher and student assessment remained largely intact, although there were some changes, like the year-round schools in Academy and more refined teacher observation in Mossville. The proverbial visitor from Mars would not find a great structural difference between these districts and most other American school systems. Our evidence suggests then that the extent of redesign in teaching that is really taking place under the rubrics of restructuring or teacher reform is relatively small. Yet even these small changes had notable, although far from revolutionary, consequences. Moreover, studies like this illustrate the difficulty of achieving even this small but feasible sort of change.

THE VALUE OF PROFESSIONALISM

Within this limited range, we have examined in detail specific versions of professionalism and bureaucracy. The most highly developed professionalism we saw consisted of:

1) Job enlargement, where teachers were paid extra to engage in training and staff development tasks.
2) Rotating assignments and the use of teachers to help select those who received the special positions.
3) Teacher participation in making major decisions about the job enlargement scheme itself.
4) Substantial decentralization of decision making as to curriculum and training so that it fell to teachers or happened through collegial interaction among teachers, staff, and administrators.

In turn, the most highly developed bureaucracy consisted of:

1) Merit-based master-teacher assignments where teachers were paid extra because they were supposed to be better.
2) Quasi-permanent positions (which could be lost if performance drops) with selection decisions made by principals and central office staff in line with strict operational criteria.
3) Teachers excluded from most decisions about the design of the master-teacher scheme.
4) No increase in participation in curriculum and training decisions along with reduced discretion in the classroom.

We are convinced by our findings in these districts and other literature that the professional design has substantial advantages over the bureaucratic. Most notably, it increases motivation because of how teachers respond to intrinsic and financial rewards. What makes teachers care about their work are the intrinsic incentives that come from successful teaching. The professional design helps teachers receive those incentives. Teachers in special positions provide their colleagues with the training and curricular support needed to improve instruction. Moreover, those who receive the special positions find the work itself rewarding because of things like task variety, increased opportunity for interaction with adults, and opportunities to help others. This is not to say that teachers will not make their teaching conform to externally determined criteria of effectiveness for financial rewards—they will. However, they externalize such changed behavior, doing it largely for the money. Moreover, their resentment about the constraints created by such a system is greater than their inspiration to teach better.

One of the ironies of intrinsic incentives is that though they can be undermined by financial rewards, they still must be bought, albeit indirectly. A major problem in getting intrinsic rewards from teaching is a lack of time. Teachers' days are normally filled with the routine aspects of working with students, correcting papers, and so forth. Teachers have outside commitments to family and other activities that must be forgone if they give more attention to their jobs. Yet the factors that truly increase a sense of accomplishment from one's work—new curricula, training opportunities, and so forth—are available only when one works longer hours. Normally, that kind of work is outside the regular contract. Teachers cannot be expected to put in the time to generate intrinsic rewards without renegotiating their work contract, and doing so requires more money. What professional job enlargement programs can do is purchase the time needed to stimulate intrinsic rewards.

Another way to look at programs to redesign teaching is as investment strategies. Bureaucratic, merit-based designs typically purchase specific behaviors or compliance with standards established by administrators or policy makers. In effect, that is all they buy. Even when the new behaviors contribute to student learning, they are not perceived as intrinsically valuable because teachers conform for the money. Professional job enlargement designs buy time that can be used to create conditions that help students learn and are rewarding to teachers. They may look "messier" and less "accountable" when teachers play an important role in deciding what developments will take place or which training and curricular opportunities they will take advantage of. Yet they can facilitate both the direct developments that improve instruction (training and so forth) and the intrinsic rewards that come from voluntary involvement with those developments. Such involvement is not likely, however, if teachers are not paid for it.

In theory, the professional design should have another advantage: it should stimulate teachers' reflective practice about teaching. The evidence from Academy, and to a lesser extent Mossville, is that these changes did encourage reflection. Some of this was deeper consideration of curricular issues. Bringing teachers together from different buildings and allowing them opportunities to interact as happened in Academy, helped them better articulate the curriculum at various grade levels. The use of teachers to develop curricula and the expectation that those teachers interact with their colleagues encouraged all involved to think through student needs more carefully. There was also greater reflection on instructional practice. Academy's and Mossville's training programs on Principles of Effective Teaching and Teacher Expectations for Student Achievement encouraged teachers to think more about how they taught. Internship programs also provided assistance for beginners who were especially positive.

Still, norms of teacher privacy limited the amount of direction senior teachers gave to their beginning colleagues, and the follow-up to training programs was not extensive. While we have considerable teacher testimony that the training offered was helpful, it is not clear that instructional practice changed radically. For such changes to occur, it seems likely that a vision of instruction more unified than was presented in Academy or accepted in Hill City must be provided. It is safe to say that the professional design observed here set the stage for more reflective practice among teachers. However, these structural changes alone are not sufficient to promote a different kind of reflection (Peterson and McCarthey 1991).

While these cases stress the benefits of the professional design, the bureaucratic one does have certain short-run advantages. Mossville illustrates that administrators who are willing to exercise their authority and have access to additional financial incentives for teachers can create specific changes in teaching behavior. In conjunction with other modifications in student accountability systems, these changes can lead to quick but modest improvements in students' basic skills. Because similar phenomena have been documented previously even without the use of merit pay (Rossman, Corbett, and Firestone 1988), it appears that bureaucratic designs can be effective in their own terms.

Yet in the long run the bureaucratic design appears to be a dead end. If professionalism supports—but is not sufficient for—substantial change in instructional practice, the bureaucratic strategy provides no basis for further development. Instead, it emphasizes compliance. It presents a standard along with a reward for meeting it. Teachers work for that extrinsic reward, not out of any intrinsic interest in improved instruction. They may think about how to meet the standard if the reward is large enough and that standard is deemed achievable, but there is no reason for deeper reflection about instruction or their students. In effect, the bureaucratic approach deflects attention away from the central educational task toward achieving the reward.

Not understanding the implications of the design decisions for teaching is a greater risk than choosing the wrong approach. The rhetoric surrounding teacher reforms and restructuring is remarkably ambiguous. With the differences between various forms of job differentiation poorly understood, it is not unusual for administrators—like the principal in our introduction—to view new forms of centralization as ways to professionalize teaching. In the same vein, administrators who advocate sharing decision-making responsibility with teachers often fail to understand the constraints they put on themselves when they seek to enact specific reforms. In this regard, Hill City is a remarkably instructive case. Like it, many districts may move only far enough in the direction of redesigning teaching to raise anxieties without doing enough to reap the benefits. They may also combine contradictory elements in a self-defeating manner.

Professionalism and Popular Reforms

What do these cases tell us about some of the reforms that have been particularly popular in this country recently? These reforms incorporated both job differentiation and changes in governance. In Chapter 1 we sorted job differentiation proposals along two dimensions. They either applied the principles of merit or job enlargement, and position changes were either permanent or temporary. Our work illustrates that merit-based programs are essentially bureaucratic, and reinforces the large volume of research that highlights their problems (e.g., Johnson 1986). Job enlargement is professional and has considerable potential for both improving practice and motivating teachers. What we did not see was permanent job-enlargement programs like the career ladder proposed by the Carnegie Forum (1986). Such programs may be too great a challenge to current definitions of real school; this study and the research of others indicates that teachers strongly resist efforts to make differences of rank permanent (Malen and Hart 1987). It may also be that they are too great a challenge to district and state budgets. In the absence of clear examples of such career ladders, it is worth noting that even temporary job-enlargement programs are difficult to achieve but worth the effort. In the long run, we suspect that permanent job-enlargement programs will be worth the effort, but they will require a major rethinking of teacher roles. Much of this rethinking will have to come from teachers themselves.

One of the most frequently discussed governance changes is site-based management, wherein many decisions once made at the district level are delegated to the building. Often, however, these programs are not intended to help teachers participate in decision-making but to overcome the inefficiencies created by overly centralized district operations (Clune and White 1989). These cases suggest two observations about site-based management. First, Hill City illustrates that when they are honestly implemented, mechanisms that incorporate teacher input into building decisions improve teacher motivation.

More important, however, teacher influence over crucial strategic decisions (i.e., those beyond the scope of the particular classroom) can be enhanced in quite different ways that do not involve site-based management at all. When such mechanisms operate at the district level, they involve teachers in decisions to which they would lack access with site-based management. Where these decisions involve curriculum—often a district-level issue—teachers become involved in issues that are central to student learning. This is important because changes to incorporate teachers into decision-making often focus on more managerial questions (Firestone, et al. 1991).

The key to teacher influence in Academy was the district-wide CEP task force. Consisting primarily of teachers, but chaired by the superintendent and with principal participation, it made many important decisions about the design of positions, criteria for selection, and so forth. Over the years, it took the lead in developing responses to changing state policy and resolving disputes that came up among teachers. These decisions were largely managerial, however.

The CEP positions were more important for involving teachers in substantive educational issues. Curriculum specialists had considerable leeway to decide what developments to make in their own areas. Committees of elementary grade-level leaders and secondary specialists had budgets that they could allocate to developing particular curricula or supporting specific events. What is especially significant about these positions from a governance viewpoint is that authority often goes with the work. By sharing training and curriculum development tasks with teachers, the central office staff, who had made these decisions in consultation with a few volunteers in the past, formally incorporated teachers into the process and in some cases turned over significant responsibility to them. The district office traded complete control for expanded and enriched programs. More curricular and training work happened because teachers were paid to do it, but as a result teachers had more influence over what was done.

These cases also suggest an important limitation to some of the thinking about professionalizing teaching: a failure to adequately consider whether and how tasks should be redistributed between newly professionalized teachers and the administrative component of the school. There is currently an almost caste-like distinction between those who teach and those who do not, with little overlap in decision-making responsibility and work between the two levels. Curriculum and training are typically central-office functions where teachers at best play an advisory role. Among the reform reports, very few have considered whether this distinction should be maintained. One notable exception is the Carnegie Forum (1986), which suggests in some places in its report that administrators are not necessary. Committees of lead teachers might replace principals and run schools. On a more pragmatic level, some states have developed mentor programs that give a few experienced teachers a minor role in helping with the induction of beginners. Such tasks provide minor support to administrators without seriously challenging the status quo.

The Academy example suggests that teachers can play a much more active role in curriculum and training than has typically been considered and that doing so can have substantial advantages for school districts. Paying teachers for such work allows a district to buy more time without making permanent commitments to additional people and at the same time incorporates additional teacher input into decisions made in this area. Yet central office staff still make two important contributions. They can see the overall district picture better than teachers if they take advantage of their access to all buildings and all faculties, and they have more time to follow events outside the district and identify important trends, ideas, and resources.

This kind of organic approach with shared responsibility across different roles is an effective way to organize the variety of functions that are needed to support classroom instruction. It is congruent with the professional ideal; yet it avoids the antiadministrative tone of parts of the Carnegie Forum report (1986), which implies that administrators are simply dispensable.

THE CHALLENGES TO BE MET

If school systems are to be redesigned, a number of challenges must be met. In some respects, these challenges are political because any serious redesign will come out of the interaction among state policy makers and the public, teachers, and administrators. The various role groups who must work together to professionalize teaching will have to rethink some basic assumptions. We begin with an issue that cuts across these groups—accountability—and then turn to problems that are more specific to teachers, state and local government, and school administrators.

Accountability

In recent decades, the value of increasing accountability has come to seem self-evident. Yet there is a serious dilemma lurking beneath the surface that has not been adequately addressed. McDonnell (1989) treats this as a choice between accountability to the public and accountability to the profession. Accountability to the public requires that educators offer proof to the larger community that students are learning and the tax money allocated to schools is well spent. As the nation has become more suspicious of government, pressure for public accountability has increased. The horse trade proposed by the National Governor's Association (1986)—stipulating that educators could have more say over how schools are run if they would be more accountable for results—is an illustration of this view.

It appears that the public supports job differentiation for teachers because it seems to provide an additional form of accountability. Suspicious of all public employees, voters resent paying the same salary to people who may be performing badly as is paid to those who are performing well. Whatever its actual problems as a strategy for motivating teachers, merit-based job differentiation is viewed as a way to ensure that more money goes to those who, it is believed, can be shown to deserve it. Creation of seemingly objective performance criteria and the use of nonteachers to inspect teachers' work are seen as ways to ensure that the public purse is not wasted. This thinking contributed to the passage of merit-pay and master-teacher programs in the states we studied and others as well. Such thinking leads to the bureaucratic redesign of teaching. This could include performance criteria that consist of assessments like Madeline Hunter's behavior-scripting techniques, student and teacher test scores, student and teacher attendance records, and other measurable and quantifiable indicators.

Accountability to the profession is based on two premises discussed earlier: that professionals are keepers of important values—in this case the welfare of children—and that only they have the knowledge to determine if those values are being adequately met. From this perspective, educators must show the value of their work to other educators, not to the public. In the mid-1980s, academic and professional reformers' proposals to redesign teaching emphasized professional accountability (Carnegie Forum 1986; Holmes Group 1986), which may be a factor contributing to researchers' growing interest in collegiality among teachers (e.g., Rosenholtz 1989). However, it is not a concept with great appeal to legislators, board members, or even some school administrators.

Accountability in professional redesign can also include a developmental approach, wherein teachers formulate a classroom program in collaboration with administrators, lead teachers, and other teachers, then work toward implementing the program. Weaknesses and strengths are discussed openly, and strategies are developed to address and remedy weaknesses and maximize strengths. Teachers work together to help each other identify and implement better classroom practice. The accountability is part of the fabric of the process, for the teacher's performance is continuously under consideration and development.

The research conducted here and most past work on teacher motivation does not speak to the public insecurity about education, which creates the demand for stronger public accountability measures. Yet it does suggest that insofar as those measures employ merit-based assessments of teacher performance, they will actually undermine the goals they are adopted to achieve. If the kind of professionalism we are advocating is to thrive and expand, at least two steps must be taken. The first, and most important, is beyond the scope of this book. Ways will have to be found to meet legitimate demands for public accountability that do not require detailed and counterproductive bureaucratic monitoring of teachers. These are likely to include finding more effective ways to monitor student progress, toughening licensing requirements to ensure that the teaching force generally becomes more talented (a step that will also enhance teacher professionalism), and generally improving educational performance.

The second step requires developing more effective professional accountability mechanisms and educating the public about their nature and effectiveness. This is likely to be a difficult step because such mechanisms are now underdeveloped. Any significant progress will require rethinking the role of professional associations in schools.

Teachers and Their Associations

Recommendations for educational improvement are typically made to policy makers and school administrators who are seen as the prime movers, but the serious professionalization of teaching will require action by teachers themselves. Among these districts, the more active teachers were in planning, the greater the professionalism that resulted. In Academy, the district that professionalized the most, teachers successfully resisted administrative proposals that were taking the district in a distinctly bureaucratic direction. In other districts as well, teachers, usually through their associations, played a major role in shaping redesign efforts (Johnson and Nelson 1987). Some of the most progressive restructuring efforts in the country have resulted from collaborative efforts between teachers' associations and school administrations (David 1989).

The challenge for teachers and their associations is to open up to new roles and responsibilities that they have avoided in the past. These new roles can have two advantages. As the evidence presented here suggests, they provide means to increase teacher motivation and effectiveness. At the same time, these very roles can provide the missing mechanisms for professional accountability.

The biggest problem that we observed in moving toward these roles was the teachers' contribution to selecting their peers for special positions in Academy. Teachers were more wary of the reviews they received from their peers than those from administrators because peer review had been used to provide malicious feedback on colleagues. Yet for professionalism to grow in education, teachers must take responsibility for such decisions and exercise it in a way that does no damage to their colleagues. Teacher selection of colleagues provides a way to differentiate jobs while avoiding the problems of merit-based appointment. Moreover, the whole idea that professionalism is based on the application of judgment in uncertain situations suggests that teachers are well placed to know how well their colleagues apply such judgment. Teacher involvement in selection for special positions is a logical extension of the idea that they participate in making decisions because of their special expertise. However, such involvement must be governed by norms of civility that are not always present today.

Teachers also oppose efforts to make permanent differentiations among their colleagues through nonrotating job-enlargement positions. Consensus on this point was overwhelming in Academy as it has been elsewhere (Malen and Hart 1987). Yet that stance constrains a development that has the potential to retain especially talented teachers, a recurring problem in education. Moreover, permanent job differentiation offers to such teachers growth opportunities that are staged to occur throughout their careers. Through the special training and development opportunities created, permanent job differentation can also extend the professional development opportunities for all teachers, including those not promoted, as was observed in Academy. A permanent cadre of teacher leaders and curriculum specialists could develop greater expertise and have even more to offer their colleagues than happens when positions rotate.

For teacher professionalism to advance, teachers and their associations will certainly have to take more responsibility for selecting colleagues for special positions and probably will need to accept more permanent differentiation among positions. While the national associations are beginning to explore such developments, there appear to be two barriers. The first is the norms of equity that currently exist among teachers. These are based on the assumption that all colleagues are roughly equally competent (both to teach and to handle whatever new responsibilities become available) and the expectation that everyone should be treated equally. Difficulty in coming to agreement about what constitutes good teaching and specific examples of good teaching contributes to these norms.

The second problem is the predominant model for teachers' associations in this country, which is based on the experience of industrial unions (Mitchell 1989). In that model, employees give up control over work in order to protect job security and access to work. This model for organizing is also based on the assumption that all workers should be treated equally. Industrial unionism has been criticized as inappropriate for education, and it has been suggested that models from craft unions, professional associations, and artists' organizations be substituted. All of these encourage teachers to take more control of and responsibility for the work they do, and several provide a basis for acceptance of both permanent job differentiation and collegial selection.

Since there is a greater openness among teachers' associations to such developments than there has been in the past, it might be useful for them and associations of administrators and school boards to work together on developing approaches for involving teachers in the selection of colleagues for special positions. Such approaches might be based on those already used in higher education and law. These formal developments will be very important for developing procedures that are fair, effective in selecting the right people, and legitimate to teachers and the public. However, even with the best-designed systems, choosing among individuals for special rewards is stressful. Insofar as professionalism is enhanced by such differentiation—and it is—the norms of teaching will have to change to accept such stress.

State and Local Government

While professionalism requires teachers to accept greater differentiation of roles and responsibility for selecting people to those roles, it also depends on increased public support. The kind of professionalism that we have seen here will need both additional financial support and a degree of policy stability that programs to redesign teaching have not yet experienced. Two kinds of financial support are needed.

The first is support for job differentiation itself. While this study corroborates past research, pointing out the drawbacks to financial incentives for teachers, it goes beyond that literature to show how money is important for motivating teachers. Money buys the time needed for training and curriculum development. A few districts might find the financial resources needed to buy such time by reducing the size of the central office staff, which currently provides such services. Since training and development have typically been underfunded, however, new money will usually be necessary. Most additional funds for those purposes should go to special positions to be filled by teachers. Without enough support to make those positions financially attractive, the training and curriculum development work needed to improve teaching and teacher motivation will not happen.

Money will also be needed for basic salary support. In many places, policy makers are using job differentiation as a substitute for across-the-board salary increases. That does not work. Schlechty (1989) points out that rewards must be provided for sustained high-quality performance, heroic efforts, and continuous performance that meets expectations, as well as for occasional special efforts. This means that all teachers should be adequately paid. For that reason, he argues that until the average teacher's salary equals that of the average college graduate's, efforts to provide differential rewards to teachers will cause morale problems. Both Mossville and Academy operated in states that funded schools and teacher salaries well below national averages, and that affected how teachers looked at the special financial rewards available to them. While the money was welcomed, there was also resentment that teachers had to do something special in order to make what they considered to be an adequate salary.

Basic salary support is needed for another reason. When regular salaries are higher, more talented people can be recruited as teachers. While job differentiation can improve the performance of people who become teachers, results will be better if one begins with a more talented base.

There is a catch-22 about these financial proposals. The public is unwilling to put more money into schools until better performance can be assured. Yet, better performance will not come about until a greater investment is made.

Financial support alone is not enough, however. To plan, both individuals and organizations need stability. Moreover, it is disruptive to devote a great deal of time fighting off threats to what is considered to be a good system. This was apparent in Mossville, where the local program was part of a state pilot program. While the pilot was five years long, our observations were conducted near the end of that period, when considerable attention was turning to the question of whether the state would allow the program to continue. Academy's program was based on legislation passed through a compromise that no one liked. Each year the legislature modified the law, and each year the district had to adjust its program in response to those changes. This was discouraging to administrators and teachers on the task force who spent a great deal of time either trying to maintain what they considered to be crucial parts of the legislation or making changes. It also created a context where rank-and-file teachers knew they could not count on the continued existence of the program. That discouraged long-term planning to achieve higher positions. Instability undermines programs by deterring long-term investments in them.

Administrative Leadership

While one of our discoveries is the decisive role of teachers in professionalizing teaching, we still find that administrative leadership is crucial. In all three districts, superintendents were catalysts for change. They either created a context in which others could initiate programs to redesign teaching or were directly involved themselves. Just as important, they maintained appropriate pressure and direction on the process, keeping it moving when obstacles or inertia threatened to slow or stop it. On the other hand, it was also clear that superintendents who tried to overcontrol the development of such programs paid a price in terms of ongoing resistance or dismissal.

Moreover, administrative openness to teacher influence certainly facilitated the exercise of that influence. The fact that Academy's superintendent was willing to work with teachers permitted the collaborative design of that program. Robert Hardwick's vacillation on teachers' influence in Hill City kept teachers from achieving their own goals and discouraged them from working on his. The kind of organic relationship between teachers and administrators that a professional model implies is undermined by the ongoing, unresolved conflicts that result from administrative opposition to teacher influence and the resulting teacher opposition to administrative agendas. Thus, an important leadership task is to set in motion the redesign process and establish a context in which teachers can have substantial influence.

Yet a process vision that incorporates teachers when decisions are made can conflict with the superintendent's own substantive reform vision. This was most apparent in Hill City, where teachers opposed the superintendent's ideas based on Sizer's thinking as discussed in his Essential Schools literature. It also occurred in Academy, where the superintendent sacrificed his interest in linking salary increases to merit in response to strong teacher preferences.

More is at stake here than the superintendent simply prevailing. A superintendent's substantive vision for educational reform is very useful in ensuring that redesign efforts will actually improve teaching. This became apparent in conversations with people knowledgeable about the policies that Mossville and Academy used to change teaching. Other districts in the same states that did not do as well tended to distribute resources so widely among teachers that they provided benefits to individuals without improving the quality of teaching. Without some kind of vision of what improved teaching should be, and determination to see it implemented, redesign programs can turn into the kind of giveaways that concern the public.

The dilemma here is how to incorporate teachers into the decision-making process while still ensuring that the resulting program is educationally sound. Here it is useful to return to Academy. In that district, both superintendents had a broad substantive vision that allowed for considerable teacher and principal initiative as long as a case could be made showing how specific proposals would support instruction. In many areas, both superintendents were executive champions who supported the initiatives of others rather than product champions with specific innovations to promote. At the same time they constantly returned to the importance of curriculum and instruction and assessed new ideas in terms of their contribution to that broad aim.

This mixed strategy of setting broad targets and encouraging individual initiative is not without problems. It is not particularly satisfying to those promoting a very specific substantive vision. The projects that result are likely to be diverse, even diffuse, as happened in Academy. Progress is likely to be slow just because people initiate such a range of ideas. Yet it has clear advantages. If done right, it does lead to a slow, steady progress to which participants become committed. Thus the results are more likely to last. This strategy also avoids the confusion and self-defeating conflicts that occurred in Hill City and the stalemate and unproductive animosities of Mossville. Moreover, it does not prevent central administrators from initiating their own specific programs and shaping the ideas of others toward a broader set of goals. What happens is centrally initiated efforts reflect the input of others and coexist with programs initiated from other sources.

FINAL THOUGHTS

This book illustrates some of the various attempts to redesign teaching. While not everything called "teacher professionalization" really is such, we believe that changes supporting true professionalization are an important part of a complete program for reforming our schools. True professionalization includes job enlargement and incorporation of teachers into a broader variety of internal decisions, always in ways that promote improved instruction.

This book also illustrates the difficulty of achieving such changes. Though considered trendsetters in their states, the districts we observed did not change the basic structure of the classroom or the formal educational process. For the reforms we advocate to take place, policy makers will have to view teachers as professionals who deserve truly adequate compensation, and provide more funding and a stable policy environment; teachers and their associations must show an increased willingness to accept professional responsibilities in their schools; and administrators must balance needs to stimulate improvement and set broad direction with needs to accept influence from a wider range of sources, and support the ideas of others as well as their own.

APPENDIX A: RESEARCH METHODS

AS AN ACKNOWLEDGMENT that qualitative studies ought to follow careful methodological techniques, this appendix provides an accounting of the procedures and processes of the study by explaining the conceptual frameworks that shaped the study and how they changed, the selection criteria and process that produced the sample, the data collection, development of the cross-site analysis, and generation of the cases.

The original problem was to understand strategic use of state reform as described in Fuhrman, Clune, and Elmore (1989) in their preliminary report on the Center for Policy Research in Education study of state reform and local response. This federally funded study tracked state-initiated education policies in six states, then documented responses to those policies in twenty-four local districts. The catalyst for the study discussed in this book was the phenomenon of active district responses when the literature suggested that none should be expected. These responses took three forms: programs that went beyond state requirements, programs implemented in anticipation of state requirements, and programs that integrated state requirements into local plans.

For the purposes of studying the phenomenon of active user districts, we developed a conceptual framework about how local will and capacity to change might affect use of state reform. This framework was content-free. The initial framework is summarized in Firestone (1989).

An important and fundamental change in direction occurred midway through the data collection as 1) it became increasingly clear that ruling coalitions in these three districts were not conclusively apparent and not as significant in the adoption and implementation of state programs as it was originally anticipated they would be; and 2) it also became clear that important changes were happening in the structure of teachers' work with attendant changes in teachers' ideas about their work in these districts, a development of considerable significance. This shift in the orienting concept of the study changed the focus of the data-collection protocol and the analysis strategy. Though district context and function continued to be a focus of data collection and ongoing analysis, the design of teacher's work and the way in which state and local policies shape that work and the consequences of such changes became more central to the study.

A qualitative case study approach was chosen because such an approach offers important advantages over quantitative methods for studying district function. Miles and Huberman (1984) offer an excellent justification for the use of qualitative rather than quantitative methods when doing education research.

> Qualitative data are attractive. They are a source of well-grounded, rich descriptions and explanations of processes occurring in local contexts. With qualitative data one can preserve chronological flow, assess local causality, and derive fruitful explanations. Then too, qualitative data are more likely to lead to serendipitous findings and to new theoretical integrations. They help researchers go beyond initial preconceptions and frameworks. (15)

The strength of qualitative case-study research methodologies is that they are sensitive to issues arising in the field and flexible enough to allow such a change in focus without compromising the integrity of the study. Whereas quantitative studies can describe who, what, where, and when, qualitative studies can tell how and why, and are superior to quantitative studies in developing explanatory power. Yin (1984) explains that when it is necessary to answer how and why questions, a case study offers the "operational links," the history needed to understand at a level not offered by frequencies and incidences.

Traditional conventions of qualitative methods warn against creating frameworks for data collection because of the belief that pre-existing frameworks will limit discovery and proscribe informational "side streets" that might lead researchers in new or different directions. However, in the event that more than one site is being studied, the need for future comparisons makes a preliminary framework for collecting data desirable. Having such a structure allows researchers to identify comparable structures and perform cross-case analysis.

Individual school districts are unique in the many ways they conduct business, but because they attempt to solve many of the same problems, analogous structures evolve across different districts. Such discrete components as central administrations, district and school administrators, teachers, students, classrooms, and so on, and organizational relationships such as those with state educational administrations, state policies, community influence and issues, and funding issues may be found in some form in almost every operating district in the country. Identifying those analogous structures in advance for all study districts can, in fact, allow researchers to identify dissimilarities, unique practices, and individual district solutions, and perceive contrasts and comparisons more efficiently.

Miles and Huberman (1984) state that

> Using the same instruments [for several studies] is the only way we can converse across studies. Otherwise, the work will be noncomparable, except in an overly global, meta-analytic form. So we need common instruments to build theory. (43)

Nevertheless, it is important for researchers to maintain attention to the possibility that prior instrumentation may limit discovery. Miles and Huberman give a strong warning:

> Predesigned and structured instruments blind the researcher to the site. If the most important phenomena or underlying constructs at work in the field are not in the instruments, they will be overlooked or misrepresented. (42)

In this study, a rather elaborate site guide (Appendix B) oriented the data collection intially. However, as we got to know more about each site, we followed leads about particular events and phenomena to be sure we well understood the particulars. Moreover, as our conceptual interests shifted to the redesign of teacher work, we attended more to the specifics of each district's reform and its consequences.

CONCEPTUAL FRAMEWORK

Considerable attention was given to the literatures of change (Corbett, Dawson, and Firestone 1984; Miles 1964; Cuban 1984; Hall

1987a, b; Berman and McLaughlin 1975; etc.); administrative and community leadership and politics (Rosenthal 1969; Burlingame 1988; Carlson 1972; etc.); and at the point that the focus of the inquiry took a different direction, the literature of teaching and restructuring (David 1989; Cohen 1990; Peterson and Commeaux 1989; Little 1982; Lortie 1975; Darling-Hammond 1984; McDonnell 1989, etc.).

The major concepts emphasized were problems of change, interactions among and around power elites, history and conditions of the district, succession of superintendents, the vision of the administration and its ability to transmit that vision, state/local relations, implementation strategies and management including the mobilization of district personnel, resource allocation and problem solving, and specific program structure.

PLANNING AND COLLABORATION

Researchers consulted extensively during the planning stages of the study to absorb the literature, and determine goals, conceptual framework, strategies, and methods. All protocols were developed collaboratively and a study consultant advised researchers with respect to appropriateness and organization. Both authors visited all districts. We conducted regular feedback sessions concerning structure, strategies, findings, and analysis at all stages of the study. This intensive consultation was pursued to ensure that both carried into the fieldwork essentially the same grounding in literature and understanding of methods and issues and that analytical issues could be fully addressed.

SITE SELECTION

The original focus of the study was the examination of districts that actively implemented state reforms. Therefore, we sought out such districts. While much could have been learned by selecting parallel districts that were not implementing state reforms, the desire to maximize limited funds dictated discovering a great deal about three user districts rather than a superficial amount about six active and nonactive districts. The ensuing change of focus may not have been possible with a different mix of study districts.

Fifty districts were considered for inclusion in the study, including the twenty-three that were part of the original Center for Policy Research in Education study of reform in six states. The candidates that were not part of the CPRE study were nominated during discovery conversations with educators in state offices, universities, state professional organizations, and other educators familiar with districts in their particular states. The criterion for selection was that the districts be active users of state teacher or curriculum reforms. That is, they either met and exceeded the state requirements, anticipated the state's requirements and preceded state programs with appropriate programs, or creatively incorporated the state's requirements into the local agenda.

Districts were also chosen based on their size and demography. Small districts were considered to be easier to manage and change and so not as useful for understanding change in larger districts, which usually have more problems and exigencies. On the other hand, it was anticipated that overly large, especially urban, districts would present problems in separating factors important to the change process from factors important to other district affairs, and in understanding the operation and context of the district in twenty days. As CPRE researchers discovered in studying large urban districts in the original study, the problems schools confronted in tending to the obstacles faced by poor urban students far overshadowed the importance of state reforms aimed at a broader range of diverse districts (Firestone et al. 1991).

Districts where students were typically from high socioeconomic status families were also eliminated from consideration because the resources available to those districts give them advantages not available to most districts. The researchers decided that districts with a broad mix of socioeconomic groups would offer the most instructive and persuasive data.

The superintendents of promising candidate districts were contacted to determine the districts' availability for the study and their appropriateness for inclusion. Local and state program documents were collected for many of them.

Of the three districts originally chosen, one dropped out before data collection could begin because the contract of the superintendent who had originally agreed to cooperate in the study was not renewed. By that time the original conceptual framework had been modified to focus on policies that redesigned teachers' work; this change created a new criterion for selection.

Hill City was selected for the study for three reasons:

1) It piloted its state's induction program, a program to assist first-year teachers in making the transition into the classroom by assign-

ing an experienced teacher who was to act as a guide to the new teacher.
2) It had indicated its intention to use its new shared governance program as a forum to develop its proposals for compliance with the state-mandated staff development act, which required districts to provide continuing professional development for teachers who had not completed master's degrees.
3) The district also planned to conform to state requirements for staff evaluation through its local program.

Mossville was selected for the study because:

1) It had lobbied the state to be a pilot in the teacher development program, which would give teachers increased pay for meeting evaluation criteria considered to indicate teaching excellence.
2) Its personnel director had been influential in the state development of the program.
3) It had fully and aggressively implemented the program, using all resources to their maximum.
4) Its outcomes were among the best of the pilot districts.

Academy was selected because:

1) It had fully and aggressively implemented the state program setting general guidelines for increased teacher pay and professional recognition but which allowed districts considerable leeway in deciding how to design its participation.
2) It had used the state program to develop its own local curriculum and instructional programs.
3) It had a reputation in the state as a lighthouse district.

DATA COLLECTION

Several steps were taken in designing the data collection. The most important was the site guide to organize and structure the fieldwork (Appendix B). First-visit interview protocols were developed and site-visit arrangements were made to coincide with as many important and pertinent district functions as possible. Information about the district and its policy were gathered in advance to orient the data collection.

Interviews

The central data collection activity was interviews. Hochschild (1981) argues that 1) intensive interviews are a device for generating insights, anomalies, and paradoxes that might not otherwise be noticed. They also 2) "fill in gaps" left by opinion polls and provide data that surveys cannot provide. In fact, Hochschild concludes that whereas poll takers must infer links between variables, interviewers can induce respondents to provide the links. 3) Finally, intensive interviews can generate findings that surveys cannot. Surveys may be able to discover correlations and variance in dimensions, but interviews can explain how and why the dimensions vary.

First-visit interviews were conducted using a broad-based protocol designed to discover district history and environment, general program structure, and key personnel. Original respondents were chosen by role from key district and program positions. Questions were structured to allow open-ended responses. Interviewers used probes and followed respondent leads as appropriate, while maintaining a general focus on the program central to study interest. Second-visit interview protocols were developed in response to first-visit data to flesh out understanding of program adoption, implementation, function, attitudes and outcomes, and to discover nuances of district/program interaction. Respondents were chosen by role from key school positions, and program participants and nonparticipants. In addition, follow-up interviews were often conducted with respondents from the first round.

The authors visited all three districts and spent a total of twenty person days in each district. As well, a number of telephone interviews were conducted. We were joined by two others on selected occasions. Interviews were conducted with 164 people from every area of district function: board members, district office administrators, building administrators, teachers, and federation and association officials (breakdowns for individual district roles are included in Table A–1). Elementary and secondary school principals and teachers were contacted—more than one per district where possible. In addition, parents, journalists, community leaders, state respondents, and others relevant to district program, history, or function were interviewed, some twice. In all, 242 interviews and meetings were transcribed and entered into the data base.

Respondents were chosen in various ways:

1) Role in the district or school: superintendent, all board members, all cabinet members, principal and teacher association presidents, PTA presidents.

TABLE A–1
Interviews Conducted

	Hill City	Mossville	Academy
Board Members Interviewed	9[1]	9[2]	7[3]
District Administrators Interviewed	6	10	9
Principals Interviewed	6	12	7
Teachers Interviewed	26	21	43
Teachers' Association Officials*	4[4]	2[5]	4[6]

[1] All 9 active members.

[2] All 7 active and 2 former members.

[3] All 5 active and 2 former members.

[4] Regional UniServ representative, past and present presidents, and president-elect.

[5] Presidents of both the NEA and AFT locals.

[6] President and president-elect, 2 former presidents (one the state NEA director).

* Numbers for association officials are also included with the numbers for teachers interviewed. They have not been added to the interview totals but are included for purposes of clarity.

2) Role in the community, such as education reporter or city manager.

3) Role with respect to the program: people with official implementation roles; selected to receive program positions; choosing not to participate in the program; receiving services from those in the program.

4) Nomination by other respondents in response to researcher requests.

   a. Principals were nominated by district administrators, teachers by building administrators to fulfill researcher criteria of broad coverage of program roles mentioned above.

   b. Others named in response to researcher requests during interviews for those important to the program.

5) People whose names were mentioned in interviews or in documents who appeared to be significant in some respect. For example, the person who brought the school desegregation suit in

Mossville, retired board members, a teacher or principal who was turned down or brought grievance, principals who were resistant, past presidents of the teachers' representative group, the UniServ representative, and so on.

Interviews consisted of approximately one-hour sessions. The interviews were open enough to allow for idiosyncratic responses and unanticipated revelations, but structured enough to allow comparisons among respondents.

Document Collection

In addition to program descriptions, the researchers also collected copies of the state policies, state reports on district programs and performance, state statistical reports of the districts, board meeting minutes and related documents, district demographics, newspaper accounts of district history and function, correspondence between the state and the district about program adoption and implementation, testing and other outcome statistics, informational newsletters, brochures, district histories, and other documents pertinent to specific districts such as a book explaining the Mossville school desegregation suits. These documents were used to establish chronology, provide additional information, confirm or disprove interview data, develop an understanding of events or programs, learn about key people, and otherwise enrich the knowledge base about the districts.

Surveys

In two of the districts a survey of state perceptions and attitudes was available. In Mossville the state commissioned a survey of teacher opinions of the program in all pilot districts. Item means were available for each district. In Academy the superintendent persuaded the researchers to conduct a survey similar to a state survey of teacher opinion. That state survey had used a sample that permitted characterizing district-to-district variation, so no data was available at the district level. It was not possible to conduct tests of statistical significance on differences between the aggregated state data and the local survey results. Financial and other constraints did not allow for the administration of a survey in Hill City.

The Academy attitude survey questionnaires were distributed by district officials familiar with research methods, who then collected the sealed questionnaires and forwarded them to the researchers. Individual respondents were given unmarked questionnaires and envelopes to ensure confidentiality. The questionnaire consisted of a series of statements about the CEP program to be ranked on a Likert-type scale with values from 1 to 5, where 1 indicated strong disagreement, 5 indicated strong agreement, and 3 indicated neutrality. Also included were demographic questions. A copy of the questionnaire, properly edited to maintain confidentiality, is included in Appendix C. Five hundred four people responded to the survey, a response rate of 70 percent. Of the respondents, 464 were teachers, a response rate of 73 percent. The survey data were analyzed using SPSS-PC version 3.0.

ANALYSIS

Interviews were analyzed using Ethnograph version 2.0, a software package allowing text data to be searched using coding schemes developed by researchers. Segments of text could be marked with more than one code, allowing flexibility in assigning codes, finding coded segments that occurred together, and using other analytic strategies. Codes were developed collaboratively by the primary researchers, and in consultation with others familiar with generic district function from other perspectives. Each primary researcher coded the other's interviews, and coding was checked for interrater agreement.

Two strategies were used in developing the cases. The first was an historical accounting of the program and of important events and changes in the district. These histories were analyzed for their contribution to the way the programs developed, and their relationship with the programs. The second strategy was the discovery of themes and patterns within the district and the program. Relationships—political, professional, social, and economic—among and within various groups in the district and between the district and the community and the state were examined. Organizational behavior and structures, leadership methods and strategies, and curricular particularities as manifested in each of the districts were assessed. All of these dimensions were analyzed as they were integrated with and influenced the shape of the program. Commonalities and dissimilarities across districts were sought to develop cross-case patterns.

Written reports were submitted to each district on completion of analysis, and response was actively solicited. Feedback sessions were conducted with district officials, board members, principals, teachers, and union officials. These were valuable for clarifying mistaken ideas, confirming accurate ones, and updating information. In one of the three districts, the relationship between the district and the teachers had deteriorated, and significant additions were made to the report.

APPENDIX B: SITE VISIT GUIDE

TABLE OF CONTENTS

I.	What Are the Conditions in the School District?	231
	District Profile—Protocol I	231
II.	What Are the Special Interests of This District?	232
	Special Interests—Protocol II	232
III.	Who Is in the Dominant Coalition?	234
	Identify Dominant Coalition—Protocol III	234
IV.	How Was the Dominant Coalition Formed?	236
	Dominant Coalition History—Protocol IV	236
V.	How Is the Dominant Coalition Defined?	237
	Dominant Coalition Dynamics—Protocol V	237
VI.	What Is the Propensity to Action of the Dominant Coalition?	238
	Propensity to Action—Protocol VI	239
VII.	What Are the Policies Involved?	239
VIII.	What Is the Fit Between the Policies and Local Goals and Objectives?	239

Fit Between Policy and Local Agenda—Protocol VIII   240

IX.   What Are the Activities to Accomplish
      District Personnel Mobilization?   240

      District Personnel Mobilization—Protocol IX   241

X.   What Functions and Linkages Are
      Being Planned and Formed?   241

      Functions and Linkages—Protocol X   242

XI–XIII. School-Site Implementation   244

XI.   What Is the School Implementation Process?   244

      School Implementation—Protocol XI   245

XII. What Are Conditions at the School?   245

      Conditions at the School—Protocol XII   245

XIII. What Are the Outcomes of Reform?   246

      Outcomes of Reform—Protocol XIII   246

XIV. What Are the Indications of Active Use?   247

      Indications of Active Use—Protocol XIV   247

I. WHAT ARE THE CONDITIONS IN THE SCHOOL DISTRICT?

Using Reform Research Protocols

School district conditions are a combination of a number of elements of district life, including demographics, networks, shared values, non-school community factors, and relationships between and among various "layers" of school people. Demographics give a quantitative district profile, but do not give any indication of the kinds of color and texture that make every district unique.

Much of the color and texture will become vivid through thorough interviewing, and through reading board minutes, newspaper files, and district histories. Other important resources are newspaper education reporters, who often have an outsiders' view of district operations, and who frequently have spent time in schools and at meetings. Meetings will also be important resources for discovering how the district conducts its official business, and for observing how people interact. In addition, driving around the community will be greatly revealing.

Demographic information should be collected from whatever available sources exist. Some districts have much of this information locally, others do not. Possible contacts include the management-information-systems person, the Chapter I office, the free- or reduced-price lunch eligibility lists, state department office, the state or local NEA or AFT chapter.

State information should be available from the state office or from publications. It is important to have state as well as local information to indicate the relative strength and standing of the district.

It is desirable to obtain the demographic information over the telephone before visiting the district, to construct context and conserve expensive field time for data collection that cannot be accomplished on the telephone. The following chart is helpful for collecting demographic information. Other conditions differ from district to district, so it is important to consider them as an important part of interviews with school people.

DISTRICT PROFILE—PROTOCOL I

	District I	*District II*	*State Average*
Population			
School enrollment			
Number of schools			
Elementary			

	District I	District II	State Average
Number of schools *(continued)*			
Middle or JHS			
High school			
AVTS			
Alternatives			
Minority percentage			
Per pupil expenditure			
Budget			
Number of teachers			
Average salary			
Average tenure			
Average education			
District capacity			
Tax base			
Market value			
Income			
Rate of growth			
Percent of students below poverty line			
Percent of students in Chapter I programs			
Dropout rate			
Percent of students enrolling in postsecondary programs			
College or university			
Vocational or technical			

II.   WHAT ARE THE SPECIAL INTERESTS OF THIS DISTRICT?
       SPECIAL INTERESTS—PROTOCOL II

Outside Pressures

Special interest groups have the express purpose of putting pressure on legislative bodies to implement some or all of their agenda. In the case of a school district, the legislative body is obviously the school board. The board business and behavior may be influenced by outside pressures, therefore it is important to know not only who the groups are, but how they affect what happens. Some of the questions to be asked are:

1. What groups or individuals become involved in school district decisions? on a regular basis? with specific issues? Giving examples might be helpful to spur people's thoughts: teachers' union or representative group; parent groups; community groups; business groups; religious groups.
2. What other activities do the groups participate in or direct?
3. Whom do the groups represent?
4. Are there shifting allegiances, or irregular patterns of participation? Are there groups which collaborate? Do certain persons or groups appear to have more access to the district leadership group's decision-making process?

Power

Some groups have more power than others to realize results from the pressure they bring to bear. Many times this imbalance will become evident during interviews and document analysis. However, clarification may be necessary. Here are some questions that will highlight the strong performers.

1. Does district leadership challenge or collaborate with the pressure group?
2. Does the group generally prevail; are they on the "right" side of the decision?
3. When does this group have the most control over decisions?

Mobility

1. How quickly can the group respond to the emergence of new issues?

Interests

The group's interests determine which fights will be chosen. Its power may depend as much on what it fights as how it fights. While its activities will probably surface in interviews and document analysis, specific questions to clarify its behavior would include:

1. What does the group mobilize for?
2. Are there particular decisions they are more likely to become involved in?

The activities of special interests will be emerging from newspaper articles and discussions with respondents about district leadership. Specific people to speak with would include upper-tier district personnel, board members, active community members, and teacher representatives who interact with the board.

These interests will include such actors as teachers' organizations, local businesses, parents, community and political interests, and others specific to the district. This set of questions is designed to identify the special interests, and to reveal their constituency bases and the scope of their power base; the nature of their participation in the decision making; the extent and nature of their influence; the evidence of that influence; the ability to mobilize and become effectual; and the variety of interests each is involved in.

III. WHO IS IN THE DOMINANT COALITION?

Determining who belongs to the dominant coalition, or district leadership, is an important precursor to analyzing the role and behavior of the coalition. After obtaining the final permission of the superintendent, and discussing the overview of the study with him or her, probe for the person who has the most inside information or is the most knowledgeable about the district, and contact that person over the telephone.

Also, contact local political activists interested in education, such as the League of Women Voters; include questions about who comprises district leadership in the interview of the newspaper reporter.

IDENTIFY DOMINANT COALITION—PROTOCOL III

District Leadership

Who are the opinion leaders in the school district?

Probe: When district leadership is mentioned, whose name(s) come to your mind?

Mention such groups as the board, the superintendent's office, the district office as a whole, city government offices, etc.

Which people determine the most about what happens in the district?

Probe: Who makes most of the decisions regarding school district activities?

Location

Where are most of the school district decisions made?

Influence Factors

Does influence on decisions within the leadership group vary depending on the kind of decision being made?

    Probe: Curriculum decisions; finance decisions; district-level hiring; any other decisions.

Stability

Are the decision makers the same for current issues as they were for issues last year?

    Probe: Which players? If not, how do the players differ?

    Look for resignations, new appointments, etc.

Communication

How do you get your information about school district decisions?

    Is it necessary to seek out information, or is it readily available?

    Is it possible to attend meetings where important decisions are made?

Roles

What positions do the influential people hold? Within the district? Outside the district?

Range of Influence

In what kinds of decisions do these groups participate in the district:

Mayor's office

City Council

Mayors' or city legislative bodies' education groups—those people whose position (i.e., appointed by the mayor to be liaison with the school district, or city council committee) is involved in local educational decisions.

County or regional education administrative unit.

Degree of Influence

Are there issues that do not get raised, or get raised in a particular way because of the political or other views of these groups?

IV. HOW WAS THE DOMINANT COALITION FORMED?

Becoming familiar with the ways in which groups involved with school district decision making and activity organization come into being is important to understanding the political and social context in which school district decisions are made. The information about the formation of dominant coalition(s) will come from interviews, newspaper articles, and informal conversations. Particularly important, as for district conditions, is locating people who have lived and worked in the district for many years. Their answers will not only give important answers about how the dominant coalition was formed, but also put present activities in the context of historical events and trends.

The questions in this protocol are not well defined because histories are unique, anecdotal, and episodic. This information is contextual and does not define the group. Therefore Protocol IV is a guide that will assist in giving texture to description.

DOMINANT COALITION HISTORY—PROTOCOL IV

Establish a critical time in the history of the district, and question people about events which led up to that critical time and what has been happening since then. Look for these particular categories in their responses.

Formation

District leadership formation
Length of operation
Continuous operation
Times when it did not appear to be functioning
A self-conscious effort to create the group
Did one person pull the group together?
Some members already working together
Existing district leadership group
Did the new one replace or join the existing one?

Political Environment

Political environment at the time of district leadership group formation

New superintendent
New city/town leader
Particular issue around which people were mobilized

Community involvement

Strength and kind of mobilization

Governing Issues:

Financial crisis
New directives or requirements
Problem within the schools that required unusual attention
Upheaval within the community

V. HOW IS THE DOMINANT COALITION (DC) DEFINED?

Separate from the issue of who the DC is, and how the coalition was formed, is the issue of their behavior with respect to school district issues and business. In order to determine when and how they operate, it is necessary to speak with members of the coalition and with others who are close observers. As with most information about the roles and behaviors of involved people, some answers will be clear from watching the district operate. However, interviews will confirm, clarify, and sometimes reinterpret what appears obvious at first glance, and sometimes clarify enigmatic behaviors and situations. It will also allow researchers to discover subtle linkages with other cultural, social, and political groups that will probably not be apparent, or that people may not think about when they are discussing the district leadership.

DOMINANT COALITION DYNAMICS—PROTOCOL V

DC Member Operation and Interaction

What are relationships among the dominant coalition?

Friction or factions among the members?
Meetings outside of formal meetings?

What is the relationship of the DC with outside agencies, such as:

The state education department and board
The state legislature
The regional administrator
The local board
The community

School-site personnel
Professional representatives

Common and Divergent Interests

What are the goals and objectives of the leadership group?

What kinds of issues do they promote in their decisions?
What programs do they support?
What actions does the group take in arrangements with the teachers?
What positions do they support about students?
Which issues and/or objectives unite/divide the district leadership group? What would or has created a debate within the group?
Are final decisions consensual?

Coalition Roles

What do different members of district leadership group do?

As members of the group?
As members of other groups in the city?

How do those roles affect the decisions that are made?

VI. WHAT IS THE PROPENSITY TO ACTION OF THE DOMINANT COALITION

One of the important assumptions of this study is that a DC is active in district affairs, and will, depending on the fit of particular policies with general goals, implement or challenge a particular state policy. Study districts have been chosen because they are user districts. The objective of this protocol is to determine the interests of a particular dominant coalition, and whether that coalition is inclined to actively pursue its interests, either by incorporating state policies into its program, or by actively opposing them at some level.

As with other research questions and protocols, many of the answers will become at least partially clear before using the following protocol. DC history, newspaper and newsletter coverage, interview responses and observations will provide important background information. The following questions will clarify, confirm, and augment existing information. Members of the DC will be the respondents.

PROPENSITY TO ACTION—PROTOCOL VI

1) What issues and goals is the district addressing and working on right now?
2) How are central office and board personnel working on those issues and goals? What plans do they have for implementing changes?
3) Does the group you work with in the district share your goals for the district? Is it active in promoting the agenda? (This also gets to the common interests of the DC, but is important here to determine whether common action taken is self-consciously directed toward furthering mutual goals.)
4) What measures have been taken in the past to further district goals? Did you sometimes find it necessary to oppose state directives to protect those goals?
5) What measures are being taken now to align the district with those goals?
6) What measures do you intend to take to align the district with those goals?

VII.   WHAT ARE THE POLICIES INVOLVED?

Are the instruments mandates, incentives or other? School organization targets?

Sources of data:
    Legislation or state DOE regulation
    District consigliere
    District superintendent

Sample strategies:
    Obtain and read a copy of the policy
    Identify the segments of the policy
    Determine how the policy is intended to be implemented
    Discuss with the superintendent
    Discuss with the consigliere

VIII. WHAT IS THE FIT BETWEEN THE POLICIES
AND LOCAL GOALS AND OBJECTIVES?

There are two perspectives from which to view this question—the dominant coalition's, and the researchers'. Whereas to the researchers the policy may look very similar to particular coalition goals and objectives, which will be reflected in the coalition interests, the coalition may hold different ideas, particularly with respect to context and intent. Therefore it is necessary to determine the apparent fit by mapping the policies onto the coalition interests and the language of DC vision, and then determining with coalition members how that fit is seen at the local level.

Coalition interests have been identified in interviews and actions associated with Protocols V and VII. The language of the coalition vision identified in Protocol X. Researcher definition of the policies will require reading both policy and attendant analysis from state education department documents, then writing an outline. Interviews with members of the coalition will answer questions about whether and to what extent there is perceived fit.

It is important in the case of divergence between researcher and coalition member perceptions to determine the nature and scope of the divergence.

FIT BETWEEN POLICY AND LOCAL AGENDA—PROTOCOL VIII

What programs are particularly impacted by [legislation or DOE policy name]? Is the impact negative or positive?

How do the requirements of the legislation assist or inhibit the district in furthering its agenda?

Probe: Can you name specific parts of the policy that are particularly useful or that provide serious obstacles?

IX. WHAT ARE THE ACTIVITIES TO ACCOMPLISH DISTRICT PERSONNEL MOBILIZATION?

A cadre of district personnel will be mobilized to implement the adopted program. Their present roles, reputation for knowledge, level of accomplishment, and level of authority are all important in considering how appropriate their appointments are, and how well they can be expected to accomplish their new task. This information will also assist in determining what tasks that were previously tended by them will either go undone, be allocated to others, or have to be fitted into their schedule.

To get an answer to this question, discover who has been assigned to implementation, interview the assignee, observe him/her at work, and speak to his/her colleagues. The following matrix will provide a framework for organizing the answers as they become clear.

The matrix will be a grid with the names of mobilized personnel at the top of columns and notes about the questions in the appropriate box.

DISTRICT PERSONNEL MOBILIZATION—PROTOCOL IX

	Name:
What assignments given?	
Present/previous assignment overlap	
Relevant knowledge and experience	
Activity level Report to whom?	
Is reported to by whom?	
Reputation?	

X. WHAT FUNCTIONS AND LINKAGES ARE BEING PLANNED AND FORMED?

To determine the effectiveness of district planning and implementation strategies, discover whether a number of critical requirements are being met. While many interviews will be required, some of the answers may be inferred from observation, as is the case in Protocol IX. In the case of the language of the vision, direct description of the program by school-site implementation staff will be necessary. Inferences about interpretation are speculative at best.

The interviews will be conducted with school-site implementation staff.

FUNCTIONS AND LINKAGES—PROTOCOL X

What is the language of the vision?

1. How would you describe the program?
   Probe: Let the person speak more freely to allow development of nuances.
2. Is your vision of the program the same as the people who originated it? Please explain.
3. Who "owns" the program?
   a. Who is mainly responsible for organizing it?
   b. Who is the leader of the program?
4. How did you become involved?
5. Are you in agreement with the intentions of the program?

Are resources being provided?

1. What kinds of new or reallocated equipment, materials, time subsidies, guidelines, technical support, etc. can you access to assist in putting the program into place?
2. Are there any parts of your job that you are unable to do because of insufficient or inappropriate resources? Can you give examples?
3. What procedures do you have to follow to obtain resources?
   a. How much time does it require to follow the procedures?
   b. Are there ways to bypass the procedures in case of emergency?
4. What is the primary use of the resources?
   a. Do they help prepare students and/or teachers to participate in the program? In what ways?
   b. Do they directly facilitate participation of students and/or teachers in the program? In what ways?

Is encouragement being provided?

1. Do important district personnel come to visit?
2. Do you feel that anyone recognizes your participation?
   a. Does anyone tell you if you have done a good job?
   b. Does anyone help you if you are having a problem?
3. Do you feel that the recognition and/or assistance is sufficient?

What are the standard procedures?

1. Besides procedures for obtaining resources, which we spoke about before, what other rules, regulations, and procedures must you follow?
   a. Which were already in place?
   b. Which are specific to this program?
   c. Who is responsible for making sure they are followed?
   d. What effect do they have on your job?
      Probe: Look for time involvement, and the "job as it says it is to be done, and the job as I think it should be done."

Is there provision for monitoring?

1. Are there ways to determine the effects of the program?
   a. Are students taking/going to take tests, or have some other kind of assessment such as teacher evaluations, diagnostics, or other?
   b. Are there assessment forms for teachers to fill out?
2. What happens to these tests/assessments?
3. Do/will you receive a report of assessment outcomes?

Is there a system for handling disturbances?

1. What happens if you experience problems with the new program?
   Probe: For example, what can you do if you don't understand a new procedure, or if something isn't happening as it should? What resources do you have for handling these and other occurrences/emergencies?
2. What are your priorities in performing your job?

What is the system for control?

1. What expectations do the district and the program planning group have for you? How do they measure your performance?
2. How do you measure your own performance?
3. What has the most influence in motivating your work?
4. What will happen if you do not do your job? (here we are looking for evidence of one of Peterson's six means of control)

What are the upward influence channels?

1. Were members of your group involved in the decision-making process?

    a.   Were they asked about their ideas and opinions?
    b.   Were they invited to meetings?
2. What has the time involvement been?
    a.   Were members of your group given sufficient time to provide opinions and ideas?
    b.   Were the time requirements too great?
3. Were their ideas and opinions included in the program plan? Are you and they satisfied with that inclusion?

XI–XIII.   SCHOOL SITE IMPLEMENTATION

This section of the instrumentation is aimed at determining what, if anything, are the outcomes of the adoption and attempted implementation of the policy or policies. Have the schools truly made the program theirs? Does the school-level program look like the program adopted and promoted by the DC? Has the DC met the needs of the school-site implementors? What, if anything, has truly happened/is happening, to practice? How is it apparent? Will the program continue in the future because it has been merged and integrated into ongoing programs?

This section contains questions to be answered by direct interview of planners and practitioners, at both the district and school levels, and by observation of practitioners at the school level. Observation and interviews at the school will reveal implementation; interviews at the district level will determine whether the implementation aligns with district/DC intentions, and whether institutionalization has taken/is taking place. The particular interviewees at the school level will be members of the school implementation staff or of the upward-influence channels, and end users. District level interviewees will be the consigliere and other members of the mobilized personnel.

This section, as indicated above, includes research Questions XI through XIII. More questions will suggest themselves based on programs specific to the program and situation. This section of the instrumentation should be redesigned during and after the pilot.

XI.   WHAT IS THE SCHOOL IMPLEMENTATION PROCESS?
SCHOOL IMPLEMENTATION—PROTOCOL XI

Who has been involved?

1. Who is participating in the program planning here?
    a.   What groups do they represent?
    b.   What are they doing?

2. What decisions have been made?
3. What is the program that has resulted?
   a. What are its salient features?
   b. How is it to be introduced into the school and the classroom?
4. Who will be responsible for overseeing the introduction?
5. What are the expected outcomes?

How closely does the school model reflect the district model?
   (This section is particularly for district personnel.)

1. Does the program follow the requirements and design of the original district program? Are there any significant variations ?

What are the similarities of the school implementation to the district implementation?
   (The answer here may be inferred by a parallel chart displaying the important topics of program implementation, descriptions of the salient district implementation in one column, and parallel features of school-site implementation in the other.)

XII. WHAT ARE CONDITIONS AT THE SCHOOL?

Part of the answer to this will be apparent in the answers to the first four questions in Protocol X. However, it will also be informative to observe and ask what resources are already available. The condition of the school with respect to resources and support is an essential consideration in assessing how well the district program is being implemented, or in fact how able the school is to implement the district program. A preliminary to this assessment is a determination about the minimum resources necessary to implement. The researchers will have to make informed projections.

CONDITIONS AT THE SCHOOL—PROTOCOL XII

1. Does the school generally have the right equipment and sufficient supplies to maintain the everyday program?
   a. Do you often have to wonder whether you will get enough textbooks or paper, for example?
   b. Are you comfortable with the provision of resources that you have?
   c. Do you ever have to struggle with other teachers or staff members for resources?

    d. Are there announcements before the end of the year that resources are getting scarce?

2. When this program was instituted, did you consider that there would be enough resources for you to implement it? Have your original estimations been supported or proven incorrect?
3. Have you received enough information to understand what you are expected to accomplish?
4. Have you received enough materials and equipment to do the job you are being asked to do in this program?
5. Do you have access to more resources should you need them? information and technical support? materials and equipment?
6. If you could have your choice of more resources to do this job, what would you ask for?

XIII. WHAT ARE THE OUTCOMES OF REFORM?

The concern here is whether all of the activity and expenditures have resulted in any meaningful change in the way business is conducted. Have teachers begun to use the program in the classroom? Have administrators changed the way they work? Are staff involved in the spirit as well as the letter of the reform and are they more motivated in their work? Have attitudes been changed?

How can one tell? The answers will be clear partly from watching the staff at their work. Researchers will ask themselves questions about what they see as well as asking staff members who were not directly involved in the implementation planning about their work and their attitudes. It is more valid to ask staff members who were not involved in the implementation planning because the implementation is successful only if the practice and attitudes of classroom teachers and school administrators are changed. The implementation planners can be asked, but they have a vested interest in specific answers.

Some questions will be direct. Others will be indirect to tease out underlying concerns and avoid answers that the respondent thinks are expected or programmed complaining that does not truly reflect the present status.

OUTCOMES OF REFORM—PROTOCOL XIII

Has practice changed or is it changing?

Start out by having the person explain what he/she teaches, how he/she teaches, what his/her values are about teaching, etc. Let the respondent talk for about five minutes, if necessary, to get a feeling for attitude about the job, commitment to the job, etc. Then begin with the questions.

1. How has the program affected you?
   Probe: Give examples.
   a. What kinds of things have happened?
   b. Have you changed the way you think about things?
   c. Have you changed the way you do things?
2. Do you look forward to coming to work?
   a. How likely are you to call in sick?
   b. What are your thoughts when you think about work?
   c. Has this changed in the last year?
3. Are you trying to do what you think the program wants you to do? Are you succeeding?
4. Were there positive effects of the program on your teaching?
   Probe: Can you explain what they were?
5. Were there negative effects of the program on your teaching?
   Probe: Can you explain what they were?
6. Are you doing things differently than you did six months ago?
   Probe: The probe should be specifically tailored to the particular program that was implemented.

XIV. WHAT ARE THE INDICATIONS OF ACTIVE USE?

The district's status as an active user will be confirmed either by indications that the district's adoption of the policy predated and anticipated this specific state requirement, that the district went above and beyond the state requirements, and/or the district used creative ways to implement the requirements while remaining within the confines of the state policy.

A determination must be made about which criteria the district may meet, then obtain answers to the appropriate questions for the criteria.

INDICATIONS OF ACTIVE USE—PROTOCOL XIV

1. Predate the state policy
   a. When was the state policy passed?
   b. Was the district program being formulated at that time?
   c. What evidence exists that the district policy was anticipating the state policy?

2. Above and beyond the state policy
   a. What are the requirements of the state policy?
   b. What are the contents of the district program?
   c. Are the additional provisions of the district program in response to the state policy?
3. Creative implementation
   a. What are the requirements of the state policy?
   b. What are the contents of the district program?
   c. Describe the ways in which the district program meets the requirements of the state policy.

APPENDIX C: JOINT ACADEMY/CPRE STUDY
OF THE ACADEMY CAREER
ENHANCEMENT PROGRAM

ACADEMY CAREER ENHANCEMENT PROGRAM
    QUESTIONNAIRE

This questionnaire is a cooperative effort of the Academy School District and the Center for Policy Research (CPRE) at Rutgers University in New Jersey. It is intended to provide information that will:

a. Help the Academy schools decide if changes are needed in the career enhancement program and provide an assessment of the ladder's effectiveness, and
b. Help CPRE better understand how educators in Academy feel about the career enhancement program as part of a study of the district that is now going on.

THE ANSWERS PROVIDED BY EACH INDIVIDUAL WILL BE KEPT CONFIDENTIAL. No one will look at the individual questionnaires except CPRE staff in New Jersey, nor will there be reports about what individuals think. The idea is to learn about the views of educators throughout the district.

Please complete the questionnaire as honestly as possible. Then put the questionnaire in the attached envelope, seal the envelope, and give it to your Career Enhancement Program Task Force Representative. That person will forward all questionnaires from your building to CPRE in New Jersey.

[101–103]

PART I: The following questions ask about the Academy career enhancement program. Please *circle* the number that indicates *the extent to which you agree* with the statements below. Remember that we want to know what the career enhancement program means to you personally.

Strongly disagree 1	Disagree somewhat 2	Neither agree nor disagree 3	Agree somewhat 4	Strongly agree 5	Deck 1 [104]

The career enhancement program provides...

1.	Incentives for good teachers to stay in the teaching profession	1	2	3	4	5	[105]
2.	Teachers with income so they do not need to take second jobs	1	2	3	4	5	
3.	More frequent teacher evaluations	1	2	3	4	5	
4.	More effective teacher evaluations	1	2	3	4	5	
5.	A comprehensive curriculum for the district	1	2	3	4	5	
6.	A cooperative work environment for teachers	1	2	3	4	5	[110]

The career enhancement program gives me...

7.	Support so I can teach my students more effectively	1	2	3	4	5
8.	The chance to interact with other teachers	1	2	3	4	5
9.	The feeling that I am more professional in my work	1	2	3	4	5
10.	Additional income	1	2	3	4	5

The career enhancement program also...

11.	Results in better curriculum materials and training for my use	1	2	3	4	5	[115]
12.	Results in better training and support for beginning teachers	1	2	3	4	5	
13.	Takes time away from family and other pursuits	1	2	3	4	5	
14.	Limits my freedom in the classroom	1	2	3	4	5	
15.	Discourages teachers from sharing ideas with others	1	2	3	4	5	
16.	Creates fear of principal evaluations	1	2	3	4	5	[120]
17.	Creates fear of or discomfort with peer review	1	2	3	4	5	

Strongly disagree 1	Disagree somewhat 2	Neither agree nor disagree 3	Agree somewhat 4	Strongly agree 5	Deck 1 [104]

The career enhancement program also...

18. Creates jealousy because some teachers are designated better than others   1   2   3   4   5

19. Creates too much competition among teachers   1   2   3   4   5

20. Has improved the overall instructional program   1   2   3   4   5

21. Has improved attention to students' academic progress   1   2   3   4   5   [125]

22. Has improved teacher leadership opportunities   1   2   3   4   5

23. Has improved the morale of teachers   1   2   3   4   5

24. The career enhancement program should be continued in my district   1   2   3   4   5

PART II: The following questions ask you about the *separate parts* of the Academy career enhancement program

EXTENDED CONTRACT COMPONENT
(Additional days added to the contract year)

The Extended Contract Component effectively increases teacher opportunities to...

25. Plan for classroom instruction   1   2   3   4   5

26. Develop curriculum   1   2   3   4   5   [130]

27. .Participate in professional development activities   1   2   3   4   5

28. Take care of critical record-keeping and paperwork tasks   1   2   3   4   5

29. Provide better instruction to students   1   2   3   4   5

30. The Extended Contract Component effectively allows the district to accomplish important district-wide planning and management tasks   1   2   3   4   5

31. The Extended Contract Component should be continued   1   2   3   4   5   [135]

PERFORMANCE BONUS COMPONENT
(Monetary bonuses awarded for excellent teaching)

The Performance Bonus Component is an effective incentive for me to...

32. Remain in the teaching profession   1   2   3   4   5

33. Care more about the quality of my teaching   1   2   3   4   5

Strongly disagree 1	Disagree somewhat 2	Neither agree nor disagree 3	Agree somewhat 4	Strongly agree 5	Deck 1 [104]

The Performance Bonus Component is an effective incentive for me to...

34. Use my professional skills more effectively   1   2   3   4   5
35. Better serve the educational needs
of students   1   2   3   4   5

The Performance Bonus Component also encourages me to...

36. Hide ideas from other teachers   1   2   3   4   5   [140]
37. Worry that bonus decisions might be made
arbitrarily by the principal or teachers   1   2   3   4   5
38. The Performance Bonus has negligible
effects on teacher performance   1   2   3   4   5

The Performance Bonus Component effectively allows the district to...

39. Retain excellent teachers   1   2   3   4   5
40. Improve the morale of teachers
in the district   1   2   3   4   5
41. My district follows fair and reasonable
procedures in administering the
Performance Bonus Component   1   2   3   4   5   [145]
42. The Performance Bonus Component
should be continued   1   2   3   4   5

JOB ENLARGEMENT
(Specialist, grade and cluster leaders, and teacher leader positions)

The Job Enlargement Component is an effective incentive for me to...

43. Remain in the teaching profession   1   2   3   4   5
44. Care more about the quality of my teaching   1   2   3   4   5
45. Use my professional skills more effectively   1   2   3   4   5
46. Develop instructional materials for myself
and others   1   2   3   4   5   [150]
47. Share leadership responsibilities in
the school   1   2   3   4   5
48. Receive pay for work that, in the past,
I did for no pay   1   2   3   4   5

The Job Enlargement Component effectively allows the district to...

49. Carry out district-wide curriculum
planning and implementation more
effectively   1   2   3   4   5
50. Carry out other district educational goals   1   2   3   4   5

Strongly disagree	Disagree somewhat	Neither agree nor disagree	Agree somewhat	Strongly agree	Deck 1 [104]
1	2	3	4	5	

The Job Enlargement Component effectively allows the district to...

51. Retain excellent teachers   1   2   3   4   5   [155]
52. My district followed fair and reasonable procedures in administering the Job Enlargement Component   1   2   3   4   5
53. The Job Enlargement Component should be continued   1   2   3   4   5

PART III: The following question asks about changes in Academy's career enhancement program that are currently under consideration.

In your opinion should the Academy career enhancement program...

54. Continue the current practice of selecting teacher leaders every two years and other positions every year   1   2   3   4   5
55. Make all positions permanent— that is, one that the incumbent holds until retirement, resignation, or removal for poor performance   1   2   3   4   5
56. Make some positions—for instance teacher leaders—permanent but not others   1   2   3   4   5   [160]
57. Continue the current practice of selecting for each position as is currently done but find a way to give incumbents permanent credit on the existing step-and-lane salary scale after they leave their position   1   2   3   4   5
58. In order to make positions permanent, revise the districts' salary schedule to take job assignments as well as experience and education into account   1   2   3   4   5

PART IV: The following questions ask about your personal background as it relates to the Career Enhancement Program

59. I am presently (circle the appropriate number)
    1. a regular classroom teacher
    2. a counselor, special education teacher, psychologist, or media specialist
    3. a building administrator (principal, assistant principal)
    4. a district office staff person (superintendent, director, supervisor)
    5. other (please specify) _____

IF YOU CIRCLED 4 OR 5 IN THE PREVIOUS ITEM SKIP TO ITEM NUMBER 69

For each of the positions listed below, please
a. circle the number that indicates if you *currently* hold it, if you held it *in the past* but do not now hold it, or if you *never* held it from 1984 to the present.
b. circle the number that indicates if you *intend to apply* for it.

	Currently hold this position	Held position in past but not now	Never held position		Yes	No
60. Teacher leader	3	2	1	|	2	1
61. Cluster or grade-level leader	3	2	1	|	2	1
62. Specialist	3	2	1 [165] |		2	1 [170]
63. Professional teacher	3	2	1	|	2	1
64. Provisional teacher	3	2	1	|	2	1

[3 blanks]

‾‾ ‾‾ ‾‾
[201-203]
Deck 2
[204]

65. In the last year, did you hold a job during the school year where you did not work for the Academy school district? Please circle the correct number.

Yes 2   No   1   [205]

66. Before the career enhancement program began, did you hold a job during the school year where you did not work for the Academy school district?

Yes 2   No   1

67. In the last year, did you hold a summer job where you did not work for the Academy school district?

Yes 2   No   1

68. Before the career enhancement program began, did you hold a summer job where you did not work for the Academy school district?

Yes 2   No   1

69. How many years of experience in education do you have?

(Fill in the blanks.) ___ ___   [210]

70. How many years have you worked in the Academy district?

(Fill in the blanks.) ___ ___

71. What is your gender? Please circle the correct number

Female   2   Male   1

72. What is your age group? Please circle the number that refers to the correct age group.

1	under 25	4	36–40	7	51–55
2	25–30	5	41–45	8	56–60
3	31–35	6	46–50	9	61 or older

73. What is your highest educational degree?

1	Pre-BA	4	MA/MS/MEd./MAT
2	BA/BS	5	Ph.D./Ed.D
3	Other		[215]

74. At what level do you teach?

1	Elementary	3	High School
2	Middle School	4	Other/Special School

NOTES

CHAPTER 1

1. In theory, teachers could participate in setting these standards. If they did, the merit principle would be more professional. In practice teachers rarely help set the standards used for determining merit.

CHAPTER 2

1. The TDP legislation covered both teachers and administrators, but in practice most attention was given to teachers. Because the focus of this book is on teachers, that is the part of the program described here.

CHAPTER 3

1. The full story illustrates the integrity of this board. The one new member who was replaced was discovered to be involved in a conflict of interest. His company was interested in holding a construction contract for the area vocational-technical school. He had used his position on the board to get an award, and when that was discovered, the president of the board steadfastly and successfully worked to have him dismissed on ethics charges.

2. UniServ representatives are employees of a state chapter of the National Education Association. Their function is to serve the local associations in a particular region, assisting in day-to-day functions and conflict resolution.

CHAPTER 4

1. Presently teachers are elected by their buildings to serve on the task force.

2. Unless otherwise specified, all figures for stipends are for the 1989–90 school year.

CHAPTER 5

1. About three-quarters of those who completed questionnaires answered this question so the response rate is particularly low.

REFERENCES

Arends, R. I. (1982). The meaning of administrative support. *Educational Administration Quarterly*. 18(4):74–92.

Bacharach, S. B., S. C. Bauer, and J. B. Shedd (eds.) (1986). *The learning workplace: The conditions and resources of teaching*. New York: Organizational Analysis and Practice.

Bacharach, S. B., and S. C. Conley (1989). Uncertainty and decisionmaking in teaching: Implications for managing line professionals. In T. J. Sergiovanni and J. H. Moore (eds.), *Schooling for tomorrow: directing reforms to issues that count* (311–328). Needham Heights, MA: Allyn and Bacon.

Bacharach, S. B., and S. M. Mitchell (1987). The generation of practical theory: Schools as political organizations. In J. W. Lorsch (ed.), *The handbook of organizational behavior* (405–418). Englewood Cliffs, NJ: Prentice-Hall.

Berman, P., and M. W. McLaughlin (1975). *Federal programs supporting educational change. The findings in review, 4*. Santa Monica, CA: RAND Corporation.

Bidwell, C. E. (1965). The school as a formal organization. In J. G. March (ed.), *Handbook of organizations* (972–1022). Chicago: Rand McNally.

Brophy, J. E., and T. L. Good (1986). Teacher behavior and student achievement. In M. C. Wittrock (ed.), *Handbook of research on teaching, 3d ed.* (328–375). New York: Macmillan.

Burlingame, M. (1988). The politics of education and educational policy: The local level. In N. J. Boyan (ed.), *Handbook of research on educational administration* (439–452). New York: Longman.

Carlson, R. O. (1972). *School superintendents: Careers and performance*. Columbus, OH: Merrill.

Carnegie Forum on Education and the Economy (May 1986). *A nation prepared: Teachers for the 21st century.* New York: Carnegie Forum.

Carnoy, M., and J. McDonnell (1989). *School district restructuring in Santa Fe, New Mexico.* New Brunswick, NJ: Center for Policy Research in Education.

Carter, K., and W. Doyle (1989). Classroom research as a resource for the graduate preparation of teachers. In A. Woolfolk (ed.), *Research perspectives on the graduate preparation of teachers* (51–68). Englewood Cliffs, NJ: Prentice-Hall.

Casner-Lotto, J. (1988). Expanding the teacher's role: Hammond's school improvement process. *Phi Delta Kappan.* 69:349–353. Janaury.

Chapman, D. W., and S. M. Hutcheson (1981). Attrition from teaching careers: A discriminant analysis. *American Educational Research Journal, 19,* 93–106.

Clark, C., and P. L. Peterson (1986). Teachers' thought processes. In M. C. Wittrock (ed.), *Handbook of research on teaching,* 3d ed. (255–296). New York: Macmillan.

Clune, W. H. and P. A. White. (1988). *School-based management: Institutional variataion, implementation, and issues for future research.* Center for Policy Research in Education.

Cohen, D. K. (1990). Revolution in one classroom. *Educational Evaluation and Policy Analysis.* 12(3):327–345.

Cohen, D. K., and D. L. Ball (1990). Policy and practice: An overview. *Educational Evaluation and Policy Analysis* 12:233–39.

Corbett, H. D., J. A. Dawson, and W. A. Firestone (1984). *School context and school change.* New York: Teachers College Press.

Cuban, L. (1976). *Urban school chiefs under fire.* Chicago: University of Chicago Press.

Cuban, L. (1989). The district superintendent and the restructuring of schools: a realistic appraisal. In T. Sergiovanni and J. H. Moore (eds.), *Schooling for tomorrow: Directing reforms to issues that count* (251–271). Needham Heights, MA: Allyn and Bacon.

Cuban, L. (1990). Reforming again, again, and again. *Educational Researcher* 19(1):3–13.

Darling-Hammond, L. (1984). Beyond the commission reports: The coming crisis in teaching. Santa Monica, CA: RAND Corporation.

Darling-Hammond, L., and B. Berry (1988). *The evolution of teacher policy.* Santa Monica, CA: RAND Corporation.

David, J. L. (1989). *Restructuring in progress: Lessons from pioneering districts.* Washington, DC: National Governors' Association.

Dewey, J. (1938). *Experience and education.* New York: Collier.

Dornbusch, S. M., and W. R. Scott (1975). *Evaluation and the exercise of authority.* San Francisco: Jossey-Bass.

Elmore, R. F. (1990). *Restructuring schools: The next generation of educational reform.* San Francisco: Jossey-Bass.

Etzioni, A. (1961). *A comparative analysis of complex organizations.* New York: Free Press.

Firestone, W. A. (1977). Participation and influence in the planning of educational change. *Journal of Applied Behavioral Science* 13:167–83.

Firestone, W. A. (1989). Using reform: Conceptualizing district initiative. *Educational Evaluation and Policy Analysis* 11(2):151–165.

Firestone, W. A., and H. D. Corbett (1988). Planned organizational change. In N. Boyan (ed.), *Handbook of research on educational administration* (321–340). New York: Longman.

Firestone, W. A., S. H. Fuhrman, and M. W. Kirst (1989). *The progress of reform: An appraisal of state education initiatives.* New Brunswick, NJ: The Center for Policy Research in Education.

Firestone, W. A., S. Rosenblum, B. D. Bader, and D. Massell (1991). *District responses to state policies in the reform decade.* New Brunswick, NJ: The Center for Policy Research in Education.

Fuhrman, S. H., W. H. Clune, and Elmore, R. F. (1988). Research on education reform: Lessons on the implementation of policy. *Teachers College Record* 90(2):237–58.

Fullan, M. G. (1982). *The meaning of educational change.* New York: Teachers College.

Fullan, M. G., S. E. Anderson, and E. E. Newton. (1986). *Support systems for implementing curriculum in school boards.* Toronto, Ontario: Ministry of Education.

Gage, N. L. (1978). *The scientific basis of the art of teaching.* New York: Teachers College Press.

Good, T. (1983). Classroom research: A decade of progress. *Educational Psychologist* 18:127–44.

Hall, G. E. (1987a). The role of district office personnel in facilitating school-based change: Hypotheses and research dilemmas. In R. Vandenberghe and G. E. Hall (eds.), *Research on internal change facilitation in schools* (163–181). Leuven, Belgium: Academic.

Hall, G. E. (1987b). Strategic sense: The key to reflective leadership in school principals. Paper presented at the conference on Reflection in Teacher Education, Houston, TX.

Hargreaves, A. (1984). Experience counts, theory doesn't: How teachers talk about their work. *Sociology Of Education* 57(4):244–253.

Hochschild, J. L. (1981) *What's fair?: American beliefs about distributive justice.* Cambridge, MA: Harvard U. Press.

The Holmes Group, Inc. (1986). *Tomorrow's teachers: A report of the Holmes Group.* East Lansing, MI: Author.

Hord, S. M., G. E. Hall, and S. M. Stiegelbauer (1983). Principals don't do it alone: The role of the consigliere. Paper presented at the annual meeting of the American Educational Research Association, Montreal.

Iannaccone, L., and F. Lutz (1970). *Politics, power, and policy.* Columbus, OH: Charles Merrill.

Johnson, S. M. (1984). Merit pay for teachers: A poor prescription for reform. *Harvard Educational Review* 54(2):175–185.

Johnson, S. M. (1986). Incentives for teachers: What motivates, what matters. *Educational Administration Quarterly* 22(3):54–79.

Johnson, S. M. (1989). Schoolwork and its reform. In J. Hannaway and R. Crowson (eds.), *The politics of reforming school administration* (95–112). New York: The Falmer Press.

Johnson, S. M. (1990). *Teachers at work: Achieving success in our schools.* New York: Basic Books.

Johnson, S. M., and N. C. W. Nelson (1987). Teaching reform in an active voice. *Phi Delta Kappan* 68:591–98.

Kasten, K. (1984). The efficacy of institutionally dispensed rewards in elementary school teaching. *Journal of Research and Development in Education* 17(4):1–13.

Kerr, N. D. [pseudonym] (1964). The school board as an agency of legitimization. *Sociology of Education* 38:34–59.

Kottkamp, R. B., E. F. Provenzo, Jr., and M. M. Cohn (1986). Stability and change in a profession: Two decades of teacher attitudes, 1964–1984. *Phi Delta Kappan* 67(8):559–567.

Lanier, J. E., and J. W. Little (1986). Research on teacher education. In M. C.

Wittrock (ed.), *Handbook of research on teaching*, 3d ed. (527–569). New York: Macmillan.

Lanier, J. E., and M. W. Sedlak (1989). Teacher efficacy and quality schooling. In T. J. Sergiovanni and J. H. Moore (eds.), *Schooling for tomorrow: Directing reforms to issues that count* (119–145). Needham Heights, MA: Allyn and Bacon.

Lawler, E. E. (1981). *Pay and organizational effectiveness: A psychological view*, 2d ed. New York: McGraw-Hill.

Lawler, E. E. (1973). *Motivation in work organizations*. Monterey, CA: Brooks/Cole.

Little, J. W. (1982). Norms of collegiality and experimentation: Workplace conditions of school success. *American Educational Research Journal* 19(3):325–340.

Lortie, D. C. (1975). *Schoolteacher: A sociological study*. Chicago: The University of Chicago Press.

Louis Harris and Associates. (1985). *The Metropolitan Life survey of former teachers in America*. New York: author.

Malen, B., and A. W. Hart (1987). Confronting reform in teacher preparation: One state's experience. *Educational Evaluation and Policy Analysis*, 9(1):9–24.

Malen, B., M. J. Murphy, and A. W. Hart (1988). Restructuring teacher compensation systems: An analysis of three incentive strategies. In K. Alexander and D. H. Monk (eds.), *Eighth Annual Yearbook of the American Education Finance Association 1987* (91–142). Cambridge, MA: Ballinger.

McCarthy, M. M. (1990). Teacher-testing programs. In J. Murphy (ed.), *The educational reform movement of the 1980s* (189–214). Berkeley, CA: McCutchan.

McDonnell, L. M. (1989). *The dilemma of teacher policy*. Santa Monica, CA: RAND Corporation.

McLaughlin, M. W., and D. Marsh (1978). Staff development and school change. *Teachers College Record* 80:69–94.

McNeil, L. (1986). *Contradictions of control: School structure and school knowledge*. New York, NY: Routledge.

Metz, M. H. (1990). Real school. In D. E. Mitchell and M. E. Goertz (eds.), *Education politics for the new century* (75–93). New York: Falmer Press.

Meyer, J. W., and B. Rowan (1977). Institutionalized organizations: Formal structure as myth and ceremony. *American Journal of Sociology* 83(2):340–363.

Miles, M. B. (1964). On temporary systems. In M. B. Miles (ed.), *Innovation in education* (437–90). New York: Teachers College Press.

Miles, M. B., and A. M. Huberman (1984). *Qualitative data analysis: A sourcebook of new methods.* Beverly Hills, CA: Sage.

Millman, J., and L. Darling-Hammond (1990). *The new handbook of teacher evaluation: Assessing elementary and secondary teachers.* Newbury Park, CA: Sage.

Mintzberg, H. (1983). *Structure in fives: Designing effective organizations.* Englewood Cliffs, NJ: Prentice-Hall.

Mitchell, D. (1989). Measuring up: Standards for evaluating school reform. In T. J. Sergiovanni and J. H. Moore (eds.), *Schooling for tomorrow: Directing reforms to issues that count* (42–60). Needham Heights, MA: Allyn and Bacon.

Mowday, R. T., L. W. Porter, and R. M. Steers (1982). *Employee-organization linkages: The psychology of commitment, absenteeism, and turnover.* New York: Academic Press.

Murnane, R. J., and D. K. Cohen (1986). Merit pay and the evaluation problem: Why most merit pay plans fail and a few survive. *Harvard Educational Review* 56(1):1–17.

Murnane, R. J., J. D. Singer, and J. B. Willett (1989). The influence of salaries and "opportunity costs" on teachers' career choices: Evidence from North Carolina. *Harvard Education Review* 59:325–46.

Murphy, M. J., and A. W. Hart (1990). Career ladders and work in schools. In J. Murphy (ed.), *The educational reform movement of the 1980s* (215–242). Berkeley, CA: McCutchan.

National Commission on Educational Excellence (1983). *A nation at risk: The imperative for educational reform.* Washington, DC: U. S. Government Printing Office.

National Education Association (1987). Status of the American public school teacher. West Haven, CT: National Education Association.

Newcombe, E. (1983). *Rewarding teachers: Issues and incentives.* Philadelphia, PA: Research for Better Schools.

Newmann, F. M., R. A. Rutter, and M. S. Smith (1989). Organizational factors that affect school sense of efficacy, community, and expectations. *Sociology of Education* 62(4):221–238.

Oldham, G. R., and J. R. Hackman (1981). Relationships between organizational structure and employee reactions: Comparing alternative frameworks. *Administrative Science Quarterly* 26(1):66–83.

Olson, L. (1988). The "restructuring" puzzle: Ideas for revamping "egg-crate" schools abound, but to what end? *Education Week* 2 November.

Passow, A. H. (1989). Present and future directions in school reform. In T. J. Sergiovanni and J. H. Moore (eds.), *Schooling for tomorrow: Directing reforms to issues that count* (13–39). Needham Heights, MA: Allyn and Bacon.

Perrow, C. B. (1970). *Organizational analysis: A sociological view.* Stony Brook, NY: The State University of New York at Stony Brook.

Peters, T. J., and R. H. Waterman (1982). *In search of excellence.* New York: Harper and Row.

Peterson, P. L., and M. A. Commeaux (1989). Assessing the teacher as a reflective professional: New perspectives on teacher evaluation. In A. E. Woolfolk (ed.), *Research perspectives on the graduate preparation of teachers* (132–152). Englewood Cliffs, NJ: Prentice-Hall.

Peterson, P. L., and S. J. McCarthey (1991). New roles and classroom practice: Preliminary findings for use in CPRE final report. Internal memorandum.

Pfeffer, J. (1978). *Organizational design.* Arlington Heights, IL: AHM.

Popkewitz, T. S., and K. Lind (1989). Teacher incentives as reforms: Teachers' work and the changing control mechanism in education. *Teachers College Record* 90(4):575–594.

Porter, A. C. (1989). External standards and good teaching: The pros and cons of telling teachers what to do. *Educational Evaluation and Policy Analysis* 11(4):343–356.

Porter, L. W., E. E. Lawler, and J. R. Hackman (1975). *Behavior in organizations.* New York: McGraw-Hill.

Ranson, S., B. Hinings, and R. Hughes (1980). The structuring of organizational structures. *Administrative Science Quarterly* 25:1–17.

Rosenholtz, S. J. (1985). Education reform strategies: Will they increase teacher commitment? *American Journal of Education* 95:534–562.

Rosenholtz, S. J. (1989). *Teachers' workplace: The social organization of schools.* New York: Longman.

Rosenshine, B. V. (1983). Teaching functions in instructional programs. *Elementary School Journal* 83(4):60–69.

Rosenthal, A. (1969). *Governing education.* Garden City, NY: Doubleday.

Rossman, G. B., H. D. Corbett, and W. A. Firestone (1988). *Change and effectiveness in schools: A cultural perspective.* Albany: SUNY Press.

Rowan, B. (1990). Commitment and control: Alternative strategies for the organizational design of schools. In C. B. Cazen and S. M. Johnson (eds.), *Review of research in education* (353–392). Washington, DC: American Educational Research Association.

Ryan, R. M., J. P. Connell, and E. L. Deci (1985). A motivational analysis of self-determination and self-regulation in education. In C. Ames and R. Ames (eds.), *Research on motivation in education*, vol 2: *The classroom milieu* (13–51). Orlando, FL: Academic Press.

Schlechty, P. (1989). Career ladders: A good idea going awry. In T. J. Sergiovanni and J. H. Moore (eds.), *Schooling for tomorrow: Directing reforms to issues that count* (356–373). Needham Heights, MA: Allyn and Bacon.

Scott, W. R. (1983). *Organizations: Rational, natural, and open systems*. Englewood Cliffs, NJ: Prentice-Hall.

Selznick, P. (1957). *Leadership in administration: A sociological interpretation*. New York: Harper and Row.

Shanker, A. (1990). The end of the traditional model of schooling—and a proposal for using incentives to restructure our public schools. *Phi Delta Kappan* 71(5):344–357.

Shulman, L. S. (1987). Knowledge and teaching: Foundations of the new reform. *Harvard Educational Review* 57(1):1–22.

Shulman, L. S. (1989). Teaching alone, learning together: Needed agendas for the new reforms. In T. J. Sergiovanni and J. H. Moore, *Schooling for tomorrow: Directing reforms to issues that count* (167–186). Needham Heights, MA: Allyn and Bacon.

Sickler, J. (1988). Teachers in charge: Empowering the professionals. *Phi Delta Kappan* 69(5):354–357.

Sirotnik, K. A., and R. W. Clark (1988). School-centered decision making and renewal. *Phi Delta Kappan* 69(9):660–64.

Sizer, T. (1984). *Horace's compromise: The dilemma of the American high school*. Boston: Houghton-Mifflin.

Slavin, R. (1987). The Hunterization of America's schools. *Instructor Magazine* 46(8):56–98.

Smith, M. S., and J. O'Day (in press). Systemic school reform. In S. H. Fuhrman and B. Malen (eds.), *The politics of curriculum and testing*. London: Falmer.

Smylie, M. A. and J. C. Smart. (1990). Teacher support for career enhancement initiatives: Program characteristics and effects on work. *Educational Evaluation and Policy Analysis*. 12(2):139–155.

Southern Regional Education Board (1990). *Paying for performance—Important questions and answers: The 1989 SREB career ladder clearinghouse report.* Atlanta, GA: Author.

Staw, B. M. (1980). Intrinsic and extrinsic motivation. In H. J. Leavitt, L. R. Pondy, and D. M. Boje (eds.), *Readings in managerial psychology* (23–61). Chicago: The University of Chicago Press.

Taylor, H., R. Leitman, and Program Planners, Inc. (1989). *The American teacher: Preparing schools for the 1990s.* Louis Harris and Associates.

Timar, T. B. (1990). The politics of school restructuring. In D. E. Mitchell and M. E. Goertz (eds.), *Education politics for the new century* (55–74). London: Falmer.

Tucker, H. J., and L. H. Zeigler (1980). *Professionals versus the public.* New York: Longman.

Tyack, D. (1974). *The one best system.* Cambridge, MA: Harvard University Press.

Weber, M. (1947). *Social and economic organization.* New York: Oxford University Press.

Weick, K. E. (1976). Educational organizations as loosely coupled systems. *Administrative Science Quarterly* 21(1):19.

Weick, K. E., and R. R. McDaniel (1989). How professional organizations work: Implications for school organization and management. In T. J. Sergiovanni and J. H. Moore (eds.), *Schooling for tomorrow: Directing reforms to issues that count* (331–354). Needham Heights, MA: Allyn and Bacon.

Wise, A. E. (1989). Professional teaching: A new paradigm for the management of education. In T. J. Sergiovanni and J. H. Moore (eds.), *Schooling for tomorrow: Directing reforms to issues that count* (301–310). Needham Heights, MA: Allyn and Bacon.

Yin, R. K. (1984). *Case study research: Design and methods.* Newbury Park, CA: Sage.

Zald, M. N. (1969). The power and functions of boards of directors: A theoretical synthesis. *American Journal of Sociology* 75(1):97–111.

Zeigler, L. H., M. K. Jennings, and G. W. Peak (1974). *Governing American schools: Political interaction in local school districts.* North Scituate, MA: Duxbury Press.

SUBJECT INDEX

A

Accountability, 2, 4, 21, 39–43, 74, 86, 102, 107, 109, 121, 190, 191, 204, 207, 211, 212, 213

Adoption, 6, 30, 33, 34, 84, 95, 150, 153

Ambiguity, 11, 25, 28, 92, 94, 106, 108; effects of, 71

Authority, 12, 24, 25, 27, 29, 31, 32, 34, 56, 77, 83, 86, 100, 102, 103, 104, 107, 114, 124, 161, 169, 170, 190, 199, 207, 209; administrators', 34, 190; teachers', 22, 24, 26, 28, 33, 69, 102, 145, 153, 157, 169, 198, 199, 206

Autonomy, 11, 12, 20, 27, 86, 113, 119, 132, 155, 160, 167, 169, 180, 199

B

Basic skills, 15, 16, 25, 41, 108, 207

Board (School): elections, 84; openness, 5, 120

Bureaucracy, 7, 14, 18, 28, 36, 89, 110, 154, 205

C

Career ladder, 8, 23, 34, 74, 132, 140, 158, 159, 164, 166, 208; Academy, 111, 120–149, 151, 152, 158–59, 161, 162, 164–166, 167, 169, 172, 174, 175, 176, 177, 184, 185, 189, 196, 200, 204, 207, 216; governance, 23, 63, 166; Mossville 47–73, 157, 160–62, 164, 167, 170, 172, 176, 179, 183, 186, 196, 200, 204, 207

Central office, 7, 81, 82, 84, 89–91, 100, 102, 103, 104, 107, 109, 110, 113, 124, 129, 148, 170, 175, 185, 188, 189, 192, 199, 205, 209, 210, 215

Coalition, 30, 31, 95

Collegiality, 104, 105, 111, 162, 181, 212

Commitment, 2, 14, 16–18, 20, 22, 23, 25, 26, 69, 79, 110, 112, 116, 127, 135, 136, 153, 156, 171, 174, 175

Communication, 48, 75, 87, 90, 93, 95, 98–100, 101, 103, 105, 141, 162, 170, 180, 198; Hill City District News, 95

Competition, 59, 60, 72, 162, 163

Conflict, 3, 28, 30, 32, 33, 77, 83, 115, 175, 182, 183, 185, 187, 188, 190, 195, 217

Consigliere, 32, 194, 195, 199

Curriculum specialists, 136, 137, 167, 169

D

Decision making, 9, 12, 17, 18, 21, 26, 29, 33, 34, 35, 74, 75, 84, 85, 87, 102, 103, 104, 105, 106, 109, 110, 111, 118, 125, 168, 171, 187, 198, 199, 200, 205, 209, 210

Decisions, 14, 30–34, 205; operational, 14, 18–19, 166, 167, 205; strategic, 14, 18, 23, 24, 27,33, 168–171, 175, 177, 186, 196, 200, 217

Design, 6, 16, 17, 24–26, 28, 64, 65, 121, 154, 155, 157, 163, 167, 168, 170, 175, 180, 181, 182, 183, 188, 199, 200, 201, 203, 205, 207, 208, 209, 216; organization, 14, 68, 149; program, 5, 129, 150, 175, 195

Direct instruction, 7, 14–16, 36, 48, 58, 155, 156, 157, 161, 167, 180

E

Empowerment, 2, 104, 106, 155, 168, 181, 200

Equity, 21, 22, 157, 214

Evaluation, 18, 19, 25, 40–42, 43, 46, 47, 48, 49, 50–58, 61, 68, 69, 70, 71, 73, 74, 85, 86, 87, 94, 95, 101, 102, 103, 104, 107, 108, 109, 110, 134, 135, 139, 140, 141, 142, 143, 160, 163, 167, 174, 179

Extended contract, 126, 128

G

Governance, 23–24, 28, 166–171, 203, 204, 208, 209

I

Implementation, 30–33, 84, 89, 90, 108, 115, 116, 117, 119, 122–124, 150, 153, 175, 183

Incentives, 14, 18–22, 25, 27, 36, 41, 47, 49, 55, 62, 71, 72, 74, 84, 89, 99, 103, 110, 121, 130, 132, 133, 138, 144, 145, 146, 155, 164, 167, 171, 174, 175, 180, 205–207, 215; extrinsic, 19, 20, 21, 28, 155, 171, 172, 180, 208; intrinsic, 2, 20, 28, 155, 171, 177, 180, 181, 205, 206, 208

Influence, 5, 8, 21, 24, 26, 27, 29–34, 64, 66, 74, 104, 110, 118, 119, 123, 125, 131, 144, 152, 153, 155, 158, 161, 163, 166, 169, 170, 171, 175–177, 182, 183, 184, 186, 188, 199, 200, 201, 202, 209–210, 216–217, 218

Interest(s), 6, 13, 22, 25, 29, 33, 36, 37, 43, 50, 77, 81, 95, 112, 136, 151, 152, 155, 156, 184, 192, 193, 208, 212, 217

J

Job differentiation, 4, 20, 21, 27, 28, 72, 154, 157, 158, 159, 163, 171, 204, 208, 211, 214, 215

Job enlargement, 4, 20–23, 27, 35, 111, 121, 124, 131, 132, 133, 140, 144, 145, 147, 155, 157, 158, 159, 162, 170, 178, 184, 186, 205, 206, 208, 209, 213, 218

K

Knowledge, 2, 12, 14–20, 23, 30, 31, 33, 40, 48, 155, 168, 180, 200, 211

L

Leadership, 45, 82, 83, 110, 114, 148–151, 153, 190, 191, 216–218

Legislation, 29, 31, 33, 47, 49, 50, 74, 121, 122, 123, 141, 183, 184, 216

M

Master teacher, 22, 85, 89–93, 104–108, 110, 122, 157, 192, 205, 211

Mentor, 59, 210

Merit pay, 3, 13, 22, 25, 27, 28, 35, 72, 92, 93, 111, 121, 124, 128, 129, 130, 131, 152, 155, 157, 158, 159, 162, 164, 167, 172, 184, 189, 193, 207, 211

Money, 20, 22, 61, 72, 73, 121, 122, 123, 125, 126, 135, 155, 171, 172–175, 177, 183, 199, 201, 206, 211, 215–216

Motivation, 2–4, 6, 12, 20, 21, 36, 66, 70, 71, 74, 75, 111, 143, 145, 154, 155, 156, 163, 171, 175, 180, 181, 182, 205, 209, 212, 213, 215

O

Outcomes, 8, 13, 16, 35, 66, 75, 85–87, 102, 103, 107, 120, 143, 154, 155, 156, 157, 180, 183

P

Participation, 4, 18, 23, 27, 84, 86, 97, 98, 103, 104, 105–106, 107, 109, 110, 111, 124, 168, 169, 183, 205

Performance bonus, 124, 129–131, 144, 152

Planning, 64, 115, 116, 119, 121, 124, 125, 126, 127, 131, 151, 152, 182, 183, 186, 187, 188, 213, 216; committees, 209, 210

Policy, 3, 4, 9, 18, 31, 32, 36, 45, 47, 75, 84, 90, 110, 111, 168, 184, 197, 209, 215, 218

Politics, 3, 6, 8, 12, 28–32, 44, 182

Principal, 24, 32–34

Process-product research, 14–16, 19

R

Reflective practice, 14–16, 25, 207

Resources, 27, 29, 31, 33, 34, 85, 86, 94, 112, 113, 126, 131, 144, 147, 178, 188, 210, 215, 217

Rewards. *See incentives*; financial, 155, 173, 216

S

Salary, 21, 22, 27, 33, 34, 36, 45, 47, 48, 71, 72, 84, 111, 116, 132, 134, 141, 159, 169, 186, 197, 198, 211, 215, 217

Selection, 23, 28, 39, 43, 48, 54, 89–93, 100, 104, 106, 108, 126, 133, 136, 138–140, 151, 153, 154, 155, 158–165, 175, 176, 178, 179, 181, 182, 186, 195, 205, 209, 213, 214

Site-based management, 2, 24, 27, 169, 209

Staff development, 18, 25, 28, 48, 63, 85, 90, 91, 109, 135, 173, 205

State influence, 33, 199, 216

Superintendent, 4, 30–34, 36–39, 42–44, 75, 76, 77, 81–82, 83, 92, 94, 95, 104, 106, 109, 110, 111, 114, 115, 118, 119, 120, 131, 150, 169, 170–171, 176, 180, 184, 185, 187, 188, 190–194, 195, 196, 197, 198, 199, 204, 209, 216, 217; selection, 48, 138, 158, 159, 164, 175

Supervision, 2, 7, 14, 19, 21, 26, 35, 50, 114, 129, 133, 134, 135, 140, 141, 142, 143, 147, 148, 149, 151, 167

T

Teacher participation, 127, 168

Teacher selection, 48, 138, 158, 159, 164, 175

Technology, 2, 13–15, 77

Thinking, 14–16, 25, 46, 72, 106, 127, 144, 148, 188, 192, 210, 211, 217

Training, 19, 21, 23, 49, 50, 53, 58–60, 61, 65, 68, 69, 71, 73, 74, 144, 146, 158, 161, 162, 168, 170, 173, 175, 189, 193, 200, 204, 205, 206, 207, 209, 210, 213, 215

U

Union, 7, 24, 33, 64, 80, 160, 170, 191, 192, 195, 198

V

Values, 2, 12, 14, 17–20, 29, 74, 76, 168, 211

AUTHOR INDEX

A

Arends, R. I., 33

B

Bacharach, S. B., 12, 18, 23, 25–27,
    29–31, 166, 169
Bader, B. D., 209
Bauer, S. C., 25
Berman, P., 18, 25
Berry, B., 21
Bidwell, C. E., 12
Brophy, J. E., 15, 16, 48
Burlingame, M., 31, 32

C

Carlson, R. O., 32
Carnegie Forum on Education and
    the Economy, 1, 12, 22, 23, 160,
    164, 208, 210, 212
Carnoy, M., 24
Carter, K., 15, 16
Casner-Lotto, J., 33
Chapman, D. W., 27
Clark, C., 16
Clark, R. W., 27, 169, 200
Clune, W. H., 24, 34, 184, 209

Cohen

Cohen, D. K., 25, 26, 30, 162, 172
Conley, S. C., 12, 18, 23, 169
Corbett, H. D. III, 33, 168, 171, 207
Cuban, L., 25, 32

D

Darling-Hammond, L., 21, 160
David, J. L., 28, 31, 33, 204, 213
Dewey, J., 3
Dornbusch, S. M., 20
Doyle, W., 15, 16

E

Elmore, R. F., 34, 184, 203
Etzioni, A., 173

F

Firestone, W. A., 3, 25, 27, 33,
    167–169, 171, 200, 207, 209
Fuhrman, S. H., 3, 34, 184
Fullan, M., 30, 32

G

Gage, N. L., 15

Good, T. 15, 16, 48

H

Hackman, J. R., 20, 178, 180
Hall, G. E., 32, 134, 194
Hargreaves, A., 25
Hart, A. W. 21, 22, 159, 163, 172, 208, 213
The Holmes Group, 22
Hord, S. M., 32, 194
Hughes, R., 12
Hutcheson, S. M., 27

I

Iannaccone, L., 39

J

Jennings, M. K., 32
Johnson, S. M., 22, 26, 27, 33, 157, 171, 180, 208, 213

K

Kasten, K., 25, 27, 28
Kerr, N. D., 30
Kirst, M. W., 3, 11
Kottkamp, R. B., 25–27

L

Lanier, J. E., 16, 168
Lawler, E. E., 20, 164, 172
Lind, K. 11, 26, 160
Little, J. W., 16, 18, 167
Lortie, D. C., 25, 27, 157, 171, 178, 180
Lutz, F., 32, 39

M

Malen, B., 21, 22, 159, 163, 172, 208, 213

Marsh, D., 168
Massell, D., 209
McCarthey, S. J., 207
McCarthy, M. M., 16
McDaniel, R. R., 12, 17, 18, 168
McDonnell, J., 168, 211
McDonnell, L. M., 24
McLaughlin, M. W., 18, 25, 168
McNeil, L., 25
Metz, M. H., 204
Meyer, J. W., 12, 31, 204
Miles, M. B., 78–80, 82
Millman, J., 159–160
Mintzberg, H., 18
Mitchell, D., 33, 160, 214
Mitchell, S. M., 29–31
Mowday, R. T., 17
Murnane, R. J., 27, 162, 172
Murphy, M. J., 21, 172

N

National Commission on Educational Excellence, 1, 13
National Education Association, 5, 77
Nelson, N. C. W., 33
Newcombe, E., 163

O

O'Day, J., 168, 169
Oldham, G. R., 20, 178, 180
Olson, L., 11

P

Passow, A. H., 2, 3
Peak, G. W., 22, 32
Perrow, C. B., 13
Peters, T. J., 201
Peterson, P. L., 16, 17, 19, 207
Pfeffer, J., 28–30
Popkewitz, T. S., 11, 25–26, 160

Porter, A. C., 17
Porter, L. W., 20, 168
Provenzo, E. F. Jr., 25

R

Ranson, S., 12, 28
Rosenblum, S., 27, 209
Rosenholtz, S. J., 18, 21, 22, 162, 167, 212
Rosenshine, B. V., 15
Rossman, G. B., 207
Rowan, B., 12, 18, 31, 167, 204
Rutter, R. A., 18
Ryan, R. M., 163, 180

S

Schlechty, P., 215
Scott, W. R., 20
Sedlak, M. W., 16, 168
Selznick, P., 17
Shanker, A., 24
Shedd, J. B., 25
Shulman, L. S., 17, 18
Sickler, J., 24, 33
Singer, J. D., 27
Sirotnik, K. A., 27, 169, 200
Sizer, T., 95, 157, 192, 217

Smart, J. C., 28
Smith, M. S., 18, 168, 169
Smylie, M. A., 28
Southern Regional Education Board, 13, 23, 34, 159
Staw, B. M., 20, 177, 178
Steers, R. M., 17
Stiegelbauer, S. M., 32, 194

T

Taylor, H., 26, 28
Timar, T. B., 204
Tucker, H. J., 32, 34
Tyack, D., 190

W

Waterman, R. H., 201
Weber, M., 18, 20
Weick, K. E., 12, 17, 18, 166, 168
White, P., 24, 43, 209
Willett, J. B., 27
Wise, A. E., 160

Z

Zald, M. N., 32
Zeigler, L. H., 32, 34